LLANDUDNO BEFORE
THE HOTELS

Llandudno Before the Hotels

10,000 B.C. – 1854 A.D.

Christopher Draper

Text: Christopher Draper

ISBN: 1-84524-095-2
978-1-84524-095-0

Cover illustration: James Field
Cover design: Sian Parri

Published by
Llygad Gwalch, Ysgubor Plas, Llwyndyrys, Pwllheli,
Gwynedd, Wales LL53 6NG.
☎ 01758 750432
✆ gai@llygadgwalch.com
Website: www.llygadgwalch.com

For William Davies (1555–1593)

Who dared to be a Daniel

CONTENTS

Illustrations

Introduction

Llandudno is the 'Queen of the Welsh Resorts', a beautiful town in a unique natural setting but it is far more than just a Victorian bathing resort. As holidaymakers arrived old Llandudno departed. A way of life evolved over millenia was swept aside by rapacious property developers.

The issues at stake in such dramatic change are immense and universal but also unique. What happened in mid-nineteenth century Llandudno has echoes in the clearance of the Great American Plains, the Scottish Highlands, Mynydd Epynt and Dyffryn Tryweryn but it was not the same. Every community has its own unique story to tell and Llandudno's twelve thousand-year history has been overlooked for too long.

Knowledge of Llandudno in prehistory is predictably patchy but I've nevertheless drawn on both geological and archaeological records to sketch a picture of Llandudno from its earliest days. No written evidence exists before Roman times and even then there is little of relevance to Llandudno and we must rely largely on archaeological accounts. As the Middle Ages advance individuals increasingly appear in our narrative as documentary evidence of their activities become available. The first half of this book (chapters 1 to 9) therefore outlines thousands of years of history whereas the second part (chapters 10 to 19) offers a more comprehensive account, culminating in a detailed description of the period 1761 to 1854 and the 'lost village' of Llandudno.

Originally the 'llan of Tudno' applied only to a restricted area of the Great Orme but from chapters 1 to 9 I have loosely interpreted 'Llandudno' as comprising the three historic parishes of Llandudno, Eglwysrhos and Llangystennin, an area known as the Creuddyn peninsula. For the latter period covered by chapters 10 to 19 I have focussed, almost exclusively, on the increasingly nucleated village of Llandudno and the area defined by its parish boundaries.

To maximise readability I have confined references and explanatory notes to a section at the back of book that also indicates where original documents and other evidence can be consulted. A detailed list of illustrations can be found on the previous pages and a summary chronology can be consulted at the end of the text. To present an easily comprehensible picture of the development of prehistoric society in the Creuddyn I have employed the familiar categories proposed by Thomsen in 1836 of 'Ages' characterised by the material exploited for tool making. This analysis is crude and exaggerates the transition from one material to another but if we appreciate that Bronze Age people still used stone tools just as we continue to write with pencils in the age of the computer the categories remain useful. I have retained the traditional cleavage of the 'Stone Age' into the Old or Paleolithic period and the New, or Neolithic Period but dispensed with a separate 'Mesolithic' category for the sake of clarity. I don't oppose more subtle ways of categorising the past I've just adopted the simplest, most comprehensible, structure capable of carrying forward the story of this particular region. Similarly I have adopted the familiar B.C. and A.D. chronology despite its historically questionable implications.

This book then is an account of human activity in and around Llandudno over the last twelve thousand years. The years before the hotels came. Ironically as I write the Victorian bathing resort that replaced the old village of Llandudno is in its turn threatened with destruction by commercial forces. Grand hotels have been torn down and replaced with characterless flats and even the last redoubt of nature, the sea, is threatened with industrialisation by turbine builders who know the price of everything and the value of nothing.

Christopher Draper,
Penrhyn Bay

Chapter One

An Ancient Landscape (350 million BC)

When the first hunter-gatherers set foot on Llandudno's limestone headlands the Earth was already ancient. Even the shimmering rock forming the Great and Little Ormes was hundreds of millions of years old. The story of Llandudno really begins back in the geological age.

Unearthing the Evidence

Until comparatively recently we had little idea of the age of the earth. In 1650, relying on biblical sources, Archbishop Ussher concluded that the world was created in 4004 BC. Darwin realised this was far too short a time-span to accommodate his theories of evolutionary change and was not alone in applying scientific analysis to the rapidly accumulating geological evidence. In 1862 physicist Sir William Thomson put the age of the earth at between 20 and 400 million years. In 1899 the Irish physicist and geologist, John Joly, settled on an age of 99 million years. In the twentieth century Ernest Rutherford's discoveries about radioactive decay pushed this date way back.

Modern Geological Analysis

Modern geologists suggest that some 4,600 million years ago dust particles orbiting the sun coalesced to form planet Earth, which for ages remained an unstable assemblage of earthquakes and erupting volcanoes.

Primitive life forms slowly emerged as products of intense chemical reactions. While violent geological activity continued at the Earth's core the surface gradually cooled down forming contorted and shifting landmasses. The face of the earth would have been quite unfamiliar to us with continents both differently shaped and dispersed than those illustrated in modern atlases. Four hundred and twenty million years ago Wales and southern Britain formed part of an entirely different landmass from northern Britain, separated by a large ocean named Lapetus. But our respective 'continents' gradually drifted together, squeezing Lapetus, until about 400 million years ago Britain was united with a collision known to geologists as the Caledonian Orogeny.

The oldest rocks in Wales pre-date the Caledonian Orogeny by 200 or 300 million years (Cambrian era) but Llandudno's characteristic limestone is much younger.

Captain Vivian's Pioneering Work

The task of discovering Llandudno's geological record was initially tackled from two different directions. In the early Victorian era mine captains employed by Llandudno mine companies began to systematically investigate, analyse and record local geological formations in pursuit of the profitable extraction of commercially valuable copper. Standing head and shoulders above colleagues in the rigour of his approach and the reliability of his findings was Cornishman William Vivian (1817-1879), one of the first to make use of the microscope in analysing minerals. Vivian served as Captain of the Old Mine from 1853 to 1860 and besides carrying out day-to-day responsibilities in the mine he continued to contribute learned papers to geological journals. In 1858 his paper *Arborescent Native Copper in the Llandudno Mine*, published in the *Quarterly Journal of the Geological Society* revealed the relationship between Llandudno's limestone beds and the nature and distribution of the veins of copper ore. Vivian's obituary acknowledged his expertise and contribution, 'Captain Vivian combined with a perfect knowledge of mining great scientific knowledge as a geologist, which enabled him to contribute many useful papers upon geological subjects . . . '

Field Club Investigations

From 1906 the initial, rather narrow, geological analyses offered by Vivian and colleagues were supplemented by detailed fieldwork undertaken by academics and enthusiasts of *Llandudno & District Field Club* (the fore-runner of the present, *Llandudno & District Historical Society*). Two or three times a week *Field Club* members rambled across the Creuddyn peninsula and beyond in pursuit of information on local fauna, flora, history and geology. The specimens collected survive in Llandudno Museum and together with the *Field Club's* research papers, published in well-illustrated *Proceedings*, continue to provide an invaluable geological resource. Much of the *Field Club's* work remains unsurpassed and supplemented with more recent studies we can now provide a narrative description of Llandudno's geological past.

Llandudno's First Inhabitants

Living organisms emerged surprisingly early in Earth's history. Fossilised limy mounds of stromatolites secreted by blue-green algae have been found in Pre-Cambrian rocks 3,500 million years old. These ancestors of modern plants used photosynthesis to produce oxygen in an otherwise anoxic atmosphere. In Wales the earliest plant fossils found comprise Silurian (420 million-year-old) specimens of *Cooksonia*, a plant-

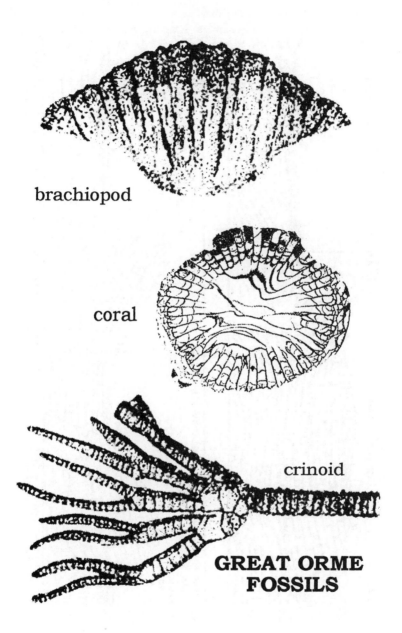

brachiopod

coral

crinoid

GREAT ORME FOSSILS

15

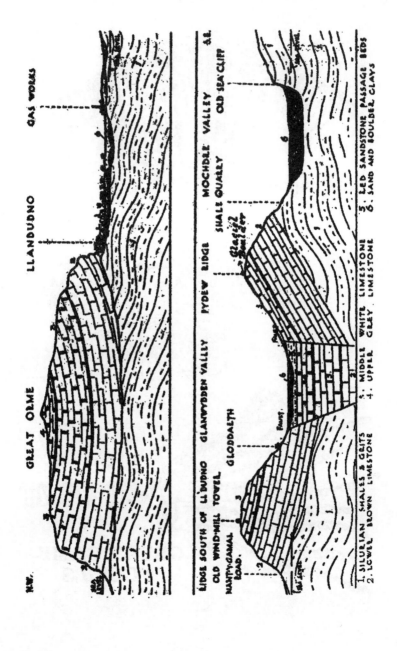

N.W.   GREAT ORME   LLANDUDNO   GAS WORKS

RIDGE SOUTH OF LL'DUDNO   GLANWYDDEN VALLEY   PYDEW RIDGE   MOCHDRE VALLEY   S.E.
OLD WIND-MILL TOWEL   SHALE QUARRY   OLD SEA CLIFF
GLODDAETH
NANT-Y-GAMAL ROAD.

1. SILURIAN SHALES & GRITS   3. MIDDLE WHITE LIMESTONE   5. RED SANDSTONE PASSAGE BEDS
2. LOWER BROWN LIMESTONE   4. UPPER GREY LIMESTONE   6. SAND AND BOULDER CLAYS

16

bearing spore capsules at the end of rigid stems.

The earliest fossilised organisms found in Llandudno are about 350 million years old (the Carboniferous era) from a time when Llandudno's characteristic limestone headlands were being formed under shallow, sub-tropical seas in conditions similar to the present day Gulf of Florida. Shallow lagoons were fringed with tall, gangling ancient plants similar to present-day *horsetails*, which were accompanied by dense mats formed by giant clubmoss, *lepidodendron*, whose fossilised remains have been recovered from Church Walks, Llandudno.

Those warm waters abounded with shellfish and corals. *Caninia*, *Lithostrotium* and *Dibunophyllum* fossils have all been found locally the first on the Little Orme, the second on the Great Orme and the third on Penrhyn Hill. Simple sponge-like creatures called crinoids and shellfish known as brachiopods flourished. Brachiopod fossils *Productus* have been recovered from the Bishop's Quarry and specimens of *Orthis* from the Little Orme. Fossilised crinoid stems have found in the area between Bryn y Bia and Penrhynside (illustrated).

Weberides and Other Animals

A particularly interesting inhabitant of Llandudno's ancient waters was trilobite *Weberides*. Trilobites, a sort of marine wood louse, spanned a vast period of geological history. Two quarryman, Robert Edward Jones and Robert Lloyd discovered a 700 million year old *Cambrian* specimen in the Penrhyn Quarry at Bethesda in 1887 but the fossilised *Weberides* subsequently discovered by members of *Llandudno Field Club* in limestone shale in the Bishop's Quarry was but half its age. Llandudno's carboniferous trilobites were at the end of a 350 million-year-long line and *Weberides* was about to follow his fellows into extinction.

When *Weberides*, along with all the other inhabitants of Llandudno's warm shallow seas expired they fell to the seabed and for almost fifty million years their calcium-rich shells and skeletal remains continued to accumulate, forming substantial deposits. This process of calcareous deposition was interrupted by sediments swept down by floods and the intermittent effects of rising and falling sea levels. This process built up bands of carboniferous limestone, in some places hundreds of metres thick.

Compression, Tilt and Fracture

Geological forces compressed, raised, tilted and fractured the layers of carboniferous limestone effectively ending the phase of carboniferous deposition. Sometime between 280 to 200 million years ago molten minerals, particularly copper-bearing ores, were forced outwards from the earth's core to fill voids in the fractured limestone. The combined effects of immense geological forces and declining sea levels eventually resulted in Llandudno's layered and copper-rich limestone being pushed above the waves to form the headlands so characteristic of the modern-day settlement, the Great and Little Ormes.

Llandudno's basic geomorphology was thus laid down in the carboniferous era leaving an environment ripe for colonisation by a variety of increasingly complex organisms. Yet the gap in the fossil record is immense. We know from wider research that around 260 million years ago there was a world-wide, mass *Permian* extinction, but we can only speculate about the type of organisms that colonised Llandudno before the last Ice Age.

Ice Ages and After Effects

A quarter of a million years ago temperatures plummeted, seas froze over and the Arctic ice-cap eventually extended to cover the whole of Wales and Northern Europe. Although there were several long periods of temperate climate when the ice receded it last returned to North Wales with a vengeance only 30,000 years ago.

This last great ice blanket cleared from Llandudno 12,000 years ago. As it departed it not only swept away most fossil records it also dramatically altered the shape of the local environment. Before the last Ice Age the River Conwy had flowed down from Snowdonia and debouched across Llandrillo marshes (the present golf course). After the Ice Age Afon Conwy followed a course to the west of the Great Orme. During the Ice Age glaciers pushed towards and over Llandudno and onwards into Snowdonia from the colder and yet more frozen north of Britain. As temperatures rose thirteen thousand years ago meltwater from Snowdonia roaring down the old course of the River Conwy was blocked at Llandrillo by a wall of still frozen sea ice. The meltwater then appears to have built up sufficient head of pressure to smash a new course through a range of low hills running from Llandudno Junction to Conwy. The small island of rock standing in the middle of the modern river that Telford used to anchor the eastern end his bridge is a vestigial element of that pre-Ice Age range of hills.

Subsequent silting blocked off most of Afon Conwy's old course and the much-reduced flow following the ancient course survives as Afon Ganol. Meanwhile as melting glaciers from the south ran up against glaciers from the north they tended to encourage liquefaction so that huge rocks borne along on their flows were deposited along their line of 'confrontation'. Numerous examples of these 'glacial erratics' remain scattered across the north-western end of the Great Orme.

As the ice departed it stripped away the soft layers of soil exposing the underlying limestone, leaving Llandudno's twin headlands as shimmering geological features; free draining, peppered with caves and attractive to passing wolves and stone age hunter-gatherers.

Chapter Two

Stone Age Hunter-Gatherers on the Great Orme (10,000 BC)

Llandudno's first human visitors arrived twelve thousand years ago, travelling west and chasing herds of horses and deer. They occupied two of Llandudno's limestone caves leaving behind archaeological evidence of their activities. They were thoroughly modern humans in body shape and intelligence, the result of four and half million years of human evolution.

Our African Ancestors
Hominids originally appeared in Africa but were understandably reluctant to move far beyond their rich, warm native lands. It took early humans four and a quarter million years to reach north Wales and around 230,000 BC hominids occupied Pontnewydd Cave in the Elwy valley, Denbighshire. Although these first Welsh men and women were not modern humans but Homo neanderthalis, they already had about half a million years experience of using a developed language, but we don't know what form this language took.

It's conceivable that these Denbighshire Neanderthals reached Llandudno during their extensive hunting expeditions but if so no evidence has been uncovered of their incursions into the Creuddyn. Perhaps Pontnewydd lay at the limit of pre-ice age hunter gathering for there is little evidence of Palaeolithic activity elsewhere in north Wales west of the Great Orme.

Post Ice Age Flora and Fauna
Until the ice began to disappear from north Wales 13,000 years ago the Creuddyn remained a rather unattractive destination for human hunter-gatherers who had retreated to the non ice-bound southern regions of Britain. As temperatures rose Arctic flora and fauna began to die out and were replaced by the animals and plants common to more temperate zones. Woolly mammoths and rhino could no longer survive and their remains were swept away by the retreating ice. Reindeer, wolves and brown bear (illustrated) lived on as temperatures rose, their skeletal remains uncovered in local caves providing solid archaeological evidence of their survival. Meanwhile the regenerating grasslands soon attracted herds of red deer, wild horses and cattle to the Creuddyn. Following

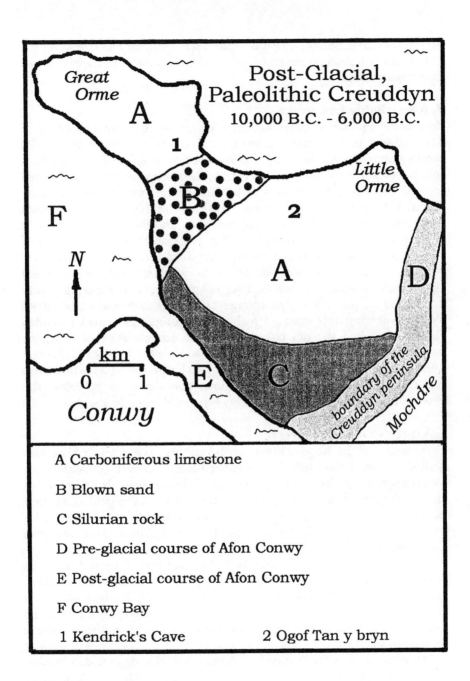

Post-Glacial, Paleolithic Creuddyn
10,000 B.C. - 6,000 B.C.

A Carboniferous limestone

B Blown sand

C Silurian rock

D Pre-glacial course of Afon Conwy

E Post-glacial course of Afon Conwy

F Conwy Bay

1 Kendrick's Cave   2 Ogof Tan y bryn

their tracks came bands of Homo Sapiens who naturally sought shelter in Llandudno's limestone caves for at least the duration of their seasonal hunter-gathering.

A Remarkable Discovery

By chance, in 1879 Thomas Kendrick uncovered extensive evidence of Llandudno's first human occupation. A discovery so significant it's worth telling the whole story. Thomas Kendrick (1821-1897) was born into poverty in a small cottage at Pant y Wennol and after his father died in 1835 the whole family was carted out of the area by the Poor Law Guardians. Nevertheless Thomas and his brother William secured employment in the Llandudno copper mines and the family returned to occupy a small terraced cottage at 4 Tan yr Ogof, on the lower slopes of the Great Orme. When the mines closed and Llandudno turned to tourism Kendrick restyled himself as 'a lapidary' and sold polished pebbles and trinkets to visitors. Ever enterprising he occupied a vacant cave situated just above his cottage as a workshop and sales outlet. Whilst enlarging this cave he realised that originally it had extended further back into the hill but over time an accumulation of stalagtitic material and breccia (limestone rubble) had eventually blocked the rear section. In digging out this material Kendrick discovered ancient human bones, stone tools and inscribed animal bones and teeth. Below the breccia he uncovered an earth and clay layer containing further bones.

Eskrigge's Observations

Fortunately whilst Kendrick was enlarging his cave workshop he was visited by an accomplished amateur geologist, Robert A Eskrigge. A Warrington cotton broker by profession, Eskrigge was also a Fellow of the Geological Society and past President of the Liverpool Geological Society (1866). Eskrigge compiled a valuable record of Kendrick's excavations in a paper included in the 1880 Proceedings of the Liverpool Geological Society.

'The limestone breccia succeeds to the clay and is from 4 to 6ft in thickness; the stones are mostly angular, and more or less cemented together by the infiltration of water through lime. In this bed, about 1 ft above the clay, were found portions of the skeletons of four human beings. The broken tibia of one skeleton and the foot of another remain to be seen in situ.'

However in a footnote, dated 5th August 1880, Eskrigge added 'further excavations have since been made' and in January 1908 G A Humphreys (referring to the latter part of Eskrigge's account) remarked that 'I am sorry to say these bones were removed later'.

Professor Boyd Dawkins' Analysis

After Eskrigge's inspection the material excavated by Kendrick was analysed by Professor William Boyd Dawkins (1837-1929) an eminent Manchester geologist with an abiding interest in Palaeolithic archaeology. Elected a Fellow of the Royal Society in 1866 Boyd Dawkins published early research into troglodytic mammalian remains in 'Cave Hunting' (1874). Professor Boyd Dawkins observed that the broken bones from the bottom earth and clay layer of Kendrick's Cave were 'in a different mineral condition from the rest and have probably been broken by the hand of man. They consist of fragments of the marrow-containing long bones of the bison.'

Recovered from the limestone layer, 'The human remains consist of portions of four skeletons at least; three adults and one child . . . The two most perfect femora measure respectively 17.9 and 17.6 inches, which according to Professor Humphrey's method, would imply that the average stature of their adult possessors was 5 feet 4.3 inches. This small stature . . . when taken with the other characters of the bones, shows that the men who buried their dead in the cave of the Great Orme's Head, belong to the small Iberic aborigines who possessed Europe west of the Rhine and north of the Mediterranean in the Neolithic Age'.

Boyd Dawkins also identified numerous animal remains in this breccia level, 'Badger, brown-bear, short-horned ox, sheep or goat, boar and horse' which he took as further evidence of his mistaken dating of human occupation to the Neolithic age. He believed the associated boulder stones had been used as hammers and possibly pot-boilers and a worn oyster shell employed as a scraper.

The professor carefully described the details of designs scratched on a number of the teeth and bones and speculated on their significance. 'The upper canines of the bear . . . are ornamented with transverse lines on the fang and have the extreme fang perforated with suspension. From the polish on the surface it is evident they were worn for some time before they were placed with the dead.'

A decorated horse jawbone, now recognised as an archeologically unique item, was meticulously noted; 'The remains of horse consist of the front part of the two lower jaws . . . the outer surface of the bone has been scraped by the hand of man in both jaws, and in one it is covered with zig-zag lines . . . In this the outer surface of the incisors is polished by friction with some soft substance and it appears to me more so than it would be naturally in the mouth of a horse. The use to which these

Brown Bear

Spotted Hyaena

Woolly Rhinoceros

articles were put by their possessors is altogether uncertain but they may have been simply ornaments or perhaps had some superstitious value.'

Thomas Kendrick's Cave of Curiosities

Boyd Dawkins' belief that Kendrick's lapidary shop had thousands of years earlier been 'used as a sepulchral vault by a family of small Iberic dwellers' supported his claim that, 'The discovery is of high interest.' Kendrick's cave finds were indeed reported in both archaeological and geological journals as well as the commercial press. Quick to capitalise on this public and scientific interest Kendrick displayed his archaeological finds at the entrance to his workshop-showroom. As business flourished he added an attractive Victorian shop front, retrieved from the redundant local branch of the National & Provincial Bank, to the front of the cave whilst the ancient cavern excavated at the rear was attractively illuminated for the benefit of customers by lanterns suspended from the roof.

Thomas Kendrick died, unmarried, of bronchial pneumonia on 26th December 1897 and was buried in St Tudno's graveyard on the Great Orme under an ornate marble headstone. Born into poverty his enterprise had enabled him to amass a considerable inheritance of £436 10s 0d that he bequeathed to his sister, Anne.

A Sadly Neglected Legacy

Following Kendrick's death in 1898 Llandudno Library Committee agreed on the importance of preserving his collection of archaeological artefacts and proposed to purchase the collection although some important items (including the decorated horse mandible) appeared to be absent from the assemblage examined eighteen years earlier by Boyd Dawkins. The Committee paid Kendrick's surviving relatives £120 with a view to creating a local museum. Sadly over the following century Llandudno treated its premier archaeological collection with indifference and neglect. It took the Library Committee until 1902 to simply place the collection in glass cases in Llandudno Library. The collection was never catalogued, no further research or conservation work was undertaken and the library display was uninspiring and uninformative to visitors. This neglect had far reaching consequences.

Destructive Dilly Dallying

Whilst Kendrick's collection gathered dust in the library a keen amateur archaeologist, Frederick Dally (1838-1914), was amassing another vitally important collection of unique artefacts from the Great Orme. Dally was a fascinating character, born in London he emigrated to British Columbia in 1862. Travelling extensively around Canada as a pioneer photographer he compiled an invaluable visual record of traditional communities before their destruction by modernity. After returning to Britain in the late 1870's he settled in Wolverhampton but frequently journeyed to Llandudno to pursue his passion for prehistory.

Dally was drawn to Llandudno by Kendrick's discoveries and after visiting him at his workshop he persuaded Kendrick to sell him several of his most important finds. A number of items missing from the collection purchased by Library Committee in 1898 later appeared in a catalogue of objects offered to the Committee following Dally's death in July 1914. This catalogue lists 82 lots of archaeological items (including the celebrated decorated horse mandible), some lots consist of as many as 40 individual artefacts.

In a letter dated 29th August 1914 Dally's son wrote from London concerning his father's collection to G A Humphreys of the Llandudno Library Committee, 'During his lifetime he frequently expressed his grave disappointment that the *Kendrick Collection* was put away in an upper room in the Free Library without attempt at classification or description, and feared, should he present (ibid) the antique relics that he had taken so much pains to collect during thirty years, these might share a similar fate. Hence my father's view was that Llandudno would probably value his collection more if they had to pay for it and he therefore wished me to ask a nominal sum of £35 (thirty-five pounds) together with the cost of removal; to Llandudno'.

Humphreys prevaricated and despite being clearly advised by Dally junior that, 'failing an early acceptance of this offer, I am charged with other arrangements for disposal of the collection' he made no satisfactory response and virtually all of Dally's vital evidence of Llandudno's ancient past has now been lost for ever.

Meanwhile the Kendrick collection lay neglected in Llandudno library until 1968 when prompted by the apparent demise of Llandudno Field Club the Librarian loaned it to a private museum in Rhos on Sea. The museum no longer operates and the whereabouts of its exhibits are unknown.

All is Not Lost

Kendrick's Cave has been much altered, we are not even sure in which of two interconnecting caverns he uncovered the most significant finds. The artefacts themselves have been dispersed but all is not lost. In recent years further excavations of Kendrick's Cave have been undertaken and efforts made to properly record, analyse, trace and even re-acquire Thomas Kendrick's original artefacts. In 1971 the British Museum (BM) traced and examined a collection of nine cattle and deer's teeth originating from Kendrick's cave and purchased locally, in the early 1930's by a Mrs Dowler of Penrhyn Bay. The BM has also identified but failed to recover a couple of inscribed and perforated bear's teeth from Kendrick's cave included in a sale catalogue at Glynllifon, Caernarfonshire in 1932.

In 1959 the BM traced the decorated horse mandible and purchased it from a young Worcester collector named J R Wright. The Museum was ignorant of the location of the mandible between 1885 and 1959 and seemed unaware of the intervening role of the Dally Collection. When, in 1914, Llandudno allowed the Dally Collection to be sold it was probably purchased by local dealer Holland before being broken up and dispersed through a series of retail sales.

Unique Importance of Kendrick's Cave
Despite the losses recent research allows us to group Kendrick's Palaeolithic finds into five main categories;
- a flint blade
- an incised horse jaw bone
- ten perforated and decorated animal teeth
- five incised metacarpals of roe deer
- the skeletal remains of four humans

Each group of finds has been ascribed to an Upper Palaeolithic date of between about 10,000 to 8,000 BC and taken together they are unique. In the opinion of Jill Cook and Roger Jacobi, of the British Museum, 'This group of finds is without parallel in north-west Europe'. They are sufficiently significant for each category to warrant separate consideration.

Flint Blade
Ignored by contemporary accounts and misdated by most modern reports, a flint blade in the British Museum Kendrick's Cave collection has recently been described by Jill Cook and Roger Jacobi as having 'a striking platform of a form known in Creswellian assemblages'. In other words its style suggests it was made around 12,000 years ago and indicates humans were present on the Great Orme as the ice was disappearing.

Analysis of the dark grey, fine-grained material comprising the blade by the British Geological Survey identifies it as Epidiorite best matched by specimens from Cornwall. If this tool originated from Cornwall it raises intriguing questions about Llandudno's earliest occupants. Had they journeyed overland from older settlements in the east, as we assumed, bringing with them tools acquired via ancient trading networks or was it possible that they had arrived by sea. Maybe they had walked from the east but acquired the blade from maritime traders calling in on the Orme?

Horse Mandible

The horse jawbone is covered with inscribed chevron patterning so extensive and effective that it is described by British Museum as 'the only piece of artwork dated to the end of the last Ice Age or Late Glacial period in Britain' (illustrated).

The decoration would have been accomplished with a sharp flint tool, probably after the horse had been butchered and eaten by the clan of hunters and their families. The beast would been a smaller, deeper jawed specimen than those we are generally familiar with today, a Wild Horse (Equus Caballus) probably resembling the extant Przewalski's horse. These creatures favoured the open steppe lands of the post glacial period and their extinction in Britain coincided with dense re-afforestation. The open landscape created by the windy free draining limestone environment of the Creuddyn would have been very attractive to herds of horses and hence their predators which inevitably included Palaeolithic hunter gatherers.

Although stone-age people had not yet learned to domesticate horses they exploited them in a variety of other ways. They made tent-like shelters from their hides as well as producing clothes and boots, wearing their teeth as decorations, their bones for making needles and harpoons tips (held firmly in place using a natural glue extracted from bones), burning their fat for illumination and consuming their flesh as a tasty food source.

Just as native Americans both exploited and revered the buffalo, Palaeolithic Llandudno man may well have preserved and decorated the horse mandible as an object of veneration.

Decorated Teeth

More than a dozen decorated animal teeth have now been recovered from Kendrick's Cave. Most were found by Kendrick himself and of these most come from ancient wild cattle and few from deer. All are decorated with lines horizontally incised across the root and perforated at the tip. They have been dated to about 10,500 BP and would originally

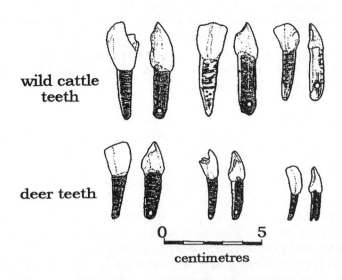

wild cattle
teeth

deer teeth

0   5
centimetres

Decorated Teeth from Kendrick's Cave

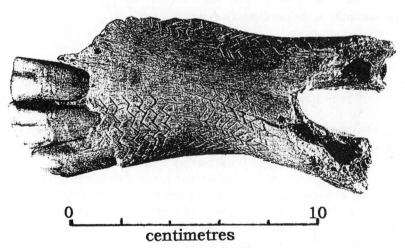

0   10
centimetres

Decorated Horse Mandible
from Kendrick's Cave

have been strung as a necklace. A wolf canine found by Melvyn Davies in 1979, is similarly decorated, perforated at the root tip and carbon dated to a similar period. Whilst perforated prehistoric teeth are commonly found in Britain decorated examples are extremely rare and confined to a few sites in the southern France, northern Spain region. These Llandudno teeth are unique in Palaeolithic Britain.

Incised Metacarpals

Variously described as 4, 5 or 6 metacarpals the collection long housed at Llandudno Library was examined by Melvyn Davies on 12th September 1986 who concluded that the incomplete fragments of bone originally came from five separate metacarpals of roe deer. These bones each carried a series of roughly parallel and unevenly spaced horizontally inscribed lines. Similar archaeological specimens have been found elsewhere, notably at Gough's Cave, Cheddar and they have been variously interpreted as tallies, calendars or gaming pieces.

Davies analysed the grouping and spacing of the marks and concluded that there was an apparent lunar significance that he suggested might be linked to observation of local tidal heights. Davies went on to remark that, 'Kendrick's Cave is a coastal cave and mussels, periwinkles and limpets have been shown by excavation to be an important part of the inhabitant's diet.'

Human Remains

Although Boyd Dawkins believed the remains belonged to four individuals more recent examination by Melvyn Davies (1991) suggests there may only have been three individuals buried, but of course some bones may have been lost over the intervening century. Davies also acknowledged that a thin-walled skull fragment might have come from a child and so could represent a fourth burial. It is suggested that these individuals may well have been buried with some ceremony as they appear to have been accompanied by significant grave goods. It is interesting to note that the horse mandible, the incised teeth and the marked metacarpals all show clear evidence of having been intentionally stained red with powdered haematite which was customarily included in ceremonial Old Stone Age burials.

Melvyn Davies's suggestion that the bone tallies may record tidal observations has received some support from recent isotopic analysis of the human bones that established beyond doubt that their original owners consumed a largely marine diet. Recent research indicates Palaeolithic man enthusiastically hunted grey seal who were forced to breed on remote islands to escape perdition.

Meanwhile Over at Tan y Bryn

Confirmation that Homo sapiens occupied Llandudno in the Upper Palaeolithic age was confirmed in 1989 after preliminary excavations were carried out by Duncan James at a cave in the grounds of Tan y Bryn, at Craig y don. Although the earth inside Ogof Tan y Bryn showed signs of disturbance it was considered to indicate only comparatively modern attempts to extract soil for garden purposes. No formal excavation had previously taken place and 'a brief 1 square metre trial sounding 20 centimetre deep in the entrance of the cave yielded eight patinated flints with hacked bone fragments from large animals'. At least two of these flints could easily be recognised as Creswellian tools suggesting that like Kendrick's Cave, Ogof Tan y Bryn was occupied around 12,000 years ago. Despite the enormous potential archaeological importance of this site no formal excavation has yet been completed.

Stone Age Llandudno

It's fair to conclude that twelve thousand years ago extended family groups of hunter-gatherers visited Llandudno. They wouldn't have been confined to just Kendrick's and Tan y Bryn caves but sheltered in countless other nooks and crannies in the local limestone. They camped under 'benders' in good weather but evidence of these and other equally ancient sites can no longer be traced. Eventually these hunter-gatherers began to corral animals instead of just chasing them and to cultivate plants where they had previously collected them from the wild.

It was no sudden change but over a few millennia farming gradually replaced hunter-gathering as the predominant lifestyle. Houses began replacing caves as the Old Stone Age gave way to the New. About 8,000 years ago Llandudno became less of a favoured seasonal hunting ground and more of an all year round Neolithic farming settlement.

Chapter Three

Llandudno's First Farmers (6,000 BC – 2,000 BC)

Eight thousand years ago all traces of tundra landscape had long since disappeared from the Creuddyn. Average temperatures rose to 17 degrees Celsius, a couple of degrees higher than today. Extensive grasslands were in many places dotted about with bilberry and juniper. Scrubby birch shrubs colonised more sheltered parts and soon small copses of birch woodlands appeared. Willow grew in damper valleys but it wasn't long before hazel became fairly common. Oak made inroads in the comparatively warm and dry early part of this period and was joined in the latter part by ash and alder as the climate became markedly more damp.

Meltwater from ancient glaciers caused sea levels to continue to rise above those experienced by Llandudno's Paleolithic visitors. As a result the Continental Shelf had been inundated and Britain had become an island. Anglesey had been isolated by the earliest meltwaters but back in the days when Kendrick's cave was first occupied the Menai Strait had been a mere river valley. By Neolithic times rising seas had transformed an inconvenient valley into a formidable tidal barrier.

In 1912 Boyd-Dawkins estimated Llandudno's Neolithic coastline extended some 3.3 miles out from its then existing limits. This now appears exaggerated but the coast certainly moved hundreds of metres inland before sea levels stabilised around 3,500 BC, leaving a coastal configuration similar to that existing today.

Evidence of the Creuddyn's Neolithic coastline appears from time to time at exceptionally low tides when fossilised tree stumps can be seen protruding from muddy sand off both Llandudno's North and West Shores. In March 1909, for example, the trunks of oak trees 51 inches in diameter were uncovered 200 yards out from the Hydropathic Hotel. These ancient offshore tree remains have, in recent years, produced carbon-dates of around 5,000 years BC proving that the coastline has altered considerably but not yet enabling mapping of the Neolithic coast with any high degree of accuracy.

Examining the Evidence

The most significant change from Paleolithic to Neolithic life was a move from hunter-gathering to farming. The Neolithic population of Wales was probably only around 2,300 people and despite the Creuddyn being a favoured settlement area it is unlikely that its population ever exceeded

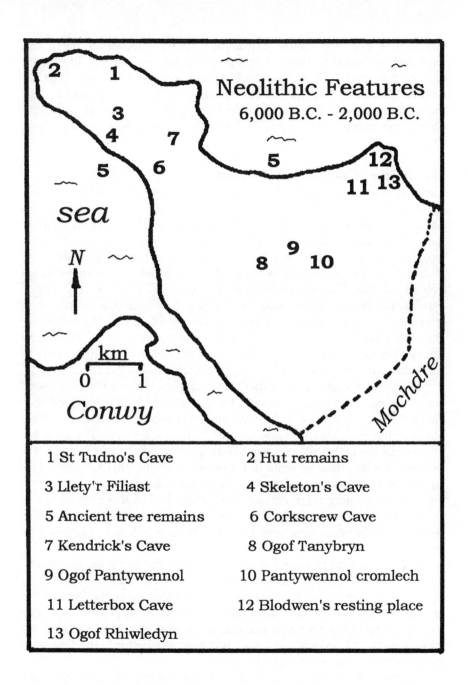

Neolithic Features
6,000 B.C. - 2,000 B.C.

sea

N

km
0   1

Conwy

Mochdre

1 St Tudno's Cave   2 Hut remains

3 Llety'r Filiast   4 Skeleton's Cave

5 Ancient tree remains   6 Corkscrew Cave

7 Kendrick's Cave   8 Ogof Tanybryn

9 Ogof Pantywennol   10 Pantywennol cromlech

11 Letterbox Cave   12 Blodwen's resting place

13 Ogof Rhiwledyn

100 in this era. Fortunately for archaeologists local caves were still exploited in Neolithic times, leaving invaluable evidence of life in the emerging agricultural era. Kendrick's Cave continued in use whilst six further limestone caverns were occupied by an expanding and increasingly settled local population. Of these, two are on the Little Orme, one in the cliffs above Bodafon Fields and three on the Great Orme.

Llandudno's First Named Resident

Llandudno's earliest 'named' resident lived on the Little Orme almost 6,000 years ago. Despite establishing that two nearby caves were occupied around that time it's not known which, if either, she called home. Nicknamed Blodwen, her skeleton was discovered in 1891 by workmen at the Little Orme quarry. Her bones had lodged about 15 metres from the surface down a narrow rock fissure. From near the bottom of this fissure quarrymen recovered a collection of ancient mammalian bones whilst near the surface they found a Bronze Age spearhead (this particular artefact will be considered in the following chapter). Details of the discovery site were recorded in a paper read to the Geological Society in London by G H Morton following his visit to the quarry and discussions with the site manager Robert Storey.

'At the north-east corner of the headland there is a remarkable boss of limestone named Trwyn y fuwch, the top of which is a hundred feet above the sea and it appears to have slipped down from a corresponding recess in the cliffs about a hundred feet higher. The principal reason for this conclusion is that the obscure bedding in the fallen mass is nearly on end and the limestone is quite unconnected with the adjacent cliffs. The fall seems to have occurred in pre-Glacial times for there is a deposit of red earth containing fragments of chert, and a bed of fine-grained white sand covered with boulder clay, one hundred and fifty yards wide between the isolated mass and the cliffs from which it is supposed to have fallen.'

Morton went on to record specific details of the findspot, 'one of the fissures in the rock was found to contain the teeth and bones of bear, hyaena, rhinoceros and other mammalia a few feet above the floor of the quarry, while some thirty or forty feet higher a skull was found, and near the top of the cliff a bronze spearhead some twelve inches in length. All these objects had probably fallen or had been washed into the fissure at different times from pre-Glacial to recent'.

All artefacts, including Blodwen, were handed over to Lawrence Lord of Bacup, Lancashire who had a proprietorial interest in the 'Little

Orme's Headland Limestone Company'. Lord gave the ancient animal bones to the Liverpool Free Museum, who promptly lost them but fortunately he donated both the spearhead and Blodwen's skeleton to his local Natural History Society, who have looked after them ever since.

Unfortunately Llandudno lost track of Blodwen and her archaeological significance wasn't appreciated until in 1995 local historian, Ken Dibble of Penrhyn Bay determined to seek her out. After contacting the Bacup Society it was agreed to temporarily transfer Blodwen from Bacup Museum to the Palaeoecological Research Unit of Manchester University to facilitate scientific analysis of the skeleton.

After 14 months of investigations in July 1996 J Roberts, D W Shimwell and M E Robinson of the Research Unit published their report, which they summarised as follows, 'The bones are thought to be from a female who died between the ages of 54 and 63 years. Her death occurred around 3,510 BC. She was approximately 5 feet tall and of a fairly robust build. Degenerative arthritis of the cervical spine and right knee and the rugged acromial ends of both her clavicles indicate that she had led a physically arduous life. More specifically, these features suggest that she was used to carrying heavy loads on her head and heavy weights with her arms extended by her sides. These heavy weights may have been water or milk containers. It is possible that she was suffering from, and perhaps died of metastatic (secondary) cancer which may have spread from a primary site in the breast.'

Ogof Rhiwledyn

Quarrying has radically altered the Neolithic era topography of the Little Orme destroying some caves and altering the accessibility of others. Ogof Rhiwledyn (SH 815 827) on the north face of the headland is now a difficult cave to approach but was probably a lot easier to enter in prehistoric times when it was used as a burial chamber. Excavations by J D Blore and Melvyn Davies recovered the remains of three children aged 4, 8-9 and 12-14 years respectively. Initially no adults were discovered because a metre thick layer of limestone accretion prevented exhaustive excavation but Melvyn Davies eventually uncovered adult bones and teeth beneath the stalagmite floor. Nevertheless the nature and deposition of artefacts uncovered suggested to Blore that the cave itself was used only for burials and occupation was otherwise confined to the entrance platform area.

Finds included an amber bead, two slate points, an antler pick and assorted animal bones. This assemblage suggests occupation at least a millenium after Blodwen's demise, right at the end of the Neolithic period. The slate points could have been leather workers' tools, the pick had been fashioned from an antler tine of a roe deer whilst amongst a variety of animal bones those of sheep and oxen displayed clear signs of butchery marks.

Letterbox Cave

Letterbox Cave (SH 814 824) is named after the wide, low shape of its opening. Situated just below and to the east of the summit of the Little Orme it was explored by Geoffrey David and pupils of St David's School, Llandudno, in June 1978. The material excavated was subsequently analysed by Melvyn Davies. The remains of ox, red deer, sheep and fox were found and a number of human bones, probably originating from a single individual aged about 17-25 years were identified.

Ogof Pant y Wennol

One kilometre south-west of Letterbox Cave at a height of 80 metres on the escarpment of a limestone ridge above Bodafon Fields, lies Ogof Pant y Wennol (SH 808 816). Excavations by Dr Kevin Mason and Melvyn Davies in 1974 supported by work completed by Tom Stone, ably assisted by Wilma and Susan Jones, between 1979-81 established this as a key Neolithic site. The remains of 4 adults and 2 babies were buried in Ogof Pant y Wennol and a wide variety of tools and animal bones recovered.

Use of the cave extended over a long period beginning maybe 11,000 BC as a shelter used by animals including a woolly rhinoceros. When humans first sought shelter around 6,000 BC they probably had to evict animal occupants.

These prehistoric residents were primarily hunters and fisherman producing small, sharp stone tools known as microliths used for cutting and scraping or attached to shafts to make arrows and spears. Occupants of Ogof Pant y Wennol shaped these microliths from both flint and a flint-like stone known as chert.

Later residents produced a characteristically Neolithic leaf-shaped arrowhead and a convex stone scraper, both of flint. Discarded flint flakes indicate cave occupants created these tools themselves in situ. Further artefacts recovered by Tom Stone include a bone needle, an antler pin and a fascinating bone tally. Typically Neolithic are recovered pottery fragments classified by archaeologists as 'Peterborough series, Ebbsfleet type' for producing pots was a Neolithic innovation along with weaving. Significantly a carefully waisted pebble excavated from Pant y wennol evidences the occupants ability to weave or at least create simple nets for the pebble appears to be a comparatively rare example (in Britain at least) of a net sinker.

As Tom Stone dug down through successive layers of cave debris he noticed that the abundance of marine shells encountered in the top layer diminished as he reached lower, very early Neolithic levels. This may well indicate that Llandudno residents consumed increasing amounts of shellfish as rising sea levels brought the coast nearer to their doorstep requiring a shorter walk to reach a convenient collection place. Interestingly, stable isotope analysis of a six thousand-year-old Ogof Pant y wennol skull shows that mid-Neolithic residents certainly still got most of their food from the land rather than from the sea.

Kendrick's Cave

Offering shelter from prevailing winds and an entrance platform facing the warming rays of the rising sun ensured Kendrick's Cave remained a desirable residence for many generations. Archaeological finds span several eras and Neolithic artefacts include bone and antler awls, antler pins, a small flint axe head, flint knives, a broken flint leaf-shaped arrowhead and potsherds.

Lloches yr Afr

Not far from Kendrick's Cave but discovered almost a century later, in October 1973, can be found a rock shelter, Lloches yr Afr (SH 779 838) alongside the Marine Drive. Originally a natural cave Lloches yr Afr was opened up to the elements and hence seriously archaeologically compromised by the construction of the Marine Drive in 1877. Nevertheless the shelter retains a rare piece of Neolithic evidence. Excavation of burnt hearth layers revealed a pit with a post-hole alongside, probably the remnant of an ancient wooden crane that held meat being cooked over a fire. Such arrangements have been found in France but this is, so far, unique in Britain. Another unusual find at Lloches yr Afr was a small pile of white, quartz pebbles whose significance remains entirely unknown.

Less uncertain is the earliest occupation of the cave for wild animals colonised Lloches yr Afr at the end of the Ice Age with a horse tibia showing clear signs of having been crunched by a hyaena.

Humans moved in as early as 7,000 BC or 8,000 BC and left behind flints and food remains including the vertebra of a fish. Limpet and mussel shells were in abundance and bone tools had been sharpened to produce effective 'winkle pickers'. Successive hearth layers contained masses of animal bones (ox, sheep, deer and pig) but nothing large, prompting Melvyn Davies to suggest that carcasses were being butchered elsewhere and the site used mainly for occasional, short term

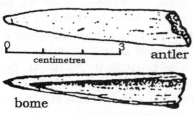
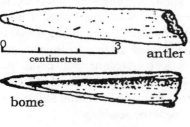

antler

bome

awls, Kendrick's Cave

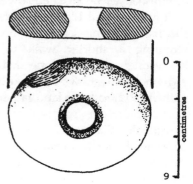

stone mace, Abbey Road

flint arrowhead,
Ogof Pant y wennol

pottery rim-sherd,
Kendrick's Cave

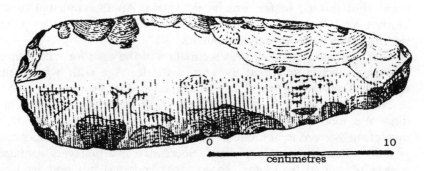

stone axe head, West Shore

shelter and snacking rather than enduring family occupation. Human use of Lloches yr Afr may have ceased around five thousand years ago with nothing later recovered than a fragment of Neolithic pottery.

Ogof Tudno

Situated west of Lloches yr Afr high and above the Marine Drive is a cave that has been much disturbed by the activities of Victorian copper miners. With at least four entrances and two names (sometimes called 'Badger's Cave') Ogof Tudno (SH 764 842) has if anything had too much recent attention but nevertheless retains indications of Neolithic occupation. Excavations in 1976-7 uncovered bone fragments of several animals including sheep, pig, goat and horse along with a quantity of limpet and mussel shells and some fish bones. Charcoal contained in the earth along with the above remains indicates human activity such as the cooking and consumption of the animals identified. With no artefacts found it seems likely that Ogof Tudno was probably used only as a temporary shelter by Neolithic hunters.

Skeleton's Cave

In the late 1850's an ancient human skeleton discovered in a cave on the Great Orme was described and illustrated in a brochure published in 1860 for William Brown who put his fascinating find on public display at Quatford Cottage. Unfortunately the bones were subsequently lost and even the findspot is now uncertain. It is now generally accepted that the skeleton was probably Neolithic and the findspot is identified as 'Skeleton's Cave' (SH 767 825) on the south-eastern slopes of the Great Orme but Brown's original brochure locates the cave at the opposite end of the Orme (although in all other respects it accurately describes 'Skeleton's Cave'). Brown's brochure is in parts more poetic than scientific, but in lieu of other evidence it's worth quoting at length, 'These bones, which consist of a human skull with the upper jaw, containing a complete set of upper teeth, the principal bones of the legs, the arm bones, a lumbar vertebra, a portion of one of the ribs, and other small human bones, were discovered in a cave on the north-west side of the Great Orme's Head'. As can be seen from the engraving included in the brochure the skull and other bones were disarticulated but bound together in a single large calcareous mass. 'The approach to the cave, which is situated about 350 feet above the level of the sea . . . is so precipitous as not to be accessible without difficulty and the mountain above is nearly perpendicular . . . The dimensions of the cave at its entrance are about five feet in length, two feet six inches in height, and two feet from the front to the back part, where a passage resembling a chimney, not visible on inspecting the cave from the outside, rises and conducts at the height of three or four feet from the floor to a dark narrow cavity six or seven yards long descending towards the west, and another, which passes upward in an oblique direction towards the east, where the bones were deposited. The head was placed with its back part downwards and the face looking upwards towards the east, and appears to have been introduced before the body and extremities.' Extrapolating from a detailed examination of the teeth it was concluded that the individual was a male 'in the prime of life'. Drawing on the fact that a Roman coin of the reign of Domitian (ruled 81-96AD) was found in a layer above the skeleton it was reasonably concluded that the bones were of a considerably earlier date.

On a more contentious, and amusing, note the brochure concludes, 'Among the numerous natural attractions at Llandudno none can be considered more interesting than these extraordinary curiosities. The phrenologist and all who are engaged in a philosophical inquiry into the progressive natural history of man, will find much to invite their investigations and the objects have been so well arranged by Mr Brown for public inspection that they may be conveniently viewed by and explained to all classes without offending the delicacy of the most fastidious; and all religious and sober-minded persons, who have studied the inspired writings of Moses must derive infinite satisfaction from observing how wonderfully the discoveries of geology confirm the history of the creation, as revealed to mankind, and recorded by him in the sacred volume of Genesis.'

Neolithic Transhumance

Neolithic residents weren't simply troglodytes. Agriculturists continued hunting and herdsmen occasionally occupied convenient caves. In upland Wales traditional patterns of seasonal change of habitation continued until the nineteenth century. Typically farmhouses adjoining lowland pastures were preferred during winter whilst dwellings alongside hill grasslands were occupied during milder summer periods. This traditional pattern of transhumance was marked by the use of hafod (summer residence) and hendre (winter dwelling). Throughout most of north Wales this facilitated best use of grazing lands but in ancient Llandudno the pattern may well have been reversed. Whereas Llandudno's lowlands may have proved too wet in winter the area's mild maritime micro-climate ensured that even on the uplands grass continued to grow, providing fertile grazing throughout the colder months. The principal dwellings of Neolithic Llandudno may well have been on the Great Orme with seasonal summer camps erected on the lowlands.

Widespread Neolithic Activity

Fortunately Neolithic life wasn't confined within roundhouses and caves and a variety of prehistoric artefacts recovered from all over the Creuddyn help build a picture of prehistoric pastimes. The range of artefacts fit comfortably into four categories; axes, holed stones, scrapers, and arrowheads.

The classic New Stone Age tool is the polished stone axe (illustrated) and nine recorded examples have been found in the Creuddyn (date of find quoted first, current location in brackets);

- Circa 1880's; A broken Graiglwyd axe 11 cm in length, with the bottom section missing, indicating an original length of approximately 18 cm, was found on the western slopes of the Vardre in the area now known as Gannock Park (Llandudno Museum)
- Circa 1886; A dark grey, finely ground stone axe was found in Llandudno in the late Victorian era. Neither the finder nor the exact location were recorded but the origin of the stone was established as Graiglwyd, Penmaenmawr (Pitt-Rivers Museum, Oxford)
- 1924?; Reverend Charles Rogerson of Nottingham found an axe, with the tip broken off, in the Bishop's Quarry on the Great Orme. Thought to have been used to break open animal bones to extract the marrow. (Llandudno Museum)
- February 1936; Fine, polished stone axe discovered at Cae'rdial, on the eastern slopes of the Vardre. The stone matches samples from Menai area. (Llandudno Museum)
- July 1936; John P Thomas of Alexandra Road, Llandudno recovered a 19 cm long polished axe from 80 cm below ground at Llanrhos, opposite Plas Mariandir, and later told reporters, 'Two of the lads were digging a drain and one of them tossed it to me saying, *What do you think of that for a funny kind of stone?'* (Llandudno Museum)
- May 1952; David Paterson discovered a 22.5 cm long, partly polished stone axe from the shingle beach near the Gogarth end of the sea wall adjoining the Great Orme. Microscopic examination by Professor Shotton of a sample of stone from the axe established its origin as the Graiglwyd quarries, Penmaenmawr (Bangor Museum?)
- Circa 1960; An axe of Graiglwyd stone was recovered from Cwm Howard by J I Platt (Llandudno Museum)

41

- 1970; Whilst engaged in horticultural work at Haulfre Gardens, Great Orme, a gardener named Mr Harris uncovered a Neolithic axe head (Retained by finder)
- 1980; A damaged, broken and water-worn handaxe was found at a depth of 1.5 metres in a newly excavated trench by Sue Jones. It measures a maximum of 10 cm by 6 cm and retains large flake marks (Retained by finder)

These finds show Llandudno's Neolithic residents realised that whilst local limestone produces excéllent cave homes it is useless for tool making. Limestone hammers would shatter on impact but fortunately an excellent, enduring stone was available not far away at Penmaenmawr. In fact stone quarried at Graiglwyd was so desirable that in Neolithic times it was traded all over Britain. One axe appears to have been fashioned from Menai stone but it is difficult to interpret its significance. Maybe the user brought it with him, perhaps its characteristics best suited a particular purpose, it could have been traded at an attractively low value, maybe the user just wanted something different or liked the colour? The possibilities are endlessly fascinating.

Holed Stones

Equally intriguing are the two holed stones discovered in Llandudno. Although both were found in the same area there was almost ninety years separating the discoveries;

- 1911; William Jones of 'Brynmor', Abbey Road found a holed stone with an hourglass perforation at a depth of just over a metre, probably whilst digging a hole in his garden. The stone (illustrated) is slightly ovoid, measuring 18cm by 15cm with a 1.2 cm hole in the middle (Llandudno Museum)
- 2001; Nigel Bannerman found a similar stone in the garden of another house in Abbey Road (Retained by finder)

Looking like modern donuts it is still a bit of a mystery how these stones were used by Neolithic people. The hole was probably made to enable the tool to be mounted on a wooden handle but why the torus shape? Decorated examples are thought to have been used as ceremonial maces, chunky, more pointed samples are referred to as 'axe-hammers' but these comparatively light-weight models would hardly impress with either their air of authority or potential for destruction or aggression.

Flint Scrapers

The use of flint scrapers for de-fleshing skins and stripping the bark from sticks is more obvious but surprisingly few have turned up over the years in the Creuddyn;

- 1935; A small hoard of Neolithic flint tools including scrapers (also a highly polished rubbing stone and a well-pitted hammer stone) was uncovered from beneath the turf, resting on the bedrock, in a valley at the north-western end of the Great Orme. Microscopic analysis of the stone scrapers revealed one to have originated from Graiglwyd whilst another, very large, round example had been fashioned from a fossil. Discarded chippings established that shaping of these stone tools had taken place on site (Previously Prestatyn Museum, present location unknown)
- 1947; Flint end scraper (illustrated) recovered from extreme north-western tip of the Great Orme by J H Morris (National Museum of Wales, NMW)
- 1957?; Unidentified find of a flint scraper on the Great Orme (NMW)
- July 1978; Duncan James found a stone scraper at the north-eastern corner of a field at Pyllau Farm, Great Orme (Untraced)

Arrowhead Finds

Finds of flint scrapers might be rare but they outnumber discoveries of flint arrowheads. Leaving aside the Pant y wennol find (see above) there are only two other recorded Creuddyn examples and both are peculiarly large.

- 1897?; William Arnold picked up a flint barbed and tanged arrowhead near St Tudno's Church, Great Orme. The artefact was 7 cm long and the colour described as, 'light whitish-grey with light yellow splashes'. (Retained by family of finder)
- 1964; Michael White of Ellesmere Port discovered an 8.4 cm long un-barbed, tanged flint arrowhead at Maesyfachrell, Great Orme (Grosvenor Museum, Chester)

The eminent archaeologist W F Grimes observed that the arrowhead discovered by William Arnold was 'exceptionally large for Wales' but then the more recently found example is even larger. Perhaps one or both examples were designed as spear points rather than arrowheads. In either case it is clear that Neolithic settlers continued hunting as well as developing farming.

Farming Evidence

Archaeological evidence from a widespread range of sites indicates that people in Wales began farming about eight thousand years ago. As indicated, hunting was not immediately abandoned and the transition was probably accomplished piecemeal from hunting through herding to finally corralling and selectively breeding beasts. Similarly gathering plants might only have finally evolved into agriculture after first nurturing plants in the wild and protecting them from animal damage. The full transition must have taken several human generations and even then aspects of hunter-gathering remained. The exact transition process remains uncertain and would likely have varied from area to area.

Several models of change are possible. Some groups may have begun by taming wild dogs to help with hunting. A successful result would have encouraged them to try and domesticate larger food animals such as wild cattle. Their domesticated dogs would have then have proved very helpful in containing and controlling cattle. Once animals were farmed and then selectively bred to improve their domesticity and food value there was no need for tribes of humans to follow wild herds. This settled existence allowed and encouraged the cultivation of plants instead of collecting whatever could be found as the tribe trecked after herds of horse, cattle and deer.

Local evidence of Neolithic farming is seen in the vestigial field boundaries associated with the roundhouses described earlier and also by charred samples of emmer wheat discovered at Pentrwyn, Great Orme by David Chapman.

Settlement Distribution

The distribution of reported finds points towards occupation of the elevated areas of Llandudno and the Creuddyn. Although the land extended further out to sea than today little evidence of Neolithic use of the flatter, coastal fringe has been found. Shellfish and fish bone finds prove people were collecting seafood but did they really not farm or build houses upon this land? Much evidence might have been destroyed but nevertheless its absence is striking. Perhaps the flatter land was simply too wet and badly drained in Neolithic times. Recent borehole investigation of Neolithic levels taken at four separate Llandudno sites, North Shore, West Shore, the Oval and Penrhyn Bay all revealed peat was being formed around 5,000 BC. This is a sure sign that the soil was so sodden that the usual cycles of vegetative decomposition could not take place. Certainly it required artificial land drainage before much of Llandudno's flatlands could be turned over to the plough or to building development in the nineteenth century.

And So To Death

Neolithic man liked Llandudno's modest uplands where he left behind impressive burial remains. The best known Creuddyn tomb, Llety'r Filiast (illustrated), is situated half way up the eastern slope of the Great Orme, at a height of 150 metres, at the end of the appropriately named, Cromlech Road. The tomb comprises four massive upright stones protruding 1.25 metres above ground, topped by a huge capstone, part of which has broken off. Llety'r Filiast translates as the 'Lair of the Greyhound Bitch' and is an ancient name drawing on the symbolism of the female greyhound in Celtic myth. Although the name is not unique in Wales it is rare for a north Wales tomb to have a folk name at all. The structure though is of a classic 'Portal Dolmen' type characterised by tall entrance stones fronting a small rectangular chamber topped off with an enormous capstone. Typical of Neolithic north Wales such tombs are also found on the eastern coast of Ireland, which is indicative of thriving cultural and maritime links.

A century ago another cromlech was recorded on the Great Orme by eminent archaeologist W Bezant Lowe. Situated a few hundred metres to the north east of Llety'r Filiast and close to Wyddfyd Farmhouse. Bezant Lowe noted that the stones comprising the tomb, 'are situated on the left of the road and at the base of a steep slope. They seem to have escaped notice, as they are, to a great extent, concealed by a rather thick growth of thorn bushes. At present, there are two upright stones, forming two sides of a chamber, and at the back of one of these is another stone which may have possibly been part of another upright. Lying flat on the ground, at the back of these, is a fourth stone, which may have been the capstone'. Modern commentators have tended to dismiss Bezant Lowe's observations but a set of large stones just north of Wyddfyd Cottage certainly fits his general description.

The remains of another possible cromlech can be located on a ledge, near the summit of a north-facing, limestone cliff about 90 metres above sea level at Pant y wennol (SH 805 815). Two massive stones stand a metre high, topped by a 1½ metre long capstone. A fourth massive stone, probably another supporting upright, lies on the ground alongside. The whole certainly gives the appearance of being a ruined cromlech and although it is not well known locally it is sometimes referred to as 'Mainc y Gynhadledd' (Conference Bench). Other artificially placed large limestone boulders lying 6 metres away may well have an association with the cromlech forming a significant Neolithic site.

Llety'r Filiast

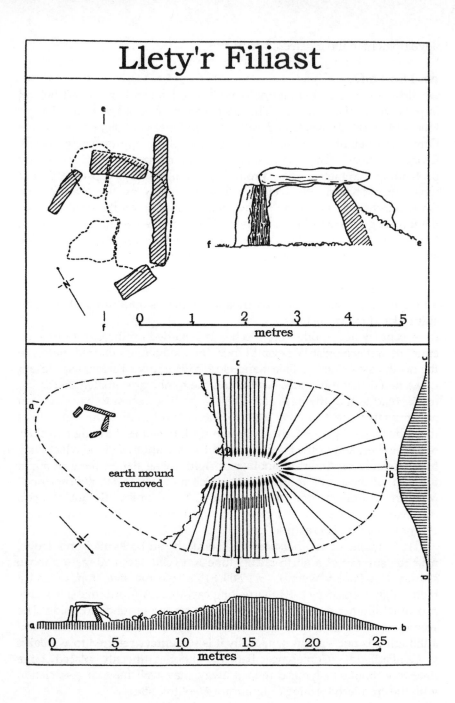

earth mound
removed

Neolithic Life in Llandudno

The wealth and variety of Llandudno finds suggests a continuity of settlement rare in Wales, where most sites of prehistoric occupation are far distant from modern towns and cities. Paleolithic hunter-gatherers came and went but from about 6,000 BC Llandudno was unlikely to have been completely abandoned although the Neolithic population of the Creuddyn is unlikely to have ever exceeded 100 people. By 2,000 BC the Creuddyn had settled into a largely agricultural way of life. With excellent stone tools available local farmers had little problem clearing woodland to make way for agriculture. Domesticated oxen pulled wooden ploughs, bees provided honey and selectively bred and specially trained dogs accompanied men on occasional hunting trips.

The Neolithic Creuddyn was probably self sufficient in food but traded local produce with adjoining clans and roving merchants in exchange for high quality stone such as flint or chert. The Creuddyn was locally favoured for its well-drained soils, convenient access to a rich harvest of seafood and mild maritime climate nevertheless Llandudno was essentially an insignificant place in New Stone Age Britain. Then, around 2,000 BC, a discovery made 5,000 years earlier in a place 2,000 miles away transformed Llandudno from a mere backwater into an ancient birthplace of Britain's prehistoric industrial revolution.

Chapter Four

Bronze Age Copper Miners (2,000 BC-500 BC)

Nine thousand years ago Neolithic people in Eastern Turkey prized an unusual orangey coloured rock obtainable at a site now known as Ergani Maden. Once shaped into beads and threaded onto leather thongs the rocks made attractive necklaces. Supplies were limited but it didn't stop experimentation and when the rock was hammered it kept an effective edge. Cold hammering was sufficient to produce a useful cutting tool from this 'native copper' but further experimentation proved heating over a fire caused the metal to become less brittle and created a more durable tool or weapon. The technique was so effective that it enabled Egyptian masons with copper tools to shape huge blocks of stone into pyramids that were the wonder of the ancient world.

With little native copper available it was thousands of years later before metal working was practised in Britain. By then people in the Balkans had learned how to smelt copper from inferior ores and how to alloy copper with tin to produce superior bronze tools. Production of this new metal began the 'Bronze Age' and effectively ended the European 'Copper Age' before it had even begun in Britain. Then around 2,000 BC the search for copper reached Llandudno, transforming it from an insignificant farming settlement into a uniquely important mining centre.

'A World Class Site'

Despite its Bronze Age significance Llandudno's ancient importance was forgotten by succeeding generations until one day in 1831 miners unexpectedly broke into ancient workings on the Great Orme. When the workers broke into the cavern, it was reported that, 'a broken stag's horn and part of two mining implements, or picks, of bronze (copper alloyed with tin), were found, one about three inches in length, which is in the possession of Mr Worthington, of Whitford, who at the period was lessee of the mines. The smaller, about one inch in length, was sent by Mr Stanley for exhibition'.

Eighteen years later, in October 1849, 'miners broke into another ancient working of considerable extent. The roof and sides were encrusted with beautiful stalactites . . . On the ground were found a number of stone mauls, of various sizes, described as weighing from 2 to 40 lb, and rudely fashioned, having been all, as their appearance suggested, used for breaking, pounding, or detaching the ore from the rock. These primitive instruments were similar to the water-worn stones or boulders found on the beach at Penmaen Mawr, from which, very probably, those most suitable for the purpose might have been selected. Great quantities of bones of animals were also found, and some of them, as the miners conjectured, had been used for working out the softer parts of the metallic veins . . . A semi-globular object, of bronze was found, about 1¼ inches in diameter, having on the concave side the stump of a shank or spike, as it appeared, by which it might have been attached to some other object. This relic, with a stone maul, had come into the possession of Lady Erskine . . . The miners at Llandudno observed, however that their predecessors of former times had been unable to work the hardest parts of the rock, in which the richest ore is found, for they have recently obtained many tons of ore of the best quality from these ancient workings. The original entrance to these caverns is not now to be traced. There were some appearances of fire and smoke upon the sides and roof of the cavern, when first discovered'.

Although stone mauls and bronze fragments recovered from these ancient workings were presented to the British Museum by William Owen Stanley, MP for Anglesey, in October 1853 no serious academic research on Llandudno's ancient copper mine was attempted for almost a century.

Most Victorian commentators simply assumed the ancient works were Roman. In an age of imperialism it seemed scarcely credible that native Britons could create such a sophisticated enterprise without the direction, engineering experience and organisational expertise of the Roman Empire. Although antiquarian Thomas Bateman (1821-61) rejected this popular attribution his argument cast further doubt on the abilities of native Britons. After examining tools from the Great Orme along with similar implements from Ecton Hill in Derbyshire Bateman declared that the, 'Romans never have used so clumsy a method of obtaining or pounding the ore'!

Veni, Vidi, Excavare?

In 1938 eminent archaeologist Oliver Davies arrived at the Great Orme's copper mine determined to discovery its ancient history. Unfortunately he found all entrances to the, by then completely abandoned, works had been effectively sealed and had to satisfy himself with an extended examination of old spoil heaps. He recovered a number of stone hammers (mauls) from mine dumps in the Pyllau area, just below the Great Orme Tram's halfway station before moving on to excavate a site at the West Shore where he found a few more. Drawing on his own expertise, interest and enthusiasm for the Roman period Davies inferred

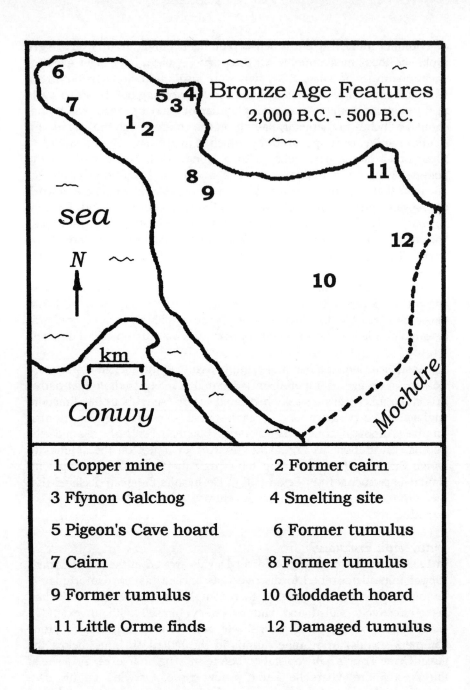

Bronze Age Features
2,000 B.C. - 500 B.C.

sea

N

km
0   1

Conwy

Mochdre

1 Copper mine   2 Former cairn

3 Ffynon Galchog   4 Smelting site

5 Pigeon's Cave hoard   6 Former tumulus

7 Cairn   8 Former tumulus

9 Former tumulus   10 Gloddaeth hoard

11 Little Orme finds   12 Damaged tumulus

that dating evidence from apparently associated coins and pottery established the ancient copper mine works as Roman. Having reinforced popular prejudice about the Roman origins of the mines Davies's view wasn't challenged as other academic archaeologists believed evidence for prehistoric mining on the Great Orme would in any case have been destroyed by later, nineteenth century, works. After all the ancient cavern discovered in 1849 had within three months been comprehensively blasted away by Victorian miners intent on extracting every last scrap of copper ore.

Duncan James Investigates

In 1976 amateur archaeologist, Duncan James decided to investigate Llandudno's long abandoned mine works for himself. After removing a mass of backfilled spoil James gained entry to two ancient galleries about 30 metres below the surface of an area known as Bryniau Poethion, just north of Davies's main Pyllau investigations. Although the prehistoric galleries had been partly reworked by later miners the unaltered sections were quite distinctive. The Victorian works showed obvious evidence of having been squarely cut with the use of iron tools and gunpowder whereas the ancient galleries were irregularly shaped and contained abandoned stone hammers, bone tools and charcoal. When this charcoal was radiocarbon dated it almost doubled the age of the mine put forward by Oliver Davies, indicating a date between about 1,300 BC and 1,000 BC. As Duncan James had suspected Llandudno's first copper miners were no abject slaves to Rome, which at that date was only an insignificant village above the Tiber, but Bronze Age excavators with a complex society of their own.

Unfortunately Duncan James's pioneering work appeared all in vain when in 1987 the local council proposed reclaiming the Pyllau site for use as a car park. When a preparatory mining survey revealed something of the extent of the ancient workings an alternative scheme was put forward to develop the mine as a public attraction. The Great Orme Bronze Age Copper Mine duly opened in 1991 and as research has continued its international importance has become firmly established.

Largest Bronze Age Copper Mine in Europe

Excavation of ancient galleries continue but archaeologists know the Bronze Age workings extend for more than 6 kilometres and go down to at least 70 metres below the surface level. Numerous samples, from various parts of the works have been carbon dated showing copper extraction took place throughout much of the Bronze Age and at least from 1,800 BC to 600 BC.

Almost 4,000 years ago work probably commenced with miners excavating open trenches running down into the naturally exposed cliff of the Pyllau Valley. Eventually it became necessary to tunnel underground following productive copper bearing veins. The ancient miners had no gunpowder to facilitate extraction but on the Orme they used firesetting techniques. Twigs and branches were carried underground and stacked against potentially productive faces. The gallery was evacuated and then the bonfire was ignited. When the fire had died down it was extinguished and cold water thrown onto the heated rock face causing it to crack. After the rock had time to cool miners would re-enter the gallery and chip away at the face that was by then much weakened making extraction of the ore much easier.

Stone Tools

Miners had a range of extraction tools at their disposal fashioned from a variety of materials. The most common were stone mauls, or hammers, used for bashing easily accessible ores from the rock face. Although more than 2,000 of these have been recovered from the surface spoil and underground workings only about 5% of them have been in any way shaped or modified before use. Varying in length from 5cm to 40cm and from 0.25kg to 29kg these stones were probably collected by the miners from the beach and carried up to the works in baskets, likely carried on their backs like rucksacks. Most mauls fit comfortably into the hand and were obviously selected as hand tools. The heaviest stones were either used two-handed or suspended in a harness and swung against the rock face. The modified hammers had been given some sort of groove to facilitate fitting to a haft or harness (illustrated).

Once the ore was extracted and taken to the surface it was pounded into fragments by process workers crouching over large dressing stones, or anvils. Around a dozen of these anvils measuring from about 40 cm to 60 cm across and 25 cm deep have been found on site with their use evidenced by wear marks. The fragmented ore was then ground on mortar stones turning it into a granular powder. Almost 30 of these stones have been recovered from surface spoil. They are typically about 30cm across, 10cm thick and have central, circular depressions on both upper and lower surfaces evidencing their use for grinding.

Bone Implements

Thousands of bones, horns and antlers, both complete and fragmentary have been recovered from surface and underground works. The overwhelming proportion coming from cattle with lesser amounts of pig, sheep/goat, deer, horse and minimal amounts of dog. Many of the bones were originally brought to the site primarily to provide food rather than mining tools with cattle bones preferred for the latter purpose. The miners selected particular bones to do specific jobs. The stronger limb bones suited chiselling work whilst the weaker rib bones made excellent gouges and scrapers. Wear marks on many bones provide vital evidence of the way in which they were used whilst some can even be matched with specific scratch marks on adjoining rock faces.

Metal Tools
Evidence of the prehistoric miners employing metal implements is much less certain. In 1868 Mine Captain William Vivian recorded the finding, underground, of a piece of an 'ancient copper implement or weapon'. Microscopic examination revealed that it was composed of about one third copper oxide, indicating a very crude form of smelting. Bronze fragments discovered underground in the nineteenth century were assumed to be burrs from chisels but metallurgical analysis has failed to establish their origin. If bronze chisels were in use the obvious question is, why has such scant evidence been recovered? It might be because bronze was so valuable it was only employed where especially difficult veins were encountered. Similarly any broken chisels would have been meticulously recovered for recasting.

Other Underground Artefacts
Although wooden tools were used in other prehistoric copper mines and an ancient oak shovel was recovered from Trecastell lead mine, in the Conwy Valley, none have been found on the Great Orme. The most likely explanation for the absence of wooden tools is that ground conditions on the Orme favour the preservation of bone but not timber. Wood was undoubtedly used in the mine as in many places impressed marks in the clay remain although the timber itself has long since decayed, leaving no material residue.

According to Owen Parry, in an article published in 1863 in Welsh in 'Y Brython', the ancient miners installed a drainage system of box-like channels comprising hazel twigs coated in clay to make them watertight. These window box like structures were affixed to the gallery walls, which they ascended in step-like fashion until they eventually reached the mine entrance. Explaining how the system operated, Parry pointed out that the clay lined hazel boxes had been 'stuck on the side of the rock, a yard and a half to two yards apart, one on top of the other, and when the lowest was filled it was emptied into the one next to it until the highest was reached, then that was emptied'.

Lighting
Evidence of how the mines were illuminated has proved extraordinarily elusive. Elsewhere ancient miners seem to have used burning narrow wooden tapers or spills either stuck in lumps of clay to keep them upright or held in the miner's teeth. With the poor preservation of wood on site nothing remains. Another possibility is that miners used basic oil lamps burning animal fat contained in small bowls. A curiously shaped, hollowed stone recovered from spoil heaps in the nineteenth century might have been just such a lamp but the bowl appears rather shallow to hold sufficient fuel.

An even more tantalising object was discovered underground in 1987. A hand-thrown earthenware pot, 24cm high and 19cm in diameter, it was initially considered nineteenth century but has recently been compared to similar pots recovered from prehistoric Austrian salt mines. Current theories suggest it might have been carried in a sling and used to convey hot charcoals underground to ignite timber for firesetting or possibly to light spills for illumination.

Washing the Processed Ores
After extraction, pounding and grinding the powdered rock was 'washed' to separate the ore from the host rock. Modern miners do the job by taking water to the extraction site but in ancient times miners found it easier to take the powdered rock to the water source. In Llandudno washing employed the use of slime pits where powdered rock was tipped into pools of water and whilst the surface material was skimmed off the heavier metallic ore concentrated at the bottom of the pool. Periodically the slime pool was drained and the concentrate scraped off the bottom, dried and then smelted.

On the Orme two springs, the 'Ffynon Rufeinig' and 'Ffynon Galchog' were traditionally said to have been used as ore washing sites by ancient miners. In 1909 John Roberts, a copper miner in Victorian times, identified Ffynon Galchog as an ancient washing site and recalled that 'many years ago tons of slime' had been recovered from around Ffynon Galchog and sent off to the smelters. The presence of mine waste at the site was established by archaeological excavations in 1990.

Investigations at Ffynon Rufeinig in 1996 recovered blue-green stained bone that provided a radiocarbon date calibrated to 1,400 BC. Other finds included small rounded nodules of the copper ores,

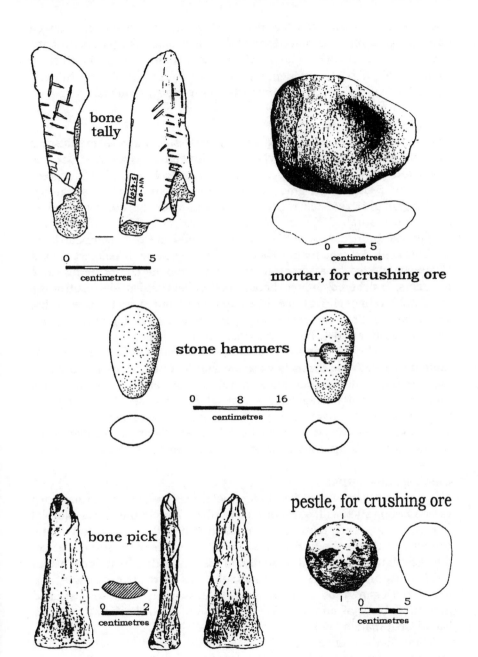

bone
tally

0   5
centimetres

mortar, for crushing ore
0   5
centimetres

stone hammers
0   8   16
centimetres

bone pick
0   2
centimetres

pestle, for crushing ore
0   5
centimetres

malachite and azurite, charcoal flecks and a flake of stone that may well have chipped off a hammerstone. Additional features identified at the site include earthworks, leats and pools that utilise a slight gradient to control water flow. The evidence leaves little doubt that Ffynon Rufeinig was indeed used as an ore washing site by Bronze Age miners.

Smelting on the Orme
Having identified the sites of extraction, processing and washing the ores the search was on to discover where smelting took place for the powdered rock had to be heated to a temperature of 1,100 degrees Celsius to produce axe-grade copper. Some commentators suggested smelting might have taken place elsewhere with the ore conveyed to areas with abundant timber for fuelling fires and tin for alloying the copper into bronze. Maybe the Llandudno ores had been shipped down to Cornwall for smelting? Then in 1995 local archaeologist David Chapman spotted an assemblage of prehistoric material, including stone hammers, butchered animal bones, pot boilers and shells protruding from an eroding cliff at the Pentrwyn headland, Great Orme. What particularly excited Chapman, an expert on ancient metal working, was the inclusion amidst burnt material in this collection of what he recognised to be fragments of copper slag. In January 1998 Chapman was funded by CADW to formally excavate the site to ascertain the nature of the eroding material and make a full record of the remains. 'This produced over 100 fragments of metal-working debris, the highest proportion of which was associated with a small, charcoal-rich feature'. The charcoal was dated to about 1,600 BC, establishing Pentrwyn as the oldest recorded copper smelting site yet discovered in Britain.

Casting the Copper
The simplest way to cast the molten metal was to pour it into flat open stone moulds such as that reported by Albert Way in the Archaeological Journal to have been found in the mine in 1849 and passed onto William Stanley and thence the British Museum. An example of the sort of flat axe this technique produced is currently on display at the Great Orme Mines (GOM). Approximately 4,500 years old this particular example was found at Deganwy by Ron Sowter. A later, slightly more sophisticated flanged flat axe of around 2,000 BC was found on the Great Orme by David Chapman in 1976.

These Early Bronze Age (EBA) axes were hafted by making a hole through a wooden handle that then tended to split in use (illustrated). Improved designs were produced in the middle and later Bronze Ages,

56

the palstave (MBA) and the socketed axe (LBA) but these both required more sophisticated casting methods. No moulds of the MBA or LBA have been recovered from the Creuddyn but numerous axes exemplifying these later designs have been discovered locally.

The Diminishing Gloddaeth Hoard

In 1686 a spectacular hoard of MBA palstaves was uncovered in a field at Gloddaeth, Edward Lhuyd recorded that, 'There were about fifty of them found under a great stone placed heads and points'. Sir Thomas Mostyn acquired the majority of the axes and preserved them at Gloddaeth Hall. However by 1912 the hoard was much diminished and its findspot inaccurately described by Bezant Lowe in volume one of, 'Heart of Northern Wales'. Lowe reported, 'A collection of seven bronze Celts at Gloddaeth, belonging to Lady Augusta Mostyn, are probably those found in 1720 at Deganwy'.

By volume two, published in 1927, a further axe had inexplicably disappeared although a photograph of the remaining six was provided. When the contents of Gloddaeth were sold off in 1935 the depleted collection was transferred to Mostyn Hall. Six years later an article published in Archaeologia Cambrensis nailed down the shifting provenance of the hoard but by then a mere five axes remained.

Isolated Axe Finds

In December 1892 a Bronze Age axe discovered in Llandudno was donated by Mr T Sheraton to the British Archaeological Association. A late Bronze Age socketed axe recovered by William Brookes from Gogarth, Great Orme was acquired by the NMGW in September 1956 whilst a MBA palstave recovered, in 1990, from Llandudno's North Shore by metal detectorist R T Gibbons is displayed at the GOM.

Although little is known of the prehistory of Pydew, Creuddyn a couple of Bronze Age axes have been recovered from the area. Around 1864 an undescribed specimen was found at Cilmeityn Bach and retained by William Owen of Llangystennin whilst in 1999 amateur archaeologist and metal detectorist, Wayne Evans turned up a MBA unlooped palstave on the Glanwydden side of Pydew. The latter can be seen at Llandudno Museum.

Two Spearheads and a Theory

Only a couple of Bronze Age spear points have been recovered from the Creuddyn. One example, found on the beach at Llandudno by R T Gibbons is displayed at GOM but the more impressive specimen is held by Bacup Museum. The Bacup spearhead (illustrated) was recovered, around 1890, from the top layer of 'red drift' soil filling the same fissure that lower down contained 'Blodwen', the Neolithic skeleton described previously. Like Blodwen the spearhead was donated to Bacup by Lawrence Lord. The slender leaf-shaped blade is 30cm long, has a maximum width of 4.5cm and was probably made around 900 BC. Although there is no obvious connection between Blodwen, who died two and a half thousand years earlier archaeologists suggest the fissure might conceivably have retained ritual significance with the spearhead having been cast in as a ceremonial offering.

Riddle of the Riddells

Theories abound on the significance of a Bronze Age find described in the 19th May 1898 edition of the Llandudno Advertiser, 'Two youths residing at *Brankleigh*, Craigydon, named Lewis and Arthur Riddell were rambling on the Great Ormeshead, when they discovered among the debris at the back of a large loose rock, near the *Pigeon's Cave*, two Decantean shoulder brooches, together with a bronze celt (or head of a battle-axe), and a dart point, also of bronze. One of the brooches, both of which are hollow, of fine gold, and in breadth about the diameter of a penny, weighs nearly three-quarters of an ounce, and is beautifully engraved with twenty-one concentric lines, whilst the other bears traces of having been enamelled' (illustrated).

This seemed unlikely to have been an isolated loss but why would anyone in the Bronze Age have deposited a collection of such valuable artefacts in a cave on the Orme? The Advertiser imaginatively sketched in the entire scenario, 'An antiquarian conjecture is that their original owner, a Pictish chieftain, lost his life and sword in battle, whereupon a fellow Decantean tribesman hid his remaining weapons and ornaments.' The reporter helpfully informed readers, 'Prior to the Roman conquest, the territory of the Decantean tribe included the Creuddyn peninsula and environs.'

A century later we recognise that the Riddells discovered not a pre-Roman, 'Decantean' collection but an earlier, Bronze Age hoard. Unfortunately modern explanations can't match the Victorian confidence in elucidating the original event.

The hoard was originally kept by Deganwy archaeologist, Dr Willoughby Gardner but was acquired, in 1956, by the NMGW. Research has established the axe as a LBA unlooped palstave, the 'dart point' as more likely a leather workers awl and the brooches as earrings or possibly 'lock rings' for fastening a cloak. The rings and axe both betray a

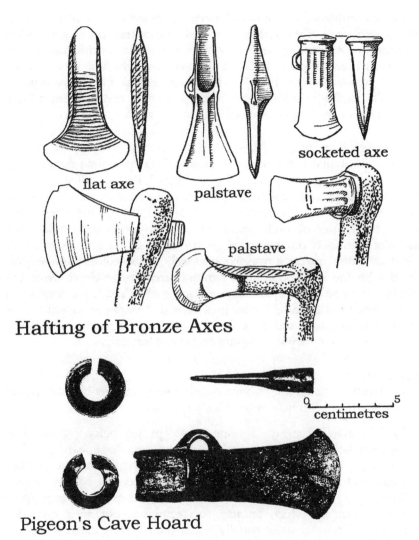

flat axe

palstave

socketed axe

palstave

Hafting of Bronze Axes

0 ⌞_____⌟ 5
centimetres

Pigeon's Cave Hoard

Little Orme Spearhead
approx 30 cms

strong Irish influence and may well have originated there. Taken together with the evidence of the awl the hoard now appears more likely to have belonged to a Bronze Age leather worker than a 'Pictish chieftain' and to have either been secreted by him in the cave from which he was for some reason unable to recover them, or to have accompanied his body as grave goods. The difficulty with the latter explanation is that no human bone finds have ever been reported from Pigeon's Cave.

Bronze Age Housing

Despite the expansive activity of Llandudno's copper mine no sign of a Bronze Age mining village has yet been located. Perhaps all sign of huts originally located alongside the mine were obliterated by the later works, maybe they remain to be discovered elsewhere on the Orme. Similarly, despite the scatter of finds across the Creuddyn no site of domestic habitation definitely datable to the Bronze Age has yet been established. It is likely that the area was continuously occupied throughout this period with the local population concentrated on the Great Orme but with farming and hunting taking place across the Creuddyn. A range of caves, wooden huts and roundhouses provided semi-permanent homes whilst tents, benders and rock shelters offered temporary or seasonal shelter for summer shepherding and occasional hunting.

In Memoriam

No evidence of distinctive Bronze Age housing remains but six ancient burial sites survived until comparatively recently;

- As Victorian property developers swept all before them local commentators recorded tantalising glimpses of a disappearing ancient landscape. John Roberts, Bryn Celyn recalled the destructive work of builders at Bryniau Poethion, Great Orme, 'When the Baptist Mission Room was built close by, in 1860, stone was used for this purpose from a carn in which an urn was founded containing cremated remains.' Carns, or more usually cairns, are typically massive earth or stone mounds, up to 20m across, raised 2m or so over Bronze Age burials. The deceased were often cremated with the ashes contained in a pottery urn. John Roberts surmised that the Bryniau Poethion ashes were the remains of a Roman soldier who had fallen in battle on the Orme but we now recognise his account as a classic Bronze Age burial. A reference by Llandudno Field Club to 'some sepulchral urns containing human ashes and bones found . . . near the cromlech on the Great Orme' appears to refer to the same site.

- John Roberts also remembered that, 'The site of Madoc Street was formerly a flat field, about the middle of which was an oval-shaped mound or small hill. This was called Y *Gorseddau*, high places or thrones. The adjoining field on the south-west side was called *Cae yr Orsedd*, Field of the Throne. At that time part of these fields were part of Pwllygwichiad farm. Mr Peter Jones (d. 1834), who was the tenant, decided to level the mound referred to, and in doing so he discovered several earthen urns containing what was believed to be cremated human remains.'
- In 1858 a Bronze Age barrow was demolished to make way for the extension of Vaughan Street to connect with Llandudno's new railway station.
- In 1912 Bezant Lowe recorded that, 'When the Marine Drive was being made round the Great Orme's Head, what was probably a round barrow, *many yards across*, and probably of the Bronze Age was destroyed. Near the centre were clear *traces of fire* but neither bones nor other relics were discovered.'
- In 1906 Llandudno Field Club recorded that, 'An urn containing ashes was excavated from a funeral mound close to the toll-gate on the Llandudno Road.' Although clearly identified on Ordnance Survey maps this Penrhyn Bay tumulus, on the corner of Marine Road, was also destroyed by developers. Within a few years of the Field Club's observations it was damaged by builders erecting Bron Derw for local solicitor, Thomas Hughes. In 2005 its destruction was completed with the demolition of Bron Derw and the erection of flats on the site.
- One Bronze Age cairn survives, on the south-western side of the Great Orme. There is no record of any finds ever having been recovered from the site and although much of the mound is considered modern the kerb stones are almost certainly original.

The Great Orme's ancient copper mine survives as eloquent testimony to the industry and inventiveness of Llandudno's Bronze Age community but around 500 BC its output slumped as knowledge of a new ubiquitous material for tool making reached north Wales.

Chapter Five

Pen Dinas Hillfort
and the Roman Occupation (500 BC – 400 AD)

From 500 BC two new factors affected life in the Creuddyn. The warm, dry climate enjoyed by the Bronze Age deteriorated and north Wales experienced a prolonged period of colder, wetter weather. The cultural and political influence of northern Europe also began to intrude as the power of Celtic tribes reached its apogee. Celtic culture dominated Europe from the Black Sea to the Channel, frustrating the imperial ambitions of Republican Rome. Celtic smiths smelted, cast and hammered iron into superb practical tools and weapons whilst Celtic craftsmen elevated metalworking from a skill to an art. Even today, the Celtic 'La Tene' style of metalwork remains unsurpassed in its subtle manipulation of symbolism and pattern. The technique emanated from Celtic central Europe but within a century its influence reached north Wales creating such pieces as the exquisite 'Cerrigydrudion Hanging Bowl'.

Celtic Creuddyn
The language of the Celts proved as distinctive and influential as their aesthetic. By 500 BC, Celtic languages were being spoken throughout Britain, although it is impossible to identify exactly how transmission occurred. In the past it was assumed that such sweeping cultural change implied invasion and domination but it is now generally accepted that the 'Celticisation' of Britain was an altogether more gradual, subtle process of acculturation. The trading of goods, ideas, skills, language and other cultural practices, probably along with a certain amount of immigration, over the years transformed Britain's Bronze Age into a Celtic Iron Age.

Celtic society was tribal with north-eastern Wales, including the Creuddyn, the preserve of the Deceangli, although territorial boundaries with the Ordovices have not been accurately mapped.

Llandudno's Iron Age Hillfort
Back in the Neolithic era farmers had practised a slash and burn agriculture, clearing trees, growing crops until the soil was exhausted and then starting the cycle again elsewhere. By the Iron Age communities were finding themselves a bit short of accessible, fertile land. As the

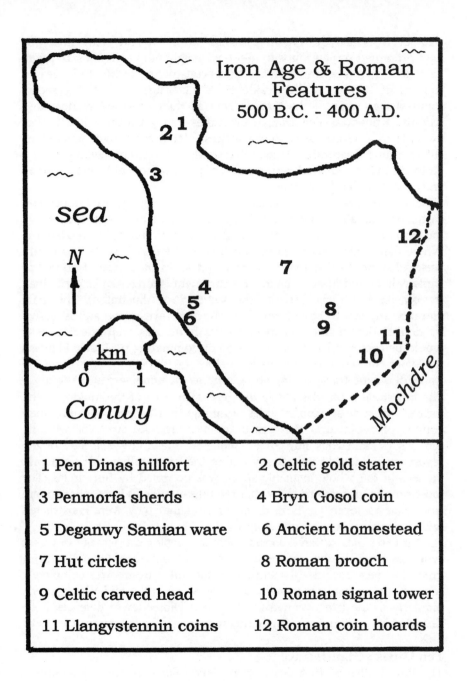

Iron Age & Roman Features
500 B.C. - 400 A.D.

sea

N

km
0 1

Conwy

Mochdre

1 Pen Dinas hillfort

2 Celtic gold stater

3 Penmorfa sherds

4 Bryn Gosol coin

5 Deganwy Samian ware

6 Ancient homestead

7 Hut circles

8 Roman brooch

9 Celtic carved head

10 Roman signal tower

11 Llangystennin coins

12 Roman coin hoards

weather worsened the growing season shortened and competition for food prompted some groups to raid their neighbours to avoid starvation. As a defensive measure Iron Age tribes constructed fortified villages on convenient hilltops. Celtic residents of Llandudno selected a rocky, south-eastern spur of the Great Orme as their most easily defended redoubt. Known as Pen Dinas (sometimes Pen y Dinas) it is a typical example of a Welsh promontory fortress, 140m high, with precipitous cliffs forming a natural protection that needed little strengthening.

In 1911 George Alfred Humphreys, of Llandudno Field Club, mapped and described Pen Dinas thus;

'The area is seven acres in extent, outlined by a rampart of stones and earth, and full advantage was taken of the rocks which protruded above the general surface, to incorporate them in this inner line of defence. Where there are no rocky cliffs, which is chiefly on the north and north-west sides, artificial defence was resorted to, in the shape of double or triple vallum and fosses. The inner escarpment is longer and steeper than the others, as will be seen by the section AA (illustrated). The main entrance appears to have been along the south-west side, and is shown by double dotted lines on the plan. Its route was well selected, as it would be commanded by a succession of dominating positions. Between the inner ramparts and the valley below, on the south side, there are traces of a wide track leading straight up to the famous rocking stone . . . The limestone protrudes above the general surface of the interior of the fortress, in almost parallel lines, running from north to south, then curving off westwards. Between these lines of rocks, are to be seen the remains of numerous hut circles, while on the north-west side of the seven acre area and immediately within the triple-vallum defence work, practically the whole available space was occupied by hut circles. The most prominent remains show that the huts – 60 or 70 in number – were from four to seven yards in diameter, and that they were constructed with concentric rings of large stones.'

Pen Dinas has suffered considerable archaeological damage in recent centuries. In 1835 the Reverend Robert Williams recorded, 'A wall of great thickness encircles the summit of the hill', but this was completely robbed out, probably to provide building stone in the mid-Victorian era. Similarly in the late twentieth century Pen Dinas' lower defences were denuded by workmen seeking hardcore as a base for the nearby car park.

Pen Dinas's Significance

The Rev. Williams' 1835 description of Pen Dinas is no longer entirely accurate but he did identify one of the most enduring riddles of Iron Age hillforts'. Were they permanently occupied or only resorted to when the community came under attack? Williams favoured the latter view, believing Pen Dinas was used, 'not for a constant residence, but only as a place of refuge on the approach of an enemy'. Most modern archaeologists would agree, identifying the absence of a reliable water supply from most hillforts as powerful evidence of their unsuitability for long-term occupation. Pen Dinas would certainly be forced to surrender, or its occupants die of desiccation, if an enemy laid siege but tribal rivalries generally incited raids rather than extended warfare. It was only in the latter part of this period, with the arrival of the Romans, that siege warfare seriously undermined the viability of hillforts.

Pen Dinas may not have had immediate access to a water source within its ancient defences but as Humphreys' map indicates there is a well sited immediately west of the fort that could have been used to provide day to day supplies for the hillfort. If a raiding party turned up they might have been satisfied by making off with a few head of the tribe's horses or cattle. If frustrated by villagers managing to get their beasts safely enclosed within the fort's defences the raiders would likely have ridden off in search of easier pickings.

Excavation Evidence
If Pen Dinas was permanently occupied excavations might uncover domestic artefacts from successive periods, if only resorted to in time of attack one might hope to recover slingshot, arrowheads, spearpoints and other assorted weapons. Unfortunately no comprehensive, archaeological excavation of Pen Dinas has ever been completed. Two limited, unpublished, excavations were undertaken, one in 1867, by W W Foulkes, and a second, by P Sirett, in 1960. Two archaeological surveys of surface features have also been completed, by G A Humphreys in 1911 (illustrated) and by Gwynedd Archaeological Trust in 1993.

Little is known of the Victorian excavation, but it is recorded that in one hut circle Foulkes uncovered the shells of limpets and snails, animal bones and a single piece of Roman Samian ware pottery. The 1960 dig investigated a single hut, about 5m in diameter, situated on the western rim of Pen Dinas. It was the specific aim of the dig to ascertain whether the fort had been permanently or just seasonally occupied. Although no formal report was published I did locate informal notes describing the finds.

Artefacts recovered included, 'A fine example of a deer horn knife handle (red deer). It was complete and undamaged but showed no trace of a blade having been in place. Judging by its condition it had been lost

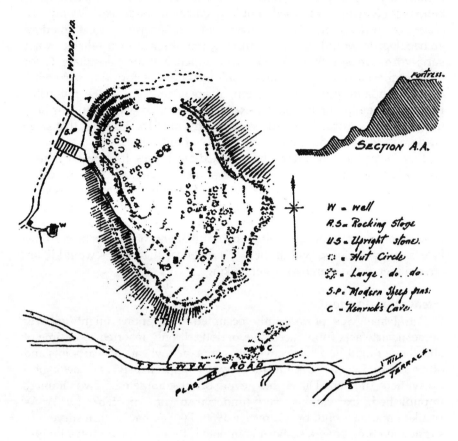

SECTION A.A.

W = well
R.S.= Rocking Stone
U.S.= Upright stone.
○ = Hut Circle
◉ = Large. do. do.
S.P.= Modern Sheep pens.
C = Kendrick's Cave.

Scale of feet.

0   100   200   300   400   500   600   700   800   900   1000/

G. A. Humphreys.
1911.

Pen y Dinas.
Great Ormes Head.

66

or misplaced by the one time owner and not deliberately discarded. An equally fine bone needle, also undamaged. A small bone button, a disc of animal bone neatly pierced in the centre.' Although several small round pot-boilers (pebbles heated in a fire and dropped into liquid to boil it in a pot that could not itself have withstood the effects of direct heat) were also found no trace of pottery was discovered. Lots of ancient food debris was found, the bones were, 'mainly those of the common Celtic sheep, mostly young animals. At one period, however a young ox made its way onto the menu, evidence of which is provided by a part of the skull and jaw together with several other bones, some of which bear knife marks. Two small but unusually fine cow horns were also recovered, both had been carefully sawn from the parent skull and were probably destined for use as knife handles or some such utensil. These horns were from the wild white cattle of the day, known now as the Chillington cattle. Other remains indicate the consumption of pigs (not apparently domesticated) and deer. There were no bird remains present. Several large horse teeth were also found but with no associated bones. Shellfish formed a large part of the diet. A vast quantity of limpet shells was uncovered, at one place a bed several inches thick had accumulated. Mussel shells were, to a lesser extent, in evidence, also several oyster shells, one of which was neatly pierced and smoothed, perhaps for use as a food scraper.'

'The hut itself consisted of a dry-stone wall, wide at the base and narrowing towards the top, probably roofed over with branches and skins, a covering that could be easily renewed at each seasonal occupation. No trace of a more permanent form of timber construction, such as a centre post was found. (Any such post would leave a soil mark or discoloration at its base even after complete disintegration). Winter winds and rain would reduce the height of the wall annually, most of the rubble falling inside the hut and thus hindering the formation of accurate strata, judging by the position of most of the food debris this in-filling was never frequently cleared out. Several small makeshift fireplaces were uncovered, at widely varying places and at different levels. All were constructed of sea washed stones, brought up from the beach for that purpose, as the local stone is particularly unsuited for use as firestone as heat causes it to crack and disintegrate.'

After laying out the finds and deconstructing the hut itself Sirett began to edge towards a conclusion, 'The excavation uncovered no occupation levels, such as are found in permanent habitations, nothing even remotely resembling a floor was located. Very few articles of human usage were found . . . The site did not, as we hoped, prove to be a permanent settlement but rather a camp used occasionally . . . by a community of herdsmen.'

Moving way beyond the evidence Sirett went on to draw several questionable conclusions but his work certainly adds weight to the idea that Pen Dinas wasn't permanently occupied. Whereas Sirret favoured the notion that it was used as a summer pasture by a community permanently based in a village further inland my own speculation leans more towards occasional use as a defensive redoubt by Iron Age residents of the Great Orme.

Iron Age Residents of the Great Orme

The remains of ancient stone huts show Iron Age occupation of the Great Orme was not confined to Pen Dinas, in four locations substantial hut-circles are evident.

- On a level shelf above the cliffs at a height of 130 metres above sea level at the far north-western tip of the Great Orme (SH 755 841) lie the remnants of at least three Iron Age houses. In 1912 Bezant Lowe could detect, 'the remains of a cluster of hut-dwellings, sufficiently numerous to form quite a *village community*. Although the Marine Drive is cut through the village, few have noticed these pre-Roman habitations. The circles are clearly visible by reason of the saucer-shaped cavities in the ground, and the large stones placed concentrically in the outer mounds. Mr G A Humphreys could not find any trace of a stone-pitched floor and from their general characteristics he considered them to be early examples.' A century later the walls have been robbed and the interiors disturbed but it is clear that the huts each originally had an external diameter of about 5.5 metres.
- Thirty metres higher and a little further inland (SH 756 838) on a level plateau are the remains of a 9.5 metre roundhouse with another, slightly smaller, hut situated 80 metres further south-south-west. A large triangular shaped field enclosure of much denuded limestone blocks appears to be contemporary with these two ancient dwellings.
- About 200 metres east of the Great Orme summit (SH 770 834), 168 metres above sea level, in an area know locally as Bryniau Poethion, can be found the relatively substantial remains of a single hut circle, 8 metres in diameter.
- On a level shelf, 125 metres above sea level on the northern side of the Great Orme at a place called Hafnant (SH 764 841), can be found another Celtic hut-circle. The external diameter is about 5.8 metres and to the east and south-west can clearly be seen the remains of field walls, field banks and terraces.

Other Creuddyn Celtic Huts

Besides the Great Orme two other Creuddyn sites retain clear evidence of Iron Age occupation, Gloddaeth and Deganwy. In Coed Gaer, above Gloddaeth Hall, can be found a small settlement comprising two hut circles. One is so distinct and impressive that some commentators dispute its authenticity, suggesting it was constructed as a Celtic folly by a now forgotten resident of Gloddaeth Hall.

The remains of the smaller structure consist of a circular depression 5m in diameter and about 60cm deep at the centre with some large limestone blocks lying near its periphery that might have originally formed part of the hut wall. The larger hut retains the base stones of a double wall, about 1.5m thick constructed from concentric circles of limestone, with an internal diameter of 8m. The 1.6m wide entrance to the hut opens to the south-east.

Although no trace of any outlying, defensive walls can be detected the huts are situated just below the ridge of the hill and sheltered from prevailing winds and inclement weather by a shallow limestone outcrop. Lying at a similar height to Pen Dinas the hut dwellers would have originally enjoyed an extensive outlook.

The Iron Age homestead at Deganwy is situated on the northern slope of the Vardre at a height of about 80m. Marked on the current Ordnance Survey map, the remains of at least three hut circles can be detected.

Significant Finds

Besides the occupation evidence three isolated discoveries on the Great Orme, at Pabo and on the Little Orme offer further clues to the early Celtic period.

According to Llandudno Field Club, 'A British gold coin was found on March 11th, 1924, by Mr Howell Idris Parry, in his garden at Llwyn Fryn, in the valley on the S W side of the ancient hill fort of Pen y Dinas (ibid). These coins are divided into two classes, uninscribed or without lettering and inscription, and inscribed with a lettered inscription, in addition to various figures and devices. These ancient British coins are rude copies of contemporary Gaulish coins, which are in turn, degenerate imitations of Greek coins current around the Mediterranean. The weight of this coin is 4 penny weights. Similar coins have been found in the south of England, but this is the first known in north Wales. The accompanying sketch map (illustrated) will give an idea of the position of the spot (A) where the coin was found.'

W F Grimes (1939) proffered a more specialist description of the coin, 'It belongs to the series introduced in the 1st century BC, apparently by the Atrebates, a Belgic tribe which in Britain occupied the middle Thames Valley. Obverse and reverse preserve something of the origin of the type in the gold stater of Philip II of Macedonia, which in the second century BC was in common use in the Roman world; but illustrate an advanced stage in the debasement due to unintelligent copying by Keltic (ibid) moneyers which began in Gaul. This is the first coin of its type to be recorded in Wales; it can only have reached here in the course of trade.'

As Grimes implies this gold stater demonstrate that two thousand years ago Llandudno was culturally linked to the wider world. Trading with Iron Age Europe brought in the language, the technology and the cultural and religious ideas of the Celts. As Francis Lynch (1991) observed a, 'feature of Celtic religion which is widespread both on the Continent and in Britain is an almost obsessive interest in heads, either actual or representational'. A feature exemplified by our second Iron Age find, discovered by local archaeologist Frank Jowett in the late twentieth century. Jowett realised that a metre long boulder set into a wall separating two gardens at Pabo had, at one end, been carved into a characteristically Celtic head. Classical writers observed that Celtic warriors would decapitate defeated enemies and return home with their heads to be displayed as trophies on the walls of their houses.

The Celt's ferocity in combat was balanced by an artistic sensitivity exemplified by a little known artefact found on the Little Orme in the late twentieth century by metal detectorist Colin Darroch. A Late Iron Age bronze harness mount (illustrated) of the mid 1st century to mid 2nd century that perfectly combines beauty and function (now housed in Llandudno Museum). The distribution of wear marks on this cheek ring, caused by the rider pulling up on the reins, suggest that it comes from the right-hand side of the bridle. With four points of attachment it's unlikely the ring became detached as the pony was being ridden but it could have easily been lost during a process of repairing or renewing the bridle. Ponies of the period were usually 12 to 13 hands high and although they had probably been used as pack animals in Llandudno in the Bronze Age this harness ring evidences the fact that the Celts introduced true horsemanship to the Creuddyn some two thousand years ago.

Tribes and Tribulation
Celtic Creuddyn evolved a way of life distinct from the Bronze Age but there was considerable continuity. Many materials and practices continued to form part of daily life but as Celtic power declined in continental Europe the Creuddyn became vulnerable to dramatic and

70

forced change imposed by the invading legions of Imperial Rome.

Gaul and northern Spain might have been Celtic in 500 BC but as the new millenium dawned continental Europe fell to the overwhelming might of Rome's armies. Whilst Rome retained central control of its legions the Celtic world comprised a disunited, aggregate of tribes sharing loose cultural affinities. Whilst Celts of the northern and western fringes of Britain attempted to retain their independence the tribal chiefs of south-eastern England increasingly developed trading and political links with agents of the Roman Empire across the Channel. By AD 43 when the Emperor Claudius set in motion the conquest of Britain the allegiance of southern England was assured and provided a convenient bridgehead for launching an assault upon Wales.

As the most notable export of the province of the Deceangli came from their metal mines their territory, which included the Creuddyn, was an important target for an Imperial army instructed to secure Britain's mineral wealth as well as to subdue hostile tribes. Invaded by troops under the control of Publius Ostorius Scapula in AD 47 the Deceangli surrendered with little resistance. In his 'Annals of Imperial Rome' Tacitus recorded the tribe's debacle, 'The army was led against the Ceangli (ibid). The country was devastated, booty collected everywhere, while the enemy declined to risk a battle, or, if he made a stealthy attempt to harass the marching columns, found his treachery punished. And now Ostorius was within measurable distance of the sea which looks towards Ireland, when an outbreak of sedition among the Brigantes recalled a leader who was firm in his resolution to attempt new conquests only when he had secured the old.'

The advance of Ostorius was halted by the resistance of two other Welsh Celtic tribes, the Ordovices and the Silures and it was only after his death that in 61 AD Anglesey was eventually captured. Even then Boudicca's uprising forced Rome to withdraw troops to put down her rebellion. In 77 AD Agricola finally secured permanent control of north Wales with the use of troops advancing from Chester. Military control of the Creuddyn was guaranteed by the erection of a Roman cavalry fort in the Conwy Valley at Caerhun, know then as Konovium.

Veni, Vidi, Vici

The Romans certainly came, saw and conquered, but the question of what else they did has puzzled local archaeologists and historians for years. Some commentators claim that the Romans worked the ancient copper mines whilst others dismiss the suggestion out of hand. The evidence is incomplete, indirect and scattered. There are no definitive

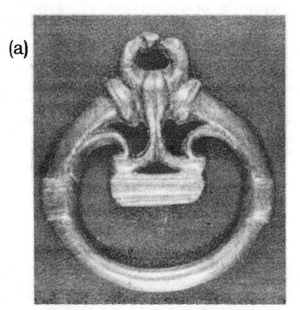

(a) Iron Age and (b) Roman
Finds from the Little Orme

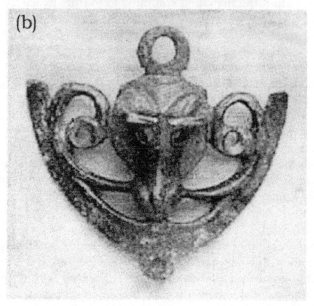

documents, no relevant mining accounts or mine plans. Neither have any characteristically Roman tools ever turned up in the mineworks. This absence of artefacts has prompted several authorities to insist that the Romans did not mine Great Orme copper. It certainly casts doubt on such an enterprise but perhaps the balance of circumstantial evidence favours an opposite conclusion.

Copper Cakes

Whilst the tools of Roman copper mining have not turned up on the Great Orme the products of just such an enterprise have been found at three other sites in the local area. In 1861 metallurgist John Percy reported that a 22lb copper cake had been found at Conwy (approx 6 km from the Great Orme). Stamped into the middle of the cake were the letters **MF** or **ME**. Percy was convinced that the copper had been smelted in the area. In 1906 the cake was acquired by the British Museum.

In 1921 two substantial fragments of copper cakes, one bearing a Roman stamp, were discovered 7 km from the Great Orme, just to the east of Bryn Euryn, Llandrillo yn Rhos. Following the demolition of the old National Schoolhouse, on Bryn Euryn Lane, workmen digging foundations for a new house unearthed an ancient skeleton that appeared to have been interred together with the copper pieces. Willoughby Gardner examined the finds and conveyed the copper to Bangor Museum for safekeeping and further investigations but sadly they disappeared without trace.

The most intriguing find is a complete copper cake, 30cm in diameter and weighing 18kg uncovered at Caerhun (15km from the Great Orme), in 1801 and acquired by the Mostyn family. If the Romans had actually mined the Great Orme the enterprise would have come under the military and financial jurisdiction of the fort at Konovium. This Caerhun cake bears the stamped inscription, 'SOCIO ROMAE' which reflects the Roman system whereby the military guaranteed the security of the works whilst the actual mining business was leased out to private partnerships (*Societates*). Impressed obliquely in smaller letters is the word, 'NATSOL' that reveals the local agent to have been a certain 'Natalius Sollers'. Unfortunately the Caerhun cake is rather similar in appearance to examples recovered from Ynys Mon and so it is just possible that the copper could have been mined there rather than on the Great Orme.

Roman Coin Finds at the Little Orme

Local finds of Roman coins are commonly cited to support to theories of Roman mining. The two most substantial hoards were buried 400m apart alongside the road running through the pass dividing the Little Orme's Head on the north from Mynydd Pentre to the south. In 1873 the road was being repaired at a point near a small farmhouse called Ty'n rhewl, opposite the entrance to the lane leading to Penrhyn Old Hall. When a section of old stone-walling was disturbed an ancient vase was exposed. Composed of reddish earthenware, glazed a dull yellowish colour on its upper parts, one-handled, somewhat pear-shaped, 38cm high and 60 cm in girth, being widest in the upper part below the neck and flanged a little outwards to the rim. The vase contained 5,032 Roman bronze coins cemented together by a green oxide into a solid mass. The finder kept his discovery to himself and it wasn't until after he died that in 1902 his nephew sold the hoard to a Manchester dealer who, without first recording details of the collection, put the coins on the market whereupon it was broken up and dispersed. Fortunately the collection was subsequently traced and expertly examined by Willoughby Gardner and W Sharp Ogden who, after successful separation and conservation treatment, identified the coins as mostly 'third brass' with a few 'second brass' and all in magnificent condition. Three thousand of the coins had been minted in Britain whilst the rest came from Gaul. The main mints represented were London, Treves, Arles and Lyon whilst of the 5,032 coins approximately 1,400 bore the image of Emperor Licinius I (307-324 AD) and 3,500 depicted Constantinus Maximus (306-337 AD). Careful analysis of the dating evidence suggests that the hoard was deposited sometime between 310 AD and 317 AD, but why was it hidden?

On the 10th January 1907 another hoard was unearthed just along the road. Willoughby Gardner recorded details of the findspot, 'on the left hand side of the road leading from Llandudno past Craigside Hydro to Colwyn Bay, opposite to the stable entrance of Simdda Hir, on Mrs Holden's property. The exact spot was in the bank, 12 yards back from the road, entering the gate just east of the ruins of the old farm buildings. The bank is at the foot of the Rhiwleden (sic) cliffs which tower 150 feet above it on the north.' Workmen were excavating soil and rubble from the Little Orme to use in the construction of Mostyn Broadway when they unearthed a collection of coins at a depth of 2 ½ ft (75cm). Mrs Holden of Simdda Hir (now 'The Craigside Inn') took possession of the 452 coins recovered whilst in the low winter light workmen continued with their delivery of two cart loads of rubble which was dumped in Llandudno onto land lying between the church and the Grand Theatre. Next morning passers-by noticed coins glinting amongst the deposited earth and soon an eager crowd were engaged in a frantic search to recover Roman coins. By the end of the day at least 100 coins had been found but some were probably taken away and a few others likely incorporated into the making of Mostyn Broadway! Fortunately the police, acting for the Treasury, rounded up most of the finds as they, at first, believed the coins were composed of precious metals and hence comprised 'Treasure Trove'. Subsequently returned to the finders most of the coins were immediately sold to dealers and interested visitors. With the help of Llandudno antique dealer, Mr F Holland, Willoughby Gardner eventually acquired 350 of the coins and succeeded in inspecting a further 100 and so ultimately a fairly comprehensive record and analysis of the hoard was made. Nearly 97% of the coins proved to be British struck money of the fascinating 'Emperor' Carausius, and this remains the largest hoard of Carausian coins ever found in Britain. Carausius was a usurper, a humbly born naval commander who claimed control of the Empire. Granted command of the Roman fleet in the Channel by Emperor Maximian in AD 286 Carausius was so outstandingly successful in defending Britain from piracy that popular acclaim spurred him on to ever more ambitious schemes. After cutting deals with the Scots and Picts he secured their support for a military attack on the Roman Governor of Britain, Quintus Bassinianus. After defeating and killing the Governor near York he marched to London and won support from the remaining Roman forces in Britain. With an island stronghold and an invincible fleet, self-proclaimed Emperor Marcus Aurelius Mausaeus Carausius extended his effective control to Gaul. Skilful in maintaining alliances, Emperor Carausius set up mints at London, Colchester and Rouen to produce his coins and the majority of the Llandudno hoard originated from London, a few came from Colchester but none from Gaul. Since gold and silver were in short supply the vast majority of Carausian coins, including all the Llandudno specimens, were of brass. After seven years of tacitly accepting the status quo Rome was growing increasingly concerned about its vulnerability to attacks from allies of its British 'Emperor'. Diocletian therefore decreed that Carausius must be crushed but before Rome could invade, Carausius's reign was ended at the treacherous and murderous hands of his own ambitious finance minister, Allectus.

This 1907 find shows an agent serving Carausius, either in a military of commercial capacity, was active in the Creuddyn between 286 AD and 293 AD. Bronze strips recovered from the soil surrounding the coins suggest that when originally hidden the hoard was contained within a metal-bound wooden box. After analysing all the evidence Willoughby Gardner felt, 'Two questions have now to be answered. First the reason for the burial of the coins in this coastal district, and secondly, the purpose for which the . . . hoards were consigned. As to the first there can be little doubt that they were buried to avoid capture by raiders from overseas, seen to be approaching the coast. It is a known fact that the Irish Sea was infested at this period by sea-rovers, as well as the southern and eastern coasts of Britain, a menace which caused the Romans to organize a fleet to protect them.'

'As to the second question, there can again be little doubt that the money constituting the Little Orme finds was consigned there from headquarters in connection with the rich copper mines in the Great Orme's Head. We know that the Romans exploited Britain in part for the sake of her mineral wealth which they worked by employing native labour. Both the hoards of 1873 and 1907 are entirely of bronze coins of small denomination. As the military were paid in silver, the finds in question must have been intended for the payment of the native miners.'

Whilst Willoughby Gardner's conclusions are suggestive he undoubtedly over-eggs the pudding and speculates way beyond the evidence. It's reasonable to conclude that the Carausian hoard was hidden at a time of uncertainty and possible unrest when, as a recognised supporter of a deposed regime, the depositer would have attracted adverse attention. In any case following Carausius's assassination coinage bearing his image was immediately demonetised. After 293 AD possession of such a coin hoard became both pointless and possibly incriminating, but neither the 1873 nor the 1907 find provide any direct evidence of Roman mining on the Great Orme. But other coin finds add further evidence to our picture of Roman activity in the Creuddyn.

Roman Coins Finds Across the Creuddyn

A small collection of Roman coins found on the Great Orme in April 1888 was recorded at the time in the 'Manchester City News' by a Dr Thomas (probably Dr Henry Thomas, proprietor of Llandudno's Hydropathic Hotel). 'Whilst working below the road near his cave on Tŷ Gwyn Road, Mr Kendrick came across an ancient fire place, and embedded in clay, he found 17 Roman coins, of the date of the Emperor Carausius. Upon the obverse is the head of the Emperor, and round it are the letters **IMP CARAVSIVS PAVC**, and upon the reverse an erect female figure, who held in her right hand a leaf; her left arm rests upon a wheel, and around the figure are the letters **HICOPH**; on another coin two figures are seated back to back at the foot of the military arms that rise between them – a helmet, breastplate and two shields suspended on an upright staff. On two of the arms are **MN, MLXXI**.' Although the report was generally accurate four of the seventeen coins were actually pre-Carausius; one

Roman Coins from the 1873
Little Orme Hoard - all British Mints

Gallienus (253-268 AD), two of Victorinus (268-293 AD) and one of Tetricus (271-273 AD) and so spanned the period 253 AD – 293 AD.

Only two other hoards have been recorded locally and both cases are problematic. Willoughby Gardner believed that two Roman coins he acquired in 1922 were the remnants of an undisclosed hoard found many years earlier by a chap called Wynne whilst grubbing up a tree in Llangystennin churchyard. WG's specimens were only slightly worn coins of Constantine I minted at Trier 307 AD and London 310 AD, respectively. Even more tantalising are reports of, 'A box of (Roman) coins found in a small lake in a garden at Penrhyn Bay in 1924' (Stamp, 1996).

Besides these five hoards nine other isolated coin finds have been recorded. The first reported discovery was made in 1849 when miners broke into an ancient cavern on the Great Orme and along with prehistoric mining tools they found a 'third brass' of Carausius. A few years later a coin of Domitian (81-96 AD) was found in a Great Orme cave along with the skeleton described in the last chapter and in 1866 the oldest coin that's turned up in the Creuddyn was discovered by the Rev. Owen Jones when lightly turning the soil over near to the Cromlech. Dally (1911) describes it as depicting the head of Apollo surrounded by rays of the sun and bearing the inscription **ROMA** which sounds as if it was a bronze Uncia struck in southern Italy between 227 BC and 187 BC. Unfortunately the son of the finder sent the coin to a friend for identification but it was never returned and was subsequently lost.

In 1890 a coin of Vespasian (68-79 AD) was dug up on the Great Orme and sometime around 1900 two coins of Constantine and Tetricus were found at the entrance to an abandoned mine adit near Gogarth farm. Twenty years later several small brass coins including one 'third brass' of Constantine were found nearby, just south of the Bishop's Palace. In 1946 Oliver Davies recovered a coin of Aurelius from the Penmorfa drainage adit.

In 1967 the 13th century masonry of Deganwy Castle was found to have incorporated five Constantinian plus other unidentified coins and in 1986 a Roman coin of AD 268-273 was found not far away in the fields of Bryn Gosol farm, Llanrhos. This wealth of coin discoveries shows local activity in the Romano-British period was not simply confined to the Great Orme however considered alongside finds of other materials a pattern emerges indicating the key importance of certain areas of the Creuddyn.

Significant Hoard of Decorative Metalwork

In 1999 metal detectorist Wayne Evans found part of a small enamelled Romano-British brooch south-east of Bryn Pydew on an ancient trackway leading to Mochdre. An interesting find but it's likely to represent no more than an isolated loss by an ancient traveller. A 1986 discovery, comprising a hoard of Roman bronze objects from the Little Orme is far more significant. Probably deposited in the late 3rd or early 4th century the collection includes 5 ox-head bucket-mounts (1 illustrated), a handle of a razor, the handle of a knife or chisel, 2 brooches and a harness ring. Three of the mounts are in the form of simple ox-heads, but the other two are more elaborate. One consists of an ox-head with a Celtic style scroll and a dolphin, commonly portrayed in Roman art, to either side. Some of the objects from the hoard appear to have been broken in antiquity and may have been collected together as scrap for re-smelting. Taken together with earlier finds the importance of the Little Orme begins to emerge, if not a significant industrial and occupation site itself the Penrhyn pass does at least appear likely to have led to metal working activity on the Great Orme.

Pieces of Pottery

Surprisingly little Roman pottery has come to light in the Creuddyn. Six years before the discovery of the 1873 'coin vase' W W Foulkes recovered a single piece of Samian pottery from his excavations at Pen Dinas hillfort. Roman pottery sherds were recovered by excavations at Deganwy Castle in 1950 and again in 1967 whilst Oliver Davies's 1948 Penmorfa dig revealed not only Romano-British pottery but also a contemporary occupation site.

One of the most impressive pieces turned up just before Christmas 1918 when, in the words of the Llandudno Advertiser, 'a workman excavating at Maes y Mor, near the Little Orme, Llandudno unearthed a well-preserved vase of Roman manufacture, similar in design to specimens found in the south of England.' The vase was acquired by local collector and antique dealer F Holland who informed the reporter that he had also recently purchased a local hotel which he intended to convert before reopening as, 'The Prince of Wales Museum'. He planned to not only exhibit the newly found Roman vase in his museum but to also have it reproduced as an item of Goss China. Holland's museum never opened but copies of the vase did appear and are still sort after by collectors of Goss ware. Unfortunately the Roman ascription was later challenged and it now appears more likely that the vase was no more than an eighteenth century import from north Africa.

End of an Era

It seems more likely than not that the Great Orme copper mines were worked on behalf of Rome by agents employing local people on a tenure offering them little alternative. Under nominal Roman occupation life continued and the Creuddyn remained lightly populated accommodating a total of maybe 100-200 people. The majority of people settled on the Great Orme with others scattered about the Creuddyn, on the Little Orme, Bryn Pydew and at Deganwy. There is no evidence to support fanciful accounts of native ambushes of Imperial troops at Nant Semper or pitched battles on Pen Dinas. It wasn't resistance from Britain but increasingly effective barbarian attacks on Rome's heartland that forced her forces to withdraw at the end of the fourth century. The Creuddyn was left vulnerable to seaborne Irish incursions but as Celtic tribalism re-emerged and native-born leaders arose the military and political significance of the Creuddyn was about to increase dramatically.

Chapter Six

Maelgwn and the Age of the Saints (400-825)

As legions supporting Macsen Wledig withdrew from Segontium the old tribal structure of the Celtic Iron Age re-emerged from the shadows. Cunedda's (c.370-430) warriors sailed from Strathclyde to stiffen local resistance to Irish incursions. Tribesmen entering the Conwy estuary probably established bases in the Creuddyn thwarting the threat of Gaelic domination. Cunedda's timely intervention protected the viability of the region's Brythonic form of the Celtic language. Without Cunedda the language of north Wales would have become Irish Gaelic rather than developing into Welsh.

After Cunedda's death the extensive lands under his control were parcelled out amongst his eight sons. Einion, the seventh son, assumed the title, 'King of Gwynedd', and rapidly established the predominant role of his kingdom. From his base at Bodysgallen ('Bod Caswallon') Einion's son and successor, Caswallon Lawhir (sometimes 'Cadwallon', c.450-517), swept the remaining Irish invaders into the sea but it was Caswallon's own son, Maelgwn, who was destined to put Deganwy on the map.

'Insularis Draco'

Maelgwn Gwynedd (c.490-549) was a supremely powerful leader. Gildas calls him, 'Insularis Draco', 'Dragon or High-King of the Island' and clearly petty kings of Britain deferred to his authority. Legend revealingly suggests how he acquired the title. The story goes that Maelgwn called together rivals for the supreme position. Inviting his fellow kings to seat themselves upon their thrones alongside him on the shoreline he asserted that he who dared remain seated longest, despite the rapidly incoming tide, surely possessed sufficient courage to justify over-lordship. Surprisingly everyone agreed and less surprisingly Maelgwn cheated, having already prepared his throne with the addition of concealed flotation units composed of waxed bird's wings. Inevitably inundation embarrassed opponents whilst floating Maelgwn to ill-deserved victory!

Gildas prefers a prosaic explanation of Maelgwn's rise to power, the systematic use of violence including the killing of his nephew and maybe even the murder of his own wife, the sister of the King of Powys. Gildas neatly summarises Maelgwn's character with a colourful phrase from Deuteronomy (32:32), 'sodden with wine pressed from the vine of

81

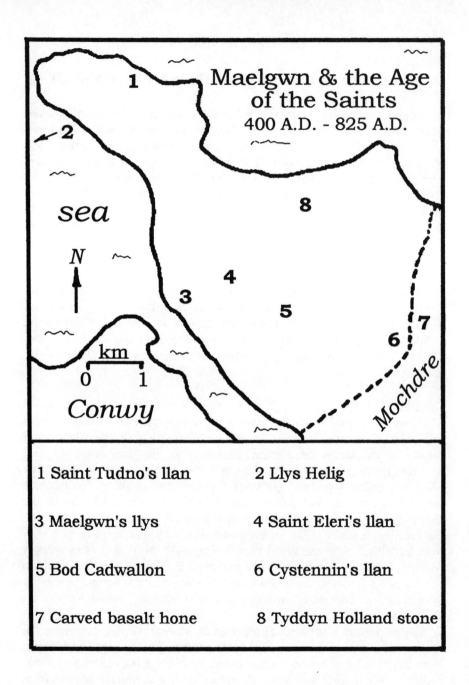

Maelgwn & the Age
of the Saints
400 A.D. - 825 A.D.

sea

N

km
0   1

Conwy

Mochdre

1 Saint Tudno's llan   2 Llys Helig

3 Maelgwn's llys   4 Saint Eleri's llan

5 Bod Cadwallon   6 Cystennin's llan

7 Carved basalt hone   8 Tyddyn Holland stone

Sodom'. Despite the dubious legends Maelgwn's dominance is clear, his strength and influence spread the power of Gwynedd, and the Creuddyn, well beyond Wales to stiffen native resistance in England against Saxon invaders.

Birthplace of a Nation

From his base at Deganwy Maelgwn pulled the petty kingdoms of Wales towards cultural and political coherence. It was hardly a unified State yet Maelgwn Gwynedd is fairly proclaimed by historians, 'Father of the Welsh Nation'. The historical details of Maelgwn's reign remain ill-defined but the basic outline is established. Similarly the detailed layout of his palace at Deganwy is unknown and archaeological evidence has been destroyed as the site has been so frequently redeveloped. Nevertheless an excavation by Leslie Alcock in 1961-2 found about a dozen sherds of east Mediterranean amphorae of a type known as Tintagel Class B, dated to c.470-600. Like Samian ware this is a sign of an elevated lifestyle for ordinary people made do with local produce. Only the rich could afford imported amphora of wine or olive oil and Maelgwn's court was a sophisticated community consuming the finest products of Bordeaux, Athens and the Black Sea. To critics who claim twelve bits of pot and a few fragments of glass offer inadequate evidence for assuming such a lifestyle Alcock suggests that good table manners might well have accompanied high status such that Maelgwn's household simply kept the place tidy. Maelgwn's well-ordered court might thus have left behind little 'rubbish' for the modern archaeologist to uncover. The absence of numismatic evidence from Maelgwn's time is unsurprising as coins were in very short supply in this period. It's likely that the luxury Mediterranean goods supplied to Maelgwn were paid for in kind rather than in cash, with local leather and timber bartered in exchange.

Alcock suggested that the inner face of a dry stone wall discovered a little way down the eastern slope of the later medieval dungeon might have originally formed part of the defences of Maelgwn's citadel. Maelgwn clearly recognised the key strategic importance of controlling the coastal crossing of Afon Conwy and in siting his court and castle at Deganwy he was probably following the lead of his father, Caswallon, who erected a watchtower at Bodysgallen to serve the same purpose.

Cultured Court

Maelgwn's military efficiency was balanced by his love of the arts. In a derogatory comment by Gildas on Maelgwn's 'knavish crew' of bards and musicians we find the first reference in Wales to the Celtic custom of poets singing the praises of their leaders. An old legend reveals Maelgwn himself wasn't above indulging in a bit of knavish behaviour with his bards and musicians. After announcing a great eisteddfod Maelgwn ensured that no boats were available to ferry the bards and musicians assembled at his palace across Afon Conwy to the festival site on Conwy Mountain. Having been forced to swim across to the competition the voices of the bards survived intact whereas the sodden instruments of the musicians sounded pitiful. As a result all the prizes went to Maelgwn's favoured poets.

Religious Patron

Maelgwn did much to promote the influence of Celtic Christianity throughout his kingdom. Until Emperor Constantine's conversion in 312 Roman prohibition effectively prevented the spread of Christian ideas in England but had lesser effect on the Celtic fringe and none at all in Ireland. Consequently following the Roman withdrawal from Britain there was an increasing traffic of Christian 'missionaries' between the Celtic lands of western Europe. Wales entered the 'Age of the Saints' with Celtic Christianity an inextricable part of a developing Welsh nation.

Maelgwn gave generously to the Church, granting to Deiniol the land on which he founded his clas, or Celtic monastery. Deiniol's settlement was enclosed by a wattle fence or 'bangor' that gave the site its name. Now crowned with a Cathedral, the building is claimed to have been in the longest continuous use of any church in Britain. Maelgwn granted land in the eastern part of his kingdom to Kentigern and Asaph but the clas they established did not exercise the same degree of authority over the Creuddyn's Christian communities as Deiniol's at Bangor.

Deiniol's settlement included a prayer house, an oratory or church, a guest house, an eating place, cells for the monks and a burial ground. Its boundary demarcated holy land within, from the secular world without. Inside there was the promise of sanctuary, both civil and spiritual, an idea synonymous with the henge-world significance of Bronze Age stone and timber circles. In the Creuddyn there is some suggestion that Maelgwn might have supported a clas founded by St Eleri (Hilary) on or near the site now occupied by the church that bears his name at Llanrhos but the evidence is difficult to reconcile. Local tradition holds that there was once some sort of monastic settlement here, a field near the church is known as 'Gardd y Monachdy' and an ancient local township bore the name 'Penclas'. Although St Eleri was active in the area and founded the church at Gwytherin he is associated with the seventh rather than the sixth century and monastic associations more likely reflect later use of the land as a grange of Aberconwy Abbey.

Struck Dead by the Yellow Plague

Whatever the origins of St Hilary's Church it is firmly associated with the later life and death of Maelgwn Gwynedd. After a career of empire building he is said to have repented of his more ruthless deeds and retired to a monastery. Perhaps this was at Llanrhos but in any case the story is that in 547 he was ensconced in St Hilary's Church whilst the deadly monster of the 'Yellow Plague' stalked the land. Unable to resist the temptation to peer out Maelgwn peeped through a key hole and was immediately spied and struck dead by the monstrous disease. An outbreak of yellow plague certainly erupted in Persia in 542 before sweeping across Europe and may well have killed Maelgwn. He was buried either in the churchyard or more poetically at the top of the nearby hill that bears his name, Bryn Maelgwn.

St Tudno

Whilst Maelgwn ruled from Deganwy a Celtic missionary, Tudno, settled on the Great Orme. One of the seven sons of Seithenyn, himself a son of a King of Dyfed, Tudno may have inhabited a cave before creating an enclosure, or llan, on the simplified pattern of a Clas. Tradition holds that the community that gathered around this llan was the beginnings of Llandudno but we now realise that whatever Tudno's role he was certainly not the first man to set foot on the Orme.

St Cystennin's, the First Church in Wales?

Near the southern boundary of the Creuddyn a llan was created by Cystennin Fendigaid ('Cystennin the Blessed'), sometimes referred to as Cystennin Gorneu (Cystennin of Cornwall). Father of the founder of Llangernw, Cystennin's saint's day is November 21st. Being the Celticised form of Constantine led confused commentators to make exaggerated claims of Llangystennin's longevity. In his 1834 'Topographical Dictionary of Wales' Lewis states, 'The church, dedicated to St Constantine, is a small plain structure, situate in a pleasing valley close to the boundary line between the counties of Carnarvon and Denbigh, and it is said to be the first Christian Church erected in Wales; it is conjectured to have been founded by Constantine the Great, who died in the year 330.'

Claims concerning the ancient foundation of the church were bolstered by the rare survival of a 'Celtic Bell' (illustrated). In the early medieval period handbells rather than the later tower-mounted type were commonly used in the Celtic church to call the faithful to prayer and the Llangystennin bell was believed to have been in use from the foundation of the church until its rebuilding in 1843. The Rev. Rees Jones, Curate of Llangystennin in the early Victorian period claimed the bell had been donated by a Welsh Princess, the wife of Constantine but more expert analysis suggests it might have been cast rather late in the 'Age of the Saints', possibly in the seventh or eighth century.

Faith Springs Eternal

Several springs and wells of the Creuddyn are enduring features of Celtic Christianity. In the Celtic Iron Age valuable artefacts were cast into lakes as offerings to the Gods. In the post-Roman era it was claimed that sacred springs were caused to gush forth from the earth by several Celtic Saints. A more prosaic explanation suggests that wandering missionaries were only likely to settle where they found a freely available source of drinking water but the more spiritually significant explanation found biblical precedent. With God's chosen people thirsting in the desert Aaron struck his staff down on the rock and sweet waters flowed forth. Cystennin's llan and later church were founded just 180 metres south of the well that until Victorian times provided water for local people. Until the provision of piped water in the nineteenth century springs and wells associated with ancient churches played a significant role in the community. Baptisms originally took place at the sacred well and even after the erection of stone churches water drawn from the Saint's well was used to fill the baptismal font. Even essentially secular ceremonies, such as the annual beating of the parish boundaries began from the sacred spring. Water from saints' wells were often credited with curative properties and occasionally the sacred character of holy wells was perverted and exploited as a 'cursing well', as at Llanelian.

The ancient significance of Ffynnon Santes Fair (Saint Mary's Well), at Llanrhos, was clouded through its later association with the Cistercians who dedicated their churches to Mary, as at Conwy. Lying just 180 metres south-west of St Hilary's Church, Saint Mary's Well was originally St Eleri's Well but unlike the church itself it never regained its original dedication. Once Llanrhos acquired piped water in 1898 the well became increasingly neglected, but fully restored by Ken Davies in 1994 and situated alongside a public footpath Eleri's ancient well remains a significant site.

The Creuddyn's third ancient church, St Tudno's on the Great Orme, also has an associated holy well that lies, overgrown and neglected, in a

Tyddyn Holland Stone

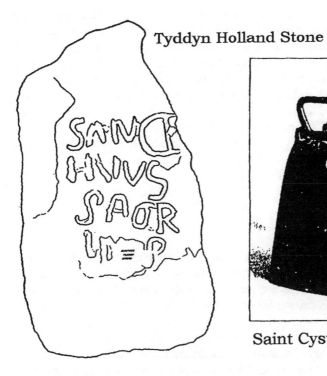

Saint Cystennin's Bell

Saint Tudno's Well

field 100 metres east-south-east of the church. Ffynnon Tudno (illustrated) was traditionally used as a source of holy water but is now inaccessible and largely forgotten. Sadwrn's Well at Brynybia, near the Little Orme fares better, it's on public land and the adjacent street, Ffynnon Sadwrn Lane, named in its honour. Although the origins of the name are disputed and no associated church or llan was founded nearby it seems likely this ancient well was dedicated to St Sadwrn (born c.485), the brother of St Illtud. Sadwrn's feast day is the 29th November.

Curative properties are traditionally associated with two ancient Great Orme wells, Ffynnon Llygaid and Ffynnon Galchog. As its name suggests Ffynnon Llygaid was revered for its waters beneficial effect on eyesight whilst water from Ffynnon Galchog, the limey well was considered good for bones and teeth.

Sanctinus the Bishop

A glimpse into the organisation of the local sixth century Celtic church is provided by a rare memorial stone (illustrated) lodged in an arched niche in the south wall at the western end of the nave of Llanrhos Church. Discovered by the cartographer and historian Lewis Morris in 1731 this stone originally stood, 'in the highway by Tyddyn Holand (sic), between Bodafon and Rhiw Leding . . . near a rock called Crai'r nodwydd dur'. According to Morris, 'There are a vast many ruins about this place, and it seems there was a town here in ye times of ye ancient Britons.' Although Holland Villa remains to mark the original findspot the 'vast many ruins' have disappeared from Bodafon fields however there are tantalisingly clues to earlier settlement on the plateau above, at Nant y gamar. The name of the farm directly above Tyddyn Holland, Castell y Gwlfryn (Castell/castle and Gwylfryn/watching place) has traditionally been associated with an early encampment overseeing incursions through the Penrhyn pass. There are elaborate, probably fanciful suggestions of archers stationed at Bryn Ifan protecting the pass from invaders but whatever Lewis Morris saw suggests that there was an ancient settlement of some kind associated with the 'Tyddyn Holland Stone'.

Morris recorded the four line, Latin script inscription as SANCT/ANVS/SACRI/ISIS which he interpreted as 'SANCTANUS SACRI ISIS' or 'Sanctinus rests here in peace' but Morris's reading has subsequently been disputed. In 1801 Richard Fenton recorded a less complete inscription and in 1877 Sir John Rhys claimed that the stone was probably a mere fragment of its original size and therefore represented only a part of the intended memorial. In 1877 Rhys suggested this might have been SANCTANUS FILIUS SACERDOTIS or

Sanctanus, son of the bishop. He even attempted to identify Sanctanus, citing an intriguing reference in the 'Liber Hymnorum' that claims, 'Bishop Sanctan made this hymn and when he was going from Clonard westward to Matoc's Island he made it'. By 1896 Rhys had re-examined the stone and revised his opinions but accurate interpretation of the clumsily cut text was not really helped by a Victorian tenant of Tyddyn Holland who 'undertook to deepen the letters for the benefit of English tourists'.

In 1950 Nash-Williams produced the definitive interpretation; SANCTINUS SACERDOS IN PACE which reads as, 'Sanctinus the Bishop Lies Here In Peace'. Sanctinus was neither Bishop of Bangor nor St Asaph yet still recognised as a Bishop. The Tyddyn Holland stone is thus a memorial to the decentralised nature of the Celtic Church. The exact role of Bishops is still unclear yet it is certain they were far more numerous in Wales in the early middle ages and they did not then preside over the huge geographically defined diocese operating today. The likelihood is that Sanctinus was attached to the religious foundation at Llanrhos and as late as 809 the Welsh annals record the death of Bishop Elfoddw the 'chief bishop in the land of Gwynedd', so clearly not the only bishop. Ironically Elfoddw was himself a key centralising agent responsible for enforcing the Roman Easter in Wales.

Sanctinus was clearly an influential Christian in a Church not yet ruled from Rome yet interestingly his memorial employs the Latin script of the long departed civil administration. In Sanctinus's time the Creuddyn practised a form of Celtic Christianity distinct from that sanctioned by Rome. To impose religious conformity in 597 Pope Gregory sent Augustine to Britain, or as Bede put it, 'so that the ignorant may be taught, the weak strengthened by persuasion, the perverse corrected by authority'.

From Celtic Christianity to Roman Catholic Control

The weak, ignorant and perverse bishops of Wales met Augustine at Chester in 603. Having previously sought the advice of a saintly hermit who had advised that if Augustine rose to greet them it would signify humility and the possibility of compromise. As they entered the appointed meeting room Augustine remained firmly seated.

The Christians of southern Ireland finally capitulated to Papal authority and complied with the Roman Easter in 630, Northumbria complied in 664, Strathclyde in 688, northern Ireland in 697 and Iona 716. Wales held out unto 768 when Bishop Elfoddw finally bent the knee to Rome.

By the end of the eighth century the Age of the Saints was over. For two centuries (c450-c650) Celtic Christianity had been characterised by ascetic missionaries with a reverence for nature and simplicity. By 800 Wales was part of a formal, hierarchical pan-European Church with the areas of influence around each llan becoming slowly more geographically defined. The Creuddyn's three llans of Tudno, Eleri and Cystennin respectively contained timber churches or oratories, probably similar to the one excavated at Llandegai in 1966, that consisted of upright poles infilled with wattle and daub, thatched with straw and with an earth floor measuring 3½ metres by 4½ metres.

If St Eleri's foundation had developed into a Clas it would initially have comprised a mixed community with married monks living alongside the single and the secular tillers of the soil and herdsmen. The monks wandered the Creuddyn and beyond propagating the message of Christ. By 800 the limitations of the Roman Church would have adversely affected the development and influence of Eleri's Clas. In 800 St Tudno's, St Eleri's and St Cystennin's all came under the spiritual oversight of the Bishop of Bangor which remained the chief Clas of the kingdom of Gwynedd whose writ reached across the Conwy to Prestatyn and Offa's Dyke.

Political Organisation

It is difficult to discern exactly how tribal society operated from the fifth to the eighth centuries but by the end of the period identifiable social and political structures began to emerge. The basic civil unit was the township and a dozen or so townships comprised the local cwmwd or commote; Gogarth, Cyngreadwr, Yr Wyddfyd, Bodafon, Rhiwledin, Penlassoc, Ganneu, Gloddaeth, Penrhyn, Trefwarth, Bodescathlan and Llanwydden. A hundred townships together formed a cantref and Creuddyn formed part of the cantref of Rhos, that in turn comprised part of the kingdom of Gwynedd. Wales lacked a formal political identity but the people west of King Offa's shared cultural links and were occasionally almost unified as subjects of the expansive Kingdom of Gwynedd.

The rulers of Gwynedd prevented Irish military incursions but did not seek to end cultural links. A beautiful basalt hone found by labourer Lawrence Davies at Llandudno Junction brickworks in the summer of 1940 appears Irish in origin and typically Celtic in design and execution. An important but insufficiently evaluated find, T D Kendrick hinted at its significance in the Antiquaries Journal, 'Outside the Celtic lands the only example known to me of a whetstone with carved masks at the end comes from the Anglo-Saxon ship-burial at Sutton Hoo'

Despite the serious danger of Saxon incursions as late as 633 Maelgwn's descendants proved so effective in battle that hopes of restoring Brythonic supremacy throughout Britain were kept alive. At the end of the sixth century the word 'Cymry' ('fellow countrymen') included the men of the North but when Cadwallon (c.590-634), King of Gwynedd, was defeated and killed by Oswald of Northumbria Wales was cut off from the remaining Celtic kingdoms of Britain. In isolation Wales's old Brythonic tongue evolved to become Welsh and the Cymry thereafter meant only the people of Wales.

Kingdom Beneath the Waves

Archaeological evidence from England suggests that sometime in the sixth century sea levels rose significantly causing flooding of the Somerset Levels and areas of East Anglia. Local tradition holds that inundation of land extending east of the present extent of the Creuddyn had a spectacularly dramatic effect with the royal palace of Lord Helig ap Glannog disappearing beneath the waves. Modern versions of the story derive from a manuscript attributed to Sir John Wynn (1553-1627) but the dearth of documentary evidence has prompted a host of antiquaries and historians to examine archaeological evidence of the submerged palace. Conveyed to the site by a local boatman in 1812, Pugh was clearly convinced, 'From the certainty of the existence of this causeway, we may venture to give credit to the existence of the remains of Helig's houses . . .'

In 1864 retired Liverpool merchant Charlton Hall organised a marine expedition to explore Llys Helig. He subsequently presented his findings to Liverpool Geological Society, informing members that, 'There did appear in the outline of the structure . . . evidence of the truth of the legend that there on that spot, now covered by the sea, and at least two miles out from the nearest land, did once stand a grand hall of magnificent dimensions, whose shape and proportions still remains distinguishable.' Charlton Hall even produced a scaled plan of Helig's lost palace.

William Ashton was particularly impressed by a trip he made to the site in 1908, claiming, 'It is quite impossible for anyone to view these 350 or more yards of strictly rectangular remains and to entertain the slightest doubt as to their having been human handiwork'. Ashton went on to elaboratedly map out his ideas in his extended study, 'Evolution of a Coastline'.

In 1913 it was the turn of journalist Horace Lees to add weight to the Llys Helig legend, publishing the results of his recent explorations in

'The Field'. Lees also raised the interesting possibility that the site might yield important artefacts. 'It is the great bank that wants investigation. Here it is where the palace must have stood with all its buildings; and any relics will be buried here beneath the stones. Seeing that the depth of water in the courtyard was about 3½ feet, is it not within the bounds of possibility that a little enterprise may bring something to light, of interest, and possibly of value?'

It seemed that seeing was believing, everyone who visited the site returned convinced that off the coast of Deganwy lay an early medieval palace beneath the waves. There was therefore understandable consternation amongst members of 'Llandudno, Colwyn Bay and District Field Club' (forerunner of 'Llandudno and District Historical Society') when, in a talk delivered in Llandudno in 1936, Dr F J North, a geologist from the National Museum of Wales, suggested that the celebrated remains of the Helig's palace were probably no more than a natural geological formation.

Taking up the gauntlet the Field Club set about organised a definitive investigation of the site. At 4.30am on Thursday 17th August 1939 a small flotilla of boats carrying an assorted bevy of experts accompanied by leading members of the Field Club set out from Deganwy beach. After locating and investigating the submerged stones the party returned to shore and began writing up their conclusions. They need hardly have bothered, the newspaper headline encapsulated their extensive observations in just six words, 'STONES NOT PALACE RUINS SAY EXPERTS'.

Several Field Club members refused to be reconciled and to this day local historians continue to investigate the site and attempt to resuscitate the legend of Llys Helig but the archaeological evidence appears as insubstantial as the historical evidence. Traditional tales of submerged kingdoms are commonly told and the legend of Llys Helig might ultimately derive from embroidered folk memories of the extensive sea level changes of the Neolithic age and should be dismissed from sensible consideration of the history of early medieval Creuddyn.

An Uncertain Future

In the seventh and eighth centuries the kingdom of Gwynedd was a noted centre of learning and culture, where scholars and men of influence would be royally entertained. Although Deganwy's supreme role was eventually eclipsed by Aberfraw, with its Castle and Llys, Deganwy remained of key importance. Unfortunately Cadwallon's defeat left the Creuddyn isolated from other Celtic regions of Britain and vulnerable to Saxon incursions from the east.

After the departure of the Romans Germanic tribes had flooded into England and once established were intent on expanding into Wales. In 812 Deganwy Castle was portentously set aflame by lightning and a decade later razed to the ground by a Mercian army led by Ceolwulf. The Mercians soon withdrew but in 825 Hywel, King of Gwynedd died and with him ended the rule of the House of Maelgwn Gwynedd. With the extinction of the royal line, political divisions in Wales, threats of further Saxon incursions and Vikings already raiding the coast of England prospects for the Creuddyn looked bleak.

Chapter Seven

Viking Raiders and Norman Colonisers (825-1284)

In 825 Merfyn Frych, the only Welsh king to come from the Isle of Man, assumed control of Gwynedd and united the kingdom against potentially overwhelming odds. Whilst Merfyn safeguarded the fortunes of the Creuddyn his son, Rhodri, who inherited the throne on Merfyn's death in 844, was the first king of Wales to be called 'Mawr'. Rhodri's claim to be known as 'the Great' rested upon his triple achievements of uniting the greater part of Wales, keeping out Saxon invaders and fighting off Viking raiders.

'The Viking Lake'

Norwegian Vikings swept down into the Irish Sea capturing Dublin in 841 and creating a major staging post for raids on Wales. The 'Black Pagans', as they were known by the Welsh, devastated Mon in 853-4 with the first of a long series of raids that ultimately gave the island its Norse name of Anglesey ('Ongulsey'). In 856 Rhodri Fawr thwarted an attack on the Creuddyn when he destroyed a Viking fleet off the coast of Llandudno. News of Rhodri's great victory over the Black Pagans travelled far and wide, it is recorded in an Irish chronicle and was applauded in the court of Charles, son of Charlemagne. Despite Rhodri's success it is a sign of the enduring presence of the Norsemen in the region that the name of their defeated leader, Horm, was bequeathed to the headland (Great Orme) beneath which he perished.

From their Dublin base the Norsemen dominated the semi-enclosed seas of the 'Viking Lake' that transported them on regular raids on Galloway, Cumbria, Man and Wales. Throughout much of his reign Rhodri rallied Welsh forces to minimise incursions but in 877 he suffered a significant defeat in a famous battle at Anglesey that the Chronicles record took place on a Sunday. He was forced to seek refuge abroad and returning to Gwynedd the following year he was attacked by the Mercian, King Ceolwulf II and killed.

Threats from East and West

Rhodri had maintained a llys at Deganwy but after his death his successsors found it increasingly difficult to preserve the integrity of the kingdom and the safety of the Creuddyn. To the east, in 921 English invaders under Edward the Elder reached Rhuddlan, which they founded as an Anglo-Saxon burgh. To the west, around 925 Norse raiders

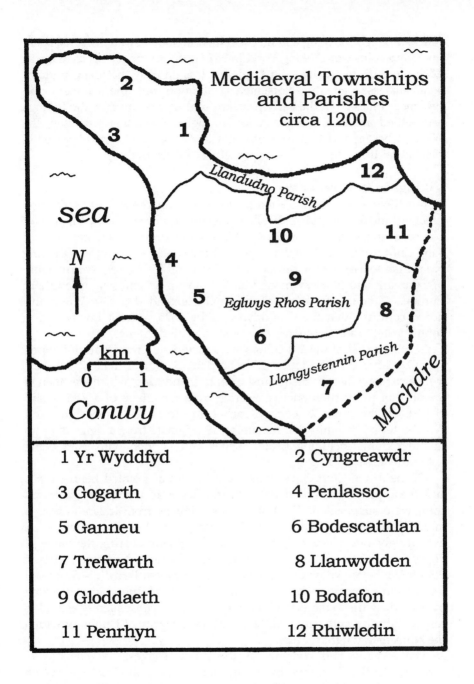

Mediaeval Townships
and Parishes
circa 1200

sea

N

km
0   1

Conwy

Llandudno Parish

Eglwys Rhos Parish

Llangystennin Parish

Mochdre

1 Yr Wyddfyd	2 Cyngreawdr
3 Gogarth	4 Penlassoc
5 Ganneu	6 Bodescathlan
7 Trefwarth	8 Llanwydden
9 Gloddaeth	10 Bodafon
11 Penrhyn	12 Rhiwledin

attacked Bangor, leaving behind booty that included Arab dirhams, hack-silver and coins from Viking York. In 987 Guthroth carried off as many as 2,000 slaves from an attack on Anglesey. It is unlikely that the Creuddyn peninsula escaped the Norsemen's attention but the earliest solid evidence comes from the early eleventh century and by then the Vikings had settled at many places across the region, including Anglesey, the Wirral, Chester, and Talacre. Norse attacks on coastal Gwynedd ceased in 993 and raiding was replaced by peaceful seaborne trading.

Vikings in the Creuddyn

In July 1979 a retired civil servant, John Smethurst Jones of Llandudno Junction and his friend and fellow metal-detectorist, Derek Blamire of Llanrhos uncovered a hoard of 204 coins (illustrated) from the time of King Cnut (c.995-1035) on the slopes of Bryn Maelgwn. Cnut was the first Norseman to assume the throne of England and his subsequent rulership of Denmark and Norway made him the most powerful king of northern Europe. Although Cnut's writ nominally extended across Wales this hoard confirms that the Creuddyn was by 1025, at least involved in a sophisticated trading network operated by settled Vikings.

Two hundred of the 204 coins are characteristic Cnut Quatrefoil types, so called after the four-lobed inner borders. No fewer than 171 of these were struck at Chester, the nearest mint to Llandudno, which was then at the peak of production after recovering from the effects of a Viking raid of 980. Of the other 29 coins 5 each come from the Shrewsbury and Winchester mints whilst the remaining 19 originate from a range of up to 14 other mints including Exeter, Lewis and London with York being noticeably absent.

Of the 4 non-Cnut-Quatrefoils 2 are known as pointed helmet types and these prove the hoard dates from after 1024 when the Quatrefoil coins were superseded. The last 2 coins originate from Ireland, one is a mere Irish copy of the usual Cnut-Quatrefoil but the other is an exceedingly rare piece, a Quatrefoil Dublin penny bearing the name of Sigtryggr Olafson on the obverse instead of Cnut's. Sigtryggr Olafson (989-1036), better known as Sihtric III 'of the Silken Beard', is described on the coin's reverse as 'King of the Irish'. He ruled Dublin until defeated by legendary Irish king Brian Boreu in 999. Boreu subsequently agreed to respect Sihtric's authority and the territorial integrity of Dublin provided the Norsemen fought for him.

The location and contents of the hoard suggest the coins were conveyed to the Creuddyn by Viking merchants from Chester intent on trading with the important Royal settlement of Deganwy. Deganwy then provided a focus for specialised craftsmen, including jewellers and silversmiths producing a range of desirable, high status trinkets. It is not difficult to imagine the circumstances under which the merchants' cash might have been buried and subsequently lost for after the death of Llywelyn ap Seisyll, King of Gwynedd in 1023 the Creuddyn was plunged into a prolonged period of chaos that ended only with the rise to power by Gruffydd ap Llywelyn in 1039.

Viking Coins on the Great Orme

On March 22nd, 1981 a student from Leeds University taking part in a field course on the Great Orme noticed a number of silver coins protruding from a molehill at Pant yr Eglwys near the north-eastern wall of the churchyard. The collection comprised three coins fused together and a single separate specimen. It is likely they originally formed part of a larger hoard that had been split and dispersed over the years by the forces of nature. The majority of the hoard had probably slipped down the cliff into the sea or possibly been found and dispersed in earlier centuries. All four coins are apparently Cnut Quatrefoils but the loose specimen is an interesting imitation that enjoyed wide currency at the time. Of the fused examples two originate from the Chester mint and one from Hereford. All four date from around 1025. The fused coins had been incompletely melted down and were probably intended to be taken to Dublin for re-coining but the process had been interrupted at a time of perceived danger.

Robert of Rhuddlan Captures Deganwy

As the Norsemen became more settled and civilised they abandoned their old beliefs and embraced Christianity. Trading relationships blossomed into full-blown alliances but the Norsemen never really took to farming and ultimately bequeathed little to the history of the Creuddyn. When Gruffyd ap Llywelyn (ruled 1039-63) gained control of Gwynedd he no longer had to beware of incursions from Dublin and was able to extend his effective rule westwards, establishing a royal residence in the previously Anglo-Saxon burgh of Rhuddlan.

Unfortunately the defeat of the Anglo-Saxons in England was only brought about by the invasion of the land hungry Normans in 1066. Conquering Wales might not have been William's immediate priority but he was imaginative enough to permit his most loyal, ambitious and adventurous barons to control the borderlands and expand their fiefdom westwards as far as they felt able.

From 1073 the swashbuckling Robert of Rhuddlan, accompanied by

Coin of
Sigtryggr
Silkbeard

Found
Bryn Maelgwn
1979

GALLOWAY

CUMBRIA

Isle of Man

"The Viking Lake"

Great
Orme

Dublin

Chester

WALES

0   miles   30

N

his faithful knight, Osbern of Orgeres, began to force his way west along the coast of north Wales and by 1078 had captured Deganwy. In 1086 Robert was recognised by the Domesday Book as 'Lord of North Wales', paying King William £40 per year for the privilege. Ordericus Vitalis tells us that, 'Robert (of Rhuddlan), enlarging his territories, erected a stone castle on mount Diganwy close to the sea.' In the course of doing so Robert, 'harried the Welsh . . . (some he) slaughtered mercilessly . . . others he kept for years in fetters, or forced into a harsh and unlawful slavery.'

The Normans advanced across the Menai Straits founding characteristic motte and bailey castles at Caernarfon, Bangor and Aberlleiniog. Having established military control the rigidly feudal and Christian Normans immediately set about formalising the structure of the Church, defining the geographical boundaries of parishes and diocese and in 1092 installing their own candidate, Herve the Breton, to the vacant see of Bangor. Many of the religious changes they effected were already in train as the native princes had tried to keep pace with trends taking place elsewhere. Despite the future ebb and flow of Welsh fortunes the centralised organisational structure favoured by the Roman Church and promoted by the Normans continued to advance, displacing the traditional forms of Celtic Christianity. The Creuddyn's three original preaching centres, or 'llans' were expanded and geographically defined to administratively split the peninsula into the newly created 'parishes' of St Tudno's, St Hilary's and St Cystennin's.

Deganwy Regained
Norman success in north Wales was limited and unsustainable. Herve, their much resented Bishop of Bangor had to beat a hasty retreat and was re-appointed to the see of Ely. Norman control of the Creuddyn was destroyed in 1093 when Robert of Rhuddlan was defeated and killed at Deganwy by a party of seaborne insurgents led by Gruffydd ap Cynan (c.1055-1137). Tradition fancifully claims Robert's head was struck off and mounted on the mast of Gruffydd's ship. Welsh control of the Creuddyn was rapidly re-established and the Normans pushed back towards Chester. Over the following two centuries the power of Gwynedd over other Welsh kingdoms waxed and waned but for most of the period the Normans were effectively excluded from the Creuddyn.

From Tribal Kingdom to Feudal Princedom
Gruffyd ap Cynan's son Owain Gwynedd (c.1100-1170) took full advantage of political divisions in England to push back Norman

incursions into Gwynedd, regaining lost territory and extending the boundaries of his kingdom eastwards to the estuary of the Dee. Unfortunately by 1157 Henry II (1133-1189) had not only restored full control in England but had secured the approval of Pope Adrian IV to stamp his authority upon Wales.

Henry rapidly advanced into Owain's kingdom but was realistic enough to accept compromise. Henry was prepared to allow Owain to rule as 'Prince of the Welsh' provided that he recognised the English King as his feudal overlord. The Norman system of landholding claimed all land as the property of the monarch who granted estates to lesser nobles on condition that they swore fealty and raised troops for the king when required. It was a rigidly hierarchical system and by accepting Henry's terms Owain kept his land but in a legal sense, delivered up his people. In accepting the role of feudal prince he was, in principle, relinquishing hopes of ever becoming king of a truly independent Wales. Gwynfor Evans neatly encapsulates Owain's approach, 'Constitutionally, the position of Wales in relation to England was being recast . . . to establish the status of a free Wales as an equal member of a confederation of feudal kingdoms recognising the overlordship of the English crown.'

King Henry's accommodation of Owain's power confirmed the leading role of Gwynedd in Wales. Put simply the princes of Gwynedd would henceforth pay homage to the king of England whilst Gwynedd could demand in its turn the fealty of all other Welsh lords.

Peace in the Creuddyn

Owain's accommodation with the English Crown did not entail submission to Canterbury for he was determined to retain some independence for the Welsh Church. Owain insisted on having his own nominee, Arthur, appointed to the see of Bangor, cunningly by-passing the claims of the Archbishop of Canterbury, by sending him to Ireland to be consecrated.

The peace and prosperity brought about by Owain encouraged Creuddyn parishioners to rebuild in stone their ancient wooden churches that had long suffered the ravages of time and the raids of the Norsemen. Of the Creuddyn's three medieval churches St Tudno's (illustrated) retains the clearest evidence of this twelfth century building work. The north wall of the nave, which incorporates a characteristically round-headed window east of the porch, formed part of a simple rectangular church erected in the age of Owain Gwynedd. The Reverend Longueville Jones writing in 1856 said, 'There are evident remains of that date in the north wall, where courses of small stones alternate with courses of larger ones, as is not uncommon in early work. This shows that the church was doubled in length by the addition of a chancel.' The twelfth century St Tudno's Church measured approximately 8 metres long by 4 metres wide and this double square box structure was typical of Welsh churches erected at the time. A screen of wooden planks probably divided the church into two halves forming a square sanctuary and a square nave.

The primitive stone baptismal font is a survival from the same period although it had been removed in the distant past and used as a trough on the nearby Glebe Farm before being restored to the church in 1855. Antiquarian H L North described it as of, 'bowl shape externally, curving in at the top and decorated with scalloping and five-leafed ornament, the leaves being connected by a stalk festooned from one to the other. Like many old Welsh fonts it is very small and could never have been used for immersion.'

Fixed to the inside of the south wall are two stone coffin lids, elaborately decorated with incised patterns that also date from the twelfth, or possibly early thirteenth century. Longueville Jones claimed, 'They possess such an elegance of design as to show that they belonged to persons of noble birth. On each of them, below the head of the cross, will be observed a buckle or brooch on either side of the stern.'

Mediaeval Townships

Underlying the Church's emerging parish system was the long-standing but evolving Welsh tribal framework, based on four main institutions, the cenedl, the tref, the cantref and the brenin corresponding to English concepts of; kindred, township, tribe and chief or king. Kin was a key concept and Gerald Cambrensis noted in the twelfth century that the Welsh, 'above all things are devoted to their clan, and will fiercely avenge any injury or dishonour suffered by those of their blood.' The tref or township was the economic unit, the area of co-operation for the production of food, by tillage of the soil, pasturage, operating fish weirs etc. The cantref was the political and judicial unit, the district within which people acted together for the trial of causes both civil and criminal and for the maintenance of the chieftain and his court. The cantref court was an assembly of the uchelwyr (or freemen) of the tribe. The brenin, the final, monarchical, element, bound the system together under one authority. In the twelfth century, chief of the Creuddyn peninsula (and much else besides) was Owain Gwynedd. The Creuddyn formed part of the geographical area of the cantref of Rhos and comprised twelve trefi, 'vills' or 'townships'. Gogarth, Cyngreawdr and Yr Wyddfyd made up the area of the Great Orme, Trefwarth and Llanwydden lay in the

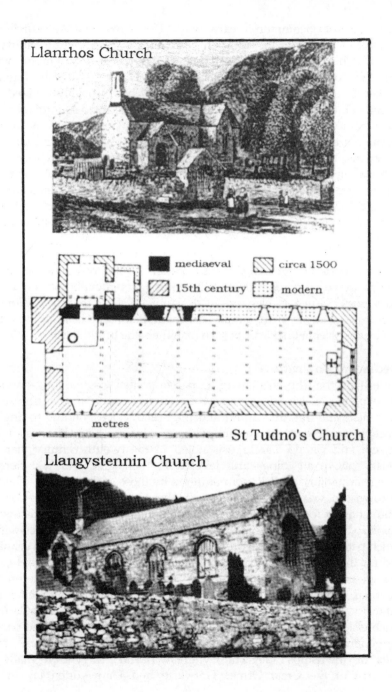

Llanrhos Church

mediaeval   circa 1500

15th century   modern

metres

St Tudno's Church

Llangystennin Church

extreme south-east whilst Penlassoc, Bodescathlan, Ganneu, Bodafon, Penrhyn, and Gloddaeth formed the geographical heartland (illustrated). The twelfth century township borders cannot be precisely drawn and the spelling of their names varied greatly with some seeming to disappear whilst new ones occasionally emerged, reflecting either shifting patterns of settlement or incomplete record keeping. Each early mediaeval cantref originally comprised a hundred townships and for administrative convenience these cantrefi were routinely divided into two or three constituent 'commotes' of which the Creuddyn was one.

From Owain Gwynedd to Llywelyn ap Iorwerth

Owain Gwynedd died in 1170 and was buried in Bangor Cathedral, where his simple arched tomb can be seen in the south wall. A constitutional moderniser in life ironically his death triggered civil war as his sons fought over the inheritance that ancient Welsh law decreed be divided between them according to 'gavelkind'. It was twenty-five years before peace returned to Gwynedd with the rise to power of Llywelyn ap Iorwerth (1173-1240).

Llywelyn adopted the pragmatic approach of Owain in his relations with King John (1167-1216). Soon after John came to power, he and Llywelyn entered into a detailed agreement that enforced the king's overlordship of Wales and stated the terms by which Llywelyn must render fealty but it also recognised the authority of Welsh law. This unique surviving document details the logical development of the process begun by Owain Gwynedd. Llywelyn did more to cement his relationship with the Crown, marrying John's illegitimate daughter, Joan, in 1205 and accompanying him on a punitive expedition into Scotland in 1209.

Unfortunately Llywelyn's relationship with John didn't stop the Marcher lords attempting to annex chunks of his land. Fed up with their incursions into the Creuddyn and impudent use of Deganwy Castle to defend their ill-gotten territorial gains Llywelyn decided to withdraw across Afon Conwy after slighting his own fortification. Randle Blondevil, the acquisitive Earl of Chester returned once more and in 1210 set about repairing Deganwy Castle for his own use. Llywelyn's men managed to evict the troublesome Earl and in retaliation carried the fight into his heartland and raided Blondevil's estates around Chester.

By that stage John was worried about Llywelyn's ever expanding ambition. He had effectively united Wales and was pushing forward into the Marches. In 1211 King John assembled an army at Chester and marched across north Wales. As John's forces advanced Llywelyn realised he would be unable to secure the Creuddyn and ordered his men to retire across the River Conwy taking with them any supplies that might be useful to the enemy and destroying everything left behind. John's forces easily gained control of Deganwy but after pitching camp on the Vardre they realised Llywelyn's scorched earth tactics had left them unable to gather sufficient supplies to sustain a prolonged campaign. The chronicles record that 'eggs commanded the price of fowls and horseflesh did duty for beef and mutton'. Starvation soon forced the army to pack up and, on Whit Monday, return to England.

Llywelyn regained Deganwy but the die was cast, peaceful co-operation with the Crown proved impossible and conflicts between Gwynedd and England followed a predictable pattern. Armies from each side would regularly march back and forth across north Wales alternately reinforcing and destroying the castle at Deganwy. Prospects for the Creuddyn looked troubled.

Deganwy and the Royal Court of Llywelyn Fawr

In 1213 Llywelyn reoccupied Deganwy Castle and completed the re-fortification work initiated by Blondevil but Deganwy was always far more than just a fort. Since the time of Maelgwn it had been the site of a royal palace (llys) providing both accommodation and administrative buildings for the itinerant court of the rulers of Gwynedd. In the twelfth and thirteenth centuries such a royal administrative complex typically included, and was supported by, a maerdref or estate that incorporated communities of the king's (of Gwynedd) bond tenants who worked the royal lands under a particularly restrictive form of tenure (tir cyfrif). The llys comprised a complex of buildings that probably included a hall, food-house and stables. The llys at Deganwy was the focus of the maerdref proving an administrative base and tax collection point for the commote of Creuddyn. Kings of Gwynedd, such as Llywelyn, periodically decamped to their Deganwy llys to meet local dignitaries and traders, dispense justice, feast and be entertained and generally consume the tax money so assiduously extracted from residents of the Creuddyn. Interestingly the modern name of the Vardre attached to the hill on which the remains of Deganwy castle are perched is a corruption of the medieval Welsh term 'maerdref'.

With the successive building, destruction and rebuilding that's occurred at Deganwy the exact layout of Llywelyn's llys can't now be mapped but excavations by Leslie Alcock in 1961-6 did find the Prince's head, or at least a contemporary representation of it in stone (copy displayed in Llandudno Museum). Alcock believed the head had been treated with some reverence and carefully concealed by soldiers serving Llywelyn's grandson in the course of a final Welsh slighting of the castle as a desperate, defensive scorched-earth tactic.

Llywelyn's Legacy

Between 1220 and 1230 Llywelyn strengthened his position by emulating Norman tactics and erecting stone castles across Snowdonia. At the time of his death in 1240 he was undisputed ruler of all 'Pura Wallia', had with impugnity hanged one of the most powerful Marcher lords and corresponded on equal terms with Phillip Augustus, King of France. Determined that his legacy would not be dissipated after his death Llywelyn had fought hard to establish primogeniture. To contain the rebellious ambitions of his eldest illegitimate son, Gruffydd, he'd kept him imprisoned in Deganwy Castle whilst he tried to ensure his crown would pass to his legitimate heir, Dafydd (c.1208-46).

In 1240 the Welsh princes were ready to accept Dafydd's accession but ironically the English King, Henry III, demanded strict adherence to Welsh inheritance law and the splitting up of Llywelyn's legacy. Henry was determined to divide and rule and prepared to take military action to impose his will. In time-honoured fashion as Henry, in 1141, advanced towards Gwynedd, Dafydd destroyed Deganwy Castle and retreated across the river.

Deganwy Castle in English Hands

Henry III took and held onto not only Deganwy Castle and the Creuddyn but the whole of Gwynedd east of the Conwy ('The Middle Country' or 'Perfeddwlad'). Dafydd signed a treaty ceding Perfeddwlad and all its fortifications to the Crown. It was a desperate retreat from the glory days of his father.

Repairs to Deganwy Castle began in the autumn of 1241 when a mandate was issued to Henry's justiciar in Ireland to have the castle safely guarded and fortified out of taxes raised in Ireland. A start was made but it wasn't until March 1244 following another directive from the king, addressed to a John Lestrange, that building work began in earnest. Henry himself arrived at Deganwy in the autumn of 1245 and observed the progress that had been made on a programme of extending and of improving the strength and sophistication of the castle that would eventually take almost a decade to complete. Most of what remains to be seen today of Deganwy Castle are the remnants of what Henry constructed in those years (illustrated). The fortifications extended across the twin hills of the Vardre, with Mansell's Tower perched on top of the smaller, eastern peak with the King's Hall with its own attached tower crowning the western hill. The area between the two peaks formed a vast open, defended parade ground, or bailey.

We can still trace the course of much of the building work from surviving documents. The donjon was begun in 1241 with progress hastened from May 1244. The King's Tower was started in May 1247 and by February 1248 the builders were ready to add the upper storey. By March 1249 they were in a position to complete the hall, adding the lead roof in October of that year. Mansell's Tower was constructed between 1247 and 1249. On 23rd August 1250 Alan le Zusch was ordered to raise the height of Mansell's Tower by 12 feet and to begin erecting a 10-foot-thick bailey wall between the two hills. Entry to the bailey was via huge entry gates, protected by massive D-shaped towers incorporating heated guardrooms in an upper storey. The northern bailey wall was finished in 1252 at cost of £1,495 13s 10d but the southern defences had to rely on natural rock formations and earthworks reinforced by timber palisades for that section never appears to have been fully completed.

Minor works and fitting out continued until about 1254 and throughout the whole of the construction period the castle was defended by a full complement of men, ammunition and 'engines of war'.

An Uneasy Peace
In 1241 Dafydd had reluctantly ceded the Perfeddwlad to Henry but had continued to rally Welsh support for reuniting Gwynedd. It was this provocation that in August 1245 brought Henry to Deganwy Castle. Henry sent a punitive raiding party across the Conwy to sack Aberconwy Abbey but his men were caught and hanged by the Welsh. Emboldened, Dafydd's troops attempted to prevent seaborne supplies getting through to Henry whose unhappy soldiers constantly complained about the cold and rain. Dafydd was prepared to negotiate and Henry guaranteed safe conduct to a party headed by Ednyfed Fychan and including Maredudd ap Rhicert and Tudur ap Madog. In October the king retreated to England but did not withdraw the garrison and retained control of the castle and the Creuddyn. Henry was determined to hold onto all lands east of Afon Conwy but Dafydd's support was growing all the time and he confidently styled himself, 'Prince of Wales'.

Then in 1246 Welsh hopes were dashed when Dafydd dropped dead at the age of 37 leaving no heir. Ironically the man who took up Dafydd's banner and carried it glory was the son of Gruffydd, his illegitimate brother who had been imprisoned in Deganwy Castle to facilitate Dafydd's own rise to power.

Days of Hope

Llywelyn ap Gruffydd's position looked fairly hopeless. Henry had proved militarily able to hold onto his lands east of the Conwy and was spending a fortune strengthening its fortifications. Llywelyn was a mere vassal of the English Crown, Wales lay battle scarred and divided and Llywelyn controlled only a portion of Gwynedd. With the Treaty of Woodstock, in 1247, Henry imposed humiliating conditions upon Llywelyn, declaring that he would retain in his own hands, 'the county of Chester with the castles of Diserth and Degannwy'. An uneasy peace was restored but contemporary chronicler Matthew Parris, felt 'Wales had been pulled down to nothing'.

Over the following eight years Llywelyn constructed a raft of secret alliances across Wales until in 1255 he felt confident enough to claim back the Perfeddwlad. In 1256 his troops began a determined siege of Deganwy Castle. The following summer a military expedition launched by Henry reached the Creuddyn and managed to relieve and re-supply the garrison but were fiercely resisted and soon forced to retreat. Llywelyn's military success rallied other Welsh princes to his flag and in 1258 they recognised him as their feudal overlord. His apparently unstoppable campaign had become a war of national liberation.

It is testament to the quality of both Henry's Deganwy fortification and his garrison troops that they resisted the siege for seven years before finally surrendering in 1263. To force submission Llywelyn must have employed a range of medieval siege engines, catapults, towers, hooked ladders and any walls not demolished during the siege were afterwards razed to the ground. Archaeological excavation reveals extensive charring amongst the foundations where pit props had first been inserted and then fired to collapse the castle walls.

But military success was not enough, Llywelyn was determined to force Henry to grant constitutional recognition to his effective power. This came in 1267 with the Treaty of Montgomery. Llywelyn acknowledged the suzerainty of Henry and agreed to pay an annual render. In return the king accepted that Llywelyn was effectively ruler of Wales with lesser princes acknowledging him as their feudal overlord.

From Triumph to Defeat

After Henry's death in November 1272 it appeared at first nothing had changed. In September 1273 Llywelyn wrote to the Justiciar of Chester thanking him for his invitation to the forthcoming coronation of Henry's son, Edward, and promising to send venison for the royal larder. But Llywelyn didn't attend when Edward I was crowned king in 1274. He

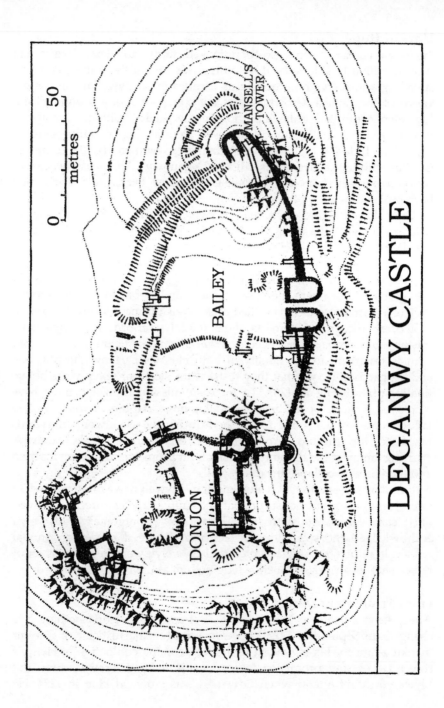

DEGANWY CASTLE

MANSELL'S TOWER

BAILEY

DONJON

0 50
metres

ceased paying his annual renders and seemed reluctant to swear fealty to the new sovereign. Exchanges passed back and forth, claiming grievances and offering excuses. When Llywelyn announced he intended to marry the daughter of Simon de Montford, Edward's declared enemy it could hardly have seemed a sign of good faith. Nor was Llywelyn reassured when Edward responded by kidnapping his bride-to-be.

On 12th November 1276 Edward's patience expired and he formally declared Llywelyn, 'a rebel and disturber of the peace'. War was inevitable.

The following year King Edward I invaded north Wales, reaching Deganwy in August. Although the castle hadn't been rebuilt since its destruction in 1263 it appears that some of the fallen and scattered stone was rapidly mortared together by his troops to create temporary defensive walls. Edward appears to have enjoyed a degree of comfort and shelter whilst resting at Deganwy as he signed surviving campaign documents, 'in castris juxta Gannou' whilst his troops undoubtedly bivouacked in tents. As he gazed out across Afon Conwy Edward decided that he would never rebuild Deganwy Castle. Following his undoubted victory he planned to control entry to the Welsh heartland by erecting a new castle across the river. In the meantime he emulated Rome's tactics and despatched a fleet to Anglesey where a team of reapers harvested the crops the Welsh armies depended on to feed them through the winter.

Llywelyn realised that he had been outmanoeuvred and offered to submit to the king's authority. Meeting at Aberconwy Abbey on the 9th November 1277 Llywelyn signed away all the gains confirmed by the Treaty of Montgomery, yet it was a kind of peace and Edward was gracious in victory. Llywelyn declared his long delayed fealty to the king and was permitted to retain control of Gwynedd west of Afon Conwy and his title, 'Prince of Wales'. Edward released Llywelyn's intended bride and even paid for the wedding but he took control of Llywelyn's lands east of Afon Conwy; the Creuddyn was again in English hands.

From Defeat to Despair
Llywelyn's limited defeat was converted into a complete disaster by the ill-judged rebellion of his disloyal brother Dafydd. In March 1282 Dafydd led an attack on the royal castle of Hawarden and called on his brother to help. Llywelyn appears to have agonised over the decision but eventually supported the attack. During the ensuing war Llywelyn was killed in a skirmish in mid-Wales amid suggestions that his traitorous brother had engineered the whole debacle to rid himself of his popular rival. If so it

ultimately did him no good.

In December 1282 Llywelyn's head was struck off and displayed on a lance at the tower of London. Dafydd was captured on Cader Idris in 1283, dragged through the streets of Shrewsbury, hanged, drawn and quartered. His head was conveyed to London, mounted on a stake and displayed alongside that of Llywelyn.

Edward trumpeted the destruction of Llywelyn's regime. He dined on plates made from Llywelyn's silver and melted down the prince's seals of office. Edward's total victory was, in 1284, cast into constitutional form with the Statute of Rhuddlan. The ancient kingdom of Gwynedd was extinguished and in its place Wales was divided up into the English system of shires.

Within months of Llywelyn's death Edward began dismantling Aberconwy Abbey and replacing it with a castle and a planted borough. Between March and June 1283 'a cartload of iron, steel and arrows from Chester was ferried across to the abbey from Deganwy . . . anchors and ships' cables were stored in the abbey . . . timber and clays were provided for building a palisade to enclose the new town.

The key strategic role the Creuddyn had enjoyed for eight hundred years was no more but Llandudno was about to gain new importance with the arrival of a key figure in Edward's administration.

Chapter Eight

Mediaeval Life in Gogarth and Gannoc (1284-1536)

In 1284 Deganwy Castle lay in ruins, stripped of its ancient role of defending the Creuddyn and the gateway to the Welsh heartlands but Edward I was not going to abandon the peninsula to the peasantry. The Creuddyn offered fertile agricultural land as well as scenic splendour, qualities much appreciated by rapacious Norman incomers.

A New Role for the Borough of Deganwy

In the mid-thirteenth century Edward's father, Henry III had planted a Norman Borough at Deganwy, adjacent to the castle he so assiduously re-fortified. The earliest documents date from 1248 when Henry ordered free burgages (plots of land) to be assigned at 'Gannoc'. The Normans created such New Towns in places of strategic importance to enable them to tax and control local populations by monopolising the marketplace as well as the battlefield. To encourage friends and fellow travellers to populate these planted Boroughs they were granted burgages on favourable terms with their safety and security assured by the adjoining military garrison.

North of the remains of the castle bailey modern archaeologists have uncovered a group of roughly rectangular enclosures that probably indicates the location of the medieval Borough of Deganwy. In 1250 Henry mandated the Justiciar of Chester to hold and publicise a market at Deganwy and in the same year an order was given to install a horse driven mill in the settlement. A millstone was discovered on the Vardre in 1948 and a semi-rotary quern turned up nearby in 1989 but in neither case could the artefact's original context be identified.

In 1252, the new Borough of Deganwy received its Royal Charter. This stipulated that 'the burgesses may enclose the said town with a dike and wall' but there is no evidence that this was ever done. Surviving pipe roll records show that between 1250 and 1255 Deganwy paid the Crown 10s per annum rental.

When Llywelyn destroyed the castle in 1263 he probably also sacked the adjacent borough but unlike the castle the town was soon rebuilt. By 1290 the market had reappeared and a list of Conwy burgesses drawn up before 1295 includes the names of six men of 'Gannou'. A rental list of 1305-6 refers to 19 properties in the town of 'Ganneu' , with the majority in the hands of English tenants. Clearly Deganwy remained a high status

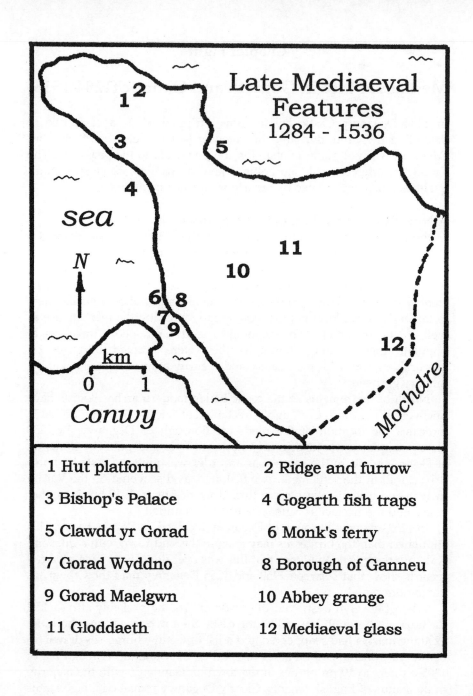

Late Mediaeval Features
1284 - 1536

sea

N

km
0 — 1

Conwy

Mochdre

1 Hut platform	2 Ridge and furrow
3 Bishop's Palace	4 Gogarth fish traps
5 Clawdd yr Gorad	6 Monk's ferry
7 Gorad Wyddno	8 Borough of Ganneu
9 Gorad Maelgwn	10 Abbey grange
11 Gloddaeth	12 Mediaeval glass

settlement even after the creation of Edward's new borough of 'Aberconway'.

Down by the Riverside

By the late thirteenth century Deganwy's raison d'etre was servicing the ferry crossing rather than the former garrison for the creation of Edward's new Conwy castle and borough had transported Deganwy's former functions across the river. It is therefore likely that buildings erected in this era gravitated westwards down the slope towards a river crossing point. The ferry was the Creuddyn's link to the region's legitimate marketplace and administrative centre of Aberconwy that was fully operational as early as 1287.

With no bridges across Afon Conwy the medieval ferry was vitally important and subject to royal decree, in 1251 for example, Henry ordered that the Friars of Bangor be allowed free passage for goods 'per Aquam de Gannoc'. The 1284 charter moving the monks to Maenan granted ownership of the ferry service to the king. A shrewd move on Edward's part because in addition to the ferry's strategic value it produced a healthy toll income, in 1284 this was worth £20 a year.

Medieval Deganwy also exploited the river with two ancient structures that can still be seen at low tide, Gorad Maelgwn and Gorad Wyddno. Gorad is the locally used name but the more correct term is 'Gored', mutated from the Welsh word 'cored' meaning 'weir'. Such fish weirs are one of the simplest, least labour-intensive and most effective ways of harvesting fish. The basic principle is that fish swim into the weir but find it difficult to swim out, particularly as the tide falls. Mediaeval weirs were typically formed by driving stakes into the sea bed and weaving slim branches in between, creating continuous hurdles strengthened at the base by piled stones forming a low foundation wall.

Huge catches were harvested from such weirs and as late as 1907 when seas were already becoming polluted and stocks overfished the fish weir just over the border of the Creuddyn at Llandrillo trapped ten tons of mackerel on one tide.

The more southerly Deganwy fish weir, Gorad Maelgwn, referred to occasionally as Goret Vailgon or the Great Weir of Gannow, was assessed in the 'Extent of the County of Caernarvon', compiled in 1284, as worth an annual rental of 40 shillings. Gorad Wyddno, the second Deganwy fish weir, named after Maelgwn's brother Gwyddno, the legendary Lord of Cantref Gwaelod was famously productive and continued in use until the early nineteenth century. By which time it had passed into the hands of the Mostyn family. In the middle ages both weirs appear to have been jointly operated by the three adjoining townships of Ganneu, Bodescathlan and Penlassoc.

Stepping Stones from Chester to Caernarfonshire

After 1284 Edward maintained the local township and commote structure but destroyed the Kingdom of Gwynedd. Since the days of Maelgwn, Gwynedd had supplied political vision, emotional determination and military might to the struggle for an independent Wales. It was therefore Edward's priority to destroy the integrity of ancient Gwynedd, it was administratively chopped into pieces. His first thought was to split Gwynedd into three new shires, Anglesey, Aberconwayshire and Cricciethshire but he settled on creating an Anglesey shire and combining the other two regions to form Caernarfonshire. This was, in many ways a conservative solution, leaving many old boundaries in operation and most ancient names unaltered. But although Gwynedd's writ had often effectively extended far to the east of Afon Conwy after the 1284 Statute of Rhuddlan the river formed the boundary of the new county of 'Caernarvonshire'. Apart from the curious anomalies of the Creuddyn and the detached townships of Maenan, Eirias, Penmaen and Llysfaen. The inclusion of Maenan in Caernarfonshire is easily explained, it resulted from Edward's decision to displace Aberconwy Abbey to make way for his new borough. To guarantee the monks' right to peaceful enjoyment of their new site at Maenan he included it within the new Crown lands of Caernarfonshire. The other detached portions of his new county are not so obviously explained. It is important to realise that post Rhuddlan, to the west of Afon Conwy lay Caernarfonshire to the east was Flintshire, and both were subject to direct rule by the Crown, whilst in between was a large swathe of land controlled by Marcher Lords. The Creuddyn, Eirias, Penmaen and Llysfaen lay along the north Wales coast like stepping stones across Marcher land. It is possible that Edward included this collection of townships in Caernarfonshire for strategic reasons. Like Hitler, Edward was keen to maintain a corridor linking territories directly under his control. He knew the Marcher lords were less than reliable allies. If insurrection erupted in the Welsh heartlands he perhaps intended to march troops across from England without having to negotiate transit rights with powerful and potentially disloyal barons. Whatever the intention the anomalous result was that although physically separated from Edward's new shire by Afon Conwy the Creuddyn peninsula was administratively attached to Caernarfonshire.

Caernarfon Rules

Caernarfonshire and Flintshire resulted from 'Rhuddlan' but Denbighshire came much later. Along its southern boundary the Creuddyn peninsula adjoined the territory of the Marcher Lords, everyone north of that boundary came under the jurisdiction of the king's sheriff at Caernarfon. The sheriff was an ancient office in England but newly created in Wales. All the financial and judicial affairs of the county were in his hands and to ensure loyalty he was paid the enormous sum of £40 per annum. Naturally Edward was anxious to reserve the position for fellow countrymen, although nominal Welshman and darling of the English establishment, Sir Gruffudd Llwyd, was appointed in 1302-05 and again 1308-9.

The chief instrument of administration was the monthly meetings of the County Court, held at Caernarfon. All important men of the county were expected to attend and adjudge a variety of matters from brewing licences to murder. Legal procedures employed a blend of English criminal law and Welsh civil law and the court was also responsible for the election of two coroners. Remarkably this whole administrative system ushered in by the Statute of Rhuddlan survived unchanged until 1536.

A Palace at Llandudno

Edward was equally keen to overhaul administration of the Church in Caernarfonshire and was fortunate to gain the loyalty of Bishop Anian (1267-1305) of Bangor. In April 1284 Bishop Anian baptised Edward's son at Caernarfon proclaiming him 'Prince of Wales'. As a reward for betraying the Welsh cause Anian was granted the Manor of Gogarth, becoming effectively Lord of Llandudno. His great palace (illustrated) now lies in ruins but when it was erected around 1300 it was the grandest house in the Creuddyn. Some claim Anian was granted the manor as early as 1277 but this rests on a confusion of Gogarth with Gogartho in Denbighshire. Whatever the exact date of the transaction it was sometime between 1284 and 1290 for taxation accounts of 1291 record Anian's ownership of the Manor and a valuation of £4 1s 8d per annum.

Anian's palace at Gogarth was erected in two phases, the first stone-built hall was almost certainly built between 1287, when construction of Conwy Castle was more or less complete, and the 1291 taxation. Even if Anian acquired the site before the Statue of Rhuddlan it is unlikely that as a high profile Anglophile he would have built his palace until he could be assured that he could, if necessary, be defended by troops rushed over from the castle garrison. Sections of a surviving wall of Anian's original hall perched on the cliff edge at Gogarth indicate that it was a two-storey building, massively constructed of local uncoursed limestone rubble, well over a metre thick and measuring 11 metres long by 7 metres wide. Dressed sandstone used for the detailing appears to have come from a quarry at Bodysgallen. Archaeological evidence suggests the building had a fireplace, a door in the north wall and a limited number of lancet windows, possibly so designed partly for defensive reasons. The hall was floored with rough stone slabs and the walls plastered internally and painted red. The building was roofed with thin Bethesda slates, similar to those employed at Conwy Castle, and plastered, or rather 'torched', internally to prevent the ingress of wind and rain. An important consideration in a building standing in such an exposed position, even before coastal erosion exacerbated the situation.

Within a decade or so of finishing the hall Anian was ready to aggrandise his palace by adding a second hall together with a set of ancillary buildings serving as kitchens, latrines etc. Uncoursed local limestone was again used but the dressed sandstone incorporated is coarser and less red than the Bodysgallen material employed previously and probably originated from the worked out Great Orme quarry. This was an even larger hall, measuring 14 metres by 9 metres, and extensive archaeological remains allow for a better understanding of the internal layout. The main hall was divided into three 4.5 metre wide bays with a span of 9 metres by huge cruck beams that supported the roof. This was an exceptional structure. The masonry work may not quite match the superb standard exemplified in a carved window frame excavated from the earlier hall but the advanced carpentry techniques employed were locally unsurpassed. Surviving slots in the Gogarth stonework point towards a pioneering use of sophisticated cruck construction and according to archaeologist Douglas Hague, Bishop Anian's carpenters created at Gogarth the widest mediaeval single spanned roof in the county.

Feudalism and the Land
In Anian's time most of the few hundred residents of the Creuddyn were farmers. Some followed specialised trades such as blacksmithing, boatbuilding or shoemaking but even craftsmen would generally still grow a few vegetables and keep a few animals. At certain times of the year, like harvest, nearly everyone would help out on the land and for many working on the king's, bishop's or some other lord's land was a feudal obligation. Farming was the basis of the Creuddyn economy and feudal obligation kept people tied to the land and to the township.

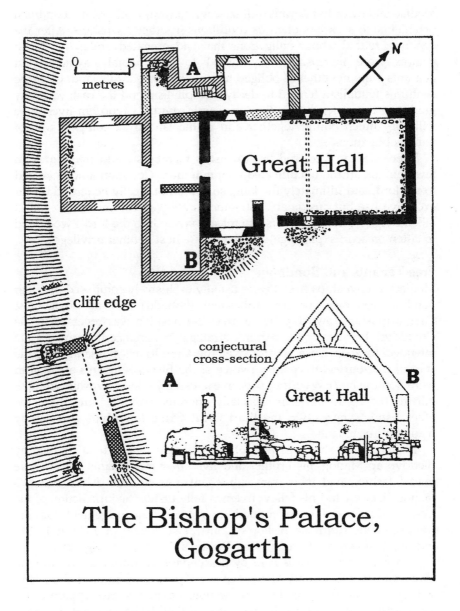

The Bishop's Palace, Gogarth

Mediaeval law didn't permit ordinary agricultural workers, the bondmen or villeins, to seek less onerous conditions in other townships. After the conquest feudal labour obligations that had operated under the Welsh princes were increasingly commuted to cash rental payments but peasants were nonetheless obliged to remain on the lord's land. Over the centuries feudalism tended to decay as capitalism and the cash economy gradually expanded but in the fourteenth century Creuddyn lives were still very much bound together and to the land by a complex web of feudal obligations.

There was no free land but township members could freely graze a few animals on the uncultivated common land. Common land belonged to the lord, and ultimately the king, so could not legally be fenced off for exclusive use but customary entitlements allowed commoners to collect fallen twigs for fuel (estovers), to release swine into the lord's woodland to fatten on acorns (pannage) and to enjoy a host of other privileges.

Free Tenants and Bondmen

Mediaeval townships (trefs) were usually exclusively composed of either bondmen (villeins) or free tribesmen (bonedd) and although most Caernarfonshire townships were 'free' the position was reversed in the Creuddyn. Because of the region's strategic importance the new regime intended to keep close control over the Creuddyn's peasantry. At the start of the fourteenth century twelve of the Bishop's tenants at Gogarth were bondmen. Yr Wyddfyd was an exclusively bond township with the villeins having to perform especially onerous manorial duties. On the other hand Cyngreadwr, the third Great Orme township, was mainly made up free tenants.

Bodafon township was part of the Bishop's manor held in 1306 by Bleddyn ap Madog, his brother and five other free tenants who in true feudal fashion had their own sub-tenants. As tenants of the Bishop's manor Bleddyn and his fellow freemen fell outside the jurisdiction of the County Court and were entitled to instead seek judgement for any transgressions from the Bishop's Court. Two letters of 1309 and 1345 indicate that in the 14th century the Bishop's Court sat at Gogarth.

Penrhyn township was held by descendants of Ednyfed Fychan who owed suit to the County Court but were permitted to hold their land without financial obligation. No rental payments are apparent for Trefwarth either and it has been suggested that the entire townships may have been sold off on privileged terms, with the township's name being a corruption of 'Trefwerth' or possibly 'Tref Iorwerth'. The majority of those living in Ganneu, Penlassoc and Bodescathlan were not free, making a total of 26 bondmen for the three townships.

Thirteen freemen of the 'Creuthin' are recorded as paying homage to Edward II following his 1307 coronation; Phelip ab Yereward, Res ab Theulin, Blethin ab David, Kenwryk Waghan, Gogan ap Hereward, Ythel ap Yropert, Goroo ab Maddoc, Blethin ab Heilin, Adam ab Heilin, Kenwrik ap Heilin, Adam ab Thomas, Goron ap Yono and Kenwrik ap Traer.

Farming the Creuddyn

In the fourteenth century there was far more arable farming in the Creuddyn than there is today. Even the Great Orme was extensively ploughed and the remains of medieval strip farming persisted and can still be identified on early Victorian maps (illustrated). Farmers were, of course, legally obliged to grind their grain at the lord's mill and Llandudno had its own windmill at least as early as the thirteenth century. It's mentioned in a manorial document of 1291 but a tax document of 1306 records that the windmill belonging to the Bishop had fallen into disrepair. The Black Prince's survey of 1352 records that the windmill was again broken and so only worth two shillings a year but if repaired would be worth twice as much but by then there were more serious troubles to contend with than a broken windmill.

The disruption caused by the conquest was followed by a noticeable deterioration in the climate. Between 1315 and 1317 there were successive failures of the harvest and in 1315 and 1348 diseases of farm animals reached epidemic proportions. An increase in arable farming and decrease in stock rearing lessened manuring of fields and causing soil infertility and crop failure. In the first half of the fourteenth century both the economy and the population of Wales was in decline and then a particularly unwelcome visitor arrived from England.

Pastuerella Pestis

In June 1348 a ship landed at Melcombe Regis, near Weymouth bearing the bacillus, Pastuerella pestis. The germ may have been carried ashore by a rat or an infected sailor but either way the Black Death had arrived in England. The bacillus survived in the saliva of the Xenopsylla cheopsis flea that was itself parasitic upon Rattus rattus, the black rat. When the flea bit into a human host its saliva infected the bloodstream with the plague bacillus. Swellings, or buboes, developed in the groin and under the armpits as the victim's skin blackened as a result of subcutaneous bleeding. Death usually followed within in a few days.

The rat flea could even travel inside bales of cloth before leaping onto

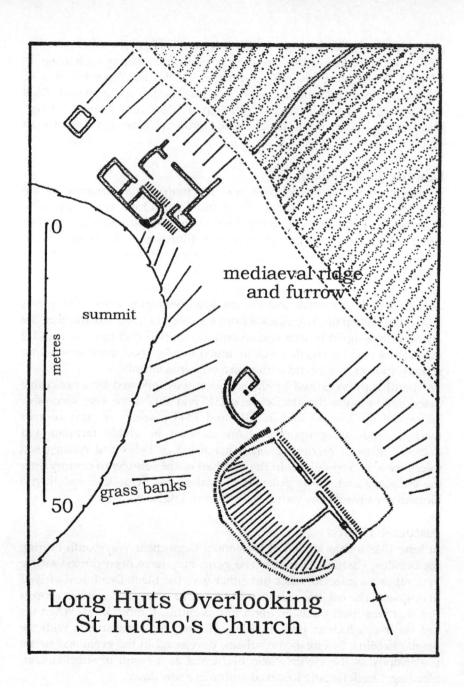

0

summit

metres

grass banks

50

mediaeval ridge
and furrow

Long Huts Overlooking
St Tudno's Church

a new human host. In March 1349 the plague reached south Wales, with deaths in Abergavenny. By June Dyffryn Clwyd was infected and by August the Black Death was killing people in the Creuddyn. The peninsula was hit comparatively hard, probably because it was more densely populated than most other parts of Wales. The annual rental value of the commote halved in 1350. In 1350-51 avowry income, payable as an annual fine on incomers to the Creuddyn seeking the protection of the feudal lord, fell to only 8d from Bleddyn ap Madog ap Robin and Dafydd ap Madog ap Meilir 'and no more for the remainder are dead by pestilence'. The Deputy-Justiciar of Caernarfonshire's records suggest Ganneu, the ancient township of Deganwy, was badly hit as the total rents and services due from bond tenants before the plague had amounted to 41s 3½d but accounts for 1351-2 show all their land had passed to the Prince for want of tenants. A letter from the Black Prince dated 20th July, 1353, makes explicit the disastrous consequence of the pestilence, cancelling the imposition of 'Staurum Princips' (Cattle Money) for a period of eleven years as 'All Gannow Died'.

Because rents were payable by townships as a unit where rents were not immediately reduced the burden of payment felt by surviving bondmen often proved intolerable, forcing them to seek a less onerous situation. Although the law hadn't formally altered, where itinerant labourers would previously have been punished and returned to their feudal lord, after the plague landlords were so desperate for labour they welcomed incomers with no questions asked.

In the latter half of the fourteenth century the Creuddyn experienced profound social change. Peasants began to realise their potential power. They would not have to wait long before they received a call to arms.

Glyndwr's Revolt

In the 1390's Richard II (1367-1400) tried to consolidate his kingdom by destroying the power of the magnates who constantly challenged his authority. Taking control of Wales, a patchwork of semi-autonomous feudal states, bishoprics, shires and territory under direct royal rule, he eliminated rivals and rewarded loyalists. This inspired many Welshmen but upset English barons who called on Henry Bolinbroke to unseat him. Confrontation took place at Conwy Castle where Richard was arrested, deposed and then imprisoned at Chester.

When a dispute arose between Anglo-Welsh nobleman, Owain ap Gruffudd ('Glyndwr') and Norman landowners, the De Grey's, the new regime conspired to frustrate the claims of the Welshman so Owain took matters into his own hands and rose up against the regime. Proclaimed by his supporters 'Prince of Wales' in September 1400 he led a successful attack on the De Grey stronghold of Ruthin. Equally effective raids on Denbigh, Rhuddlan, Flint, Hawarden and Holt swiftly followed.

Owain had spent his youth studying law in London and had probably witnessed the peasants' revolt of 1381. As Welshmen rallied to his cause Owain's revolt soon took on the character of a popular national uprising. Two brothers of the Tudor family of Anglesey, Gwilym and Rhys ap Tudor who had previously served as archers in Richard's campaigns in Ireland threw in their lot with Owain's struggle against Henry and his English armies. Employing small scale guerilla tactics on Good Friday, 1401, the Tudors led a group of forty rebels into Conwy Castle whilst the garrison was attending religious services in the chapel. They kept control of the stronghold for six months before withdrawing under safe passage with a sizeable ransom.

With the garrison disabled it was time for the men of the Creuddyn to act. The plague had snapped many of the links in the feudal chain holding down the peasantry and with Conwy in rebel hands the Bishop's Palace was an obvious target. Since Edward's invasion the Bishops of Bangor had acted as English lords and it was time to even the score. By 1401 the earlier of the two halls at Gogarth had become the Bishop's personal quarters and it appears to have received the full force of rebel anger. The Bishop realised he was a likely target and had special features installed in the building to increase the security of his quarters, jambs were modified to prevent doors being lifted off their hinges but it was all to no avail. In late 1401 or early 1402 a raiding party called and fired the building. It was left gutted and uninhabitable. In a popular expression of opposition to the Bishop's collaboration with the Crown in 1402 rebels also burnt down his cathedral at Bangor.

In 1402 Glydwr captured his old enemy Reynald de Grey in an ambush at Ruthin and held him for a year until Henry handed over a substantial ransom. The French and Bretons supported Owain and his campaign appeared unstoppable. In 1404 he boldly convened a national parliament at Machynlleth where he proposed an independent, unified Welsh State with two national universities, one in north Wales and the other in the south. The Welsh Church was declared independent of Canterbury and he proposed the legal system should revert to the traditional principles of Hywel Dda.

Owain negotiated a 'Tripartite Indenture' with Edmund Mortimer and the Earl of Northumberland to depose Henry and divide England and Wales up between themselves and in 1405 he was within a whisker of carrying it off. A combined Franco-Welsh force swept victoriously through south Wales and advanced to engage the English army in an apparently decisive battle at Woodbury Hill, near Worcester. For eight days the two sides stared at each other across a potential battlefield and then mysteriously both sides withdrew.

Owain's hour had passed and as his French support began to ebb away the focus of English tactics moved from punitive military raids to economic blockades. Welsh trading links were disrupted and weapons were in short supply. His campaign was running out of steam and in 1407 a thousand men from all over Flintshire appeared before the Chief Justice of the county and agreed to pay a communal fine for previously supporting Glyndwr. Slowly other areas followed suit until even his castles surrendered to the English. In 1410 Owain attempted a last ditch raid into Shropshire but it went terribly wrong and one of his most faithful commanders, Rhys Ddu was captured and executed.

In one of the final flashes of revolt in 1412 Owain captured and ransomed a leading Welsh supporter of Henry's, Dafydd Gam but that was the last time he was ever seen in public. Owain simply disappeared from history and as the dying embers of rebellion were extinguished in the Creuddyn the Bishop of Bangor rebuilt his palace at Gogarth. Records reveal that the Bishop's manor was fully operational by 1438 but his original hall was never reconstructed to its former elevated status. It seems unlikely that any Bishop ever again occupied it as his private quarters. Hague suggests successive Bishops felt insecure in the Creuddyn and remained reluctant to return.

Before the Glyndwr uprising the Palace offered the Bishop high status accommodation and a private judicial court. Within a century it lay abandoned and collapsed into ruins. In 1536-9 Leland described the once grand palace as 'almost clene downe by the sea' and although storms and coastal erosion undoubtedly took their toll, Canterbury's disregard for the Welsh Church and the English clergy's cynical exploitation of the episcopal post led to serious neglect. Most of the twelve Englishman appointed Bishop of Bangor between 1417 and 1541 held more remunerative posts elsewhere and seldom visited Wales and rarely, if ever, set foot in the Creuddyn. Hague remarks that 'At the end of the 15th century, the reconstruction of the Cathedral (Bangor) was commenced by bishops Dean and Skeffyngton . . . from then on, Gogarth was completely eclipsed'. But declining episcopal influence opened up new opportunities for the House of Gloddaeth.

Origins of Gloddaeth

The Gloddaeth Estate originated from an early thirteenth century land grant made by Llywelyn ap Iorwerth to Madog ap Mabon. Madog held the land on a rather unusual tenure that committed him to provide military support for the Prince even on campaigns beyond the borders of Gwynedd. The emphasis on military, rather than a more commercial form of tenure reflects the overriding strategic importance of the Creuddyn. Despite past support for the Welsh princes after their final downfall the House of Gloddaeth wasted little time in switching allegiance to the Crown. Documents record that on 3rd July 1298 Gloddaeth and Morfa Rhianedd passed down to one of Madog ap Mabon's decendants, Madog Gloddaith (sic) ap Madog ap Fychan, a man who would rise to play a leading role in the regime of Edward II. The first reference to Madog Gloddaith's tenure of office comes from 1319 when he was 'farming' the raglotry of Creuddyn and the bailiwick of the detached township of Penmaen, Llysfaen and Eirias (in other words he leased the right to collect Crown taxes in these areas, for a fixed fee, pocketing the surplus). In the following decade he served for several periods as under-sheriff and acting high sheriff of Caernarfonshire. In 1324 he was paid by the Crown for escorting troops to Portsmouth en route to Gascony and in 1336 he was appointed to guard the north Wales coast and arrest any ships needed for the king's service. In 1341 he was directed, with three others, to raise 100 spearmen and 200 archers from north Wales to go to Carlisle in readiness for the king's Scottish campaign. On 5th August 1343 Madog Gloddaith travelled to Caernarfon to declare his fealty to the king's son, Edward, the newly ordained Prince of Wales.

The following two generations at Gloddaeth enjoyed similarly privileged appointments and although they suffered the enduring restrictions applied to Welsh landholding and commercial activities they could hardly be considered downtrodden victims. It seems surprising then that Madog Gloddaith's grandson, Rhys ap Gruffudd ap Madog Gloddaith, played a prominent part in the Glyndwr revolt. What exactly prompted him to shift from trusted official to rebel is unknown but distant kinship links with the descendants of Ednyfed Fychan might have obliged him to act on residual feelings of tribal loyalty. In any case a 1406 list of 2,000 north Wales men pardoned by Henry IV after appealing for amnesty for previously supporting Glyndwr is followed by a list of obdurate outlaws that includes Rhys ap Gruffudd ap Madog Gloddaith. Records of an inquisition held at Prestatyn on 2nd October 1406 also cites Rhys's continuing rebellion but by the year end he had returned to the loyalist fold, repented to the Crown and paid a substantial fine to amend for earlier revolt. There is no record of Rhys's activities after 1406 but the

Gloddaith family never again held office in the principality.

Rhys's son Gruffydd (d.1480) and his wife Sioned had eight children but in 1448 seven fell victim to the plague leaving only Margaret (d.1532) to inherit the Gloddaeth Estate with its hall and 185 acres as well as a further 27 acres and four tenements in the townships of Rhiwledin and Cyngreawdr.

Margaret's Historic Union

In 1457 Margaret married Hywel ab Ieuan Fychan (d.1468), previously of Mostyn Hall, and so united two powerful Estates. It was an historic step for the Mostyns held Gloddaeth and expanded its landholding until they gained effective control of the Creuddyn. Since Llywelyn's original Gloddaeth grant, Madog's successors had been content to preserve the extent of the estate but Margaret was more expansive. She bought several parcels of land, sometimes in conjunction with her husband and sometimes with her son, Richard ap Hywel. Her final land purchase was made in 1528, just four years before her death. When Richard died in 1540 his Creuddyn lands amounted to 191 acres at Gloddaeth and 34 acres at Cyngreawdr and Rhiwledin, a modest expansion of the estate his mother had inherited.

The Acquisitive Mostyns

The Mostyns claimed descent from the old royal houses of Wales but were as anxious to demonstrate their loyalty to the English Crown as their new in-laws at Gloddaeth. The original Mostyn Estate had been founded in the fourteenth century by Tudor ap Ithel Fychan, originally of Halkyn, who systematically bought up parcels of land in Flintshire. He overstepped the mark when he purchased land at Whitford because the law decreed it was reserved for English colonists. As a consequence Tudor was fined and his Whitford land was confiscated. His successors at Mostyn cultivated better relations with the colonial regime. Ieuan Fychan (d.1457), for example, was educated in the households of several great English lords, fought at Agincourt and was so trusted by the Crown that he was freed from the legal restrictions applied to all other Welshmen. He was appointed to represent the Crown as Steward of the Court of the Manor of Mostyn and in 1454, on behalf of the colonial authority, he arrested Henry de Wirral, the Abbot of Basingwerke. By then, according to Mostyn agent and chronicler, George Hiller, his estates 'amounted to about 3,000 acres and he is known to have drained the marshes at Mostyn, mined the coal, and thought to have owned ships which traded from Mostyn to Ireland and Brittany'. It was Ieuan Fychan's son, Hywel (d.1468), who carried the family name to the Creuddyn and on marrying Margaret, planted it firmly at Gloddaeth Hall.

Troubled Times

Late fifteenth century Creuddyn was a place for lawless opportunism. The subtle network of obligations and loyalties that characterised tribal society had atrophied, feudalism had collapsed and yet the English legal system was not fully applicable or efficiently administered. This presented unparalleled opportunities for the enterprising and avaricious but few protections for the delicate and dispossessed. Like vultures, English barons and, increasingly, wealthy Welshmen fought over the decaying corpse of the feudal system greedily buying up land abandoned by bondmen who had voted with their feet.

When Edward IV died, unexpectedly, in 1483 he left behind a disputed succession. After defeating Edward's younger brother, Richard at Bosworth Field, Henry Richmond (1457-1509), a man born at Pembroke Castle became King Henry VII of England. The accession of Henry Tudor opened up the possibility of royal preferment for previously excluded Welshmen. Indeed Henry duly appointed Richard ap Hywel of Gloddaeth as an attendant at the Royal Court. Shrewdly realising the opportunities for advancement in London were uncertain and limited compared to those opening up in Tudor Wales Richard declined, proudly declaring 'I dwell among my own people'.

Despite Henry Tudor's twenty-four year reign he did little to alter the colonial administration of Wales but his son was to pursue a far more radical approach. In 1536 King Henry VIII would sweep away the creaking system of administration ushered in at Rhuddlan in 1284. Society in the Creuddyn was about to be shaken to its roots.

Chapter Nine

Uchelwyr to Country Gentlemen (1536-1760)

The Tudor monarchy raised the hopes of many in Wales. Unprecedented opportunities drew the Welsh gentry to the colleges of Oxford, the Inns of Court and to the Royal Household. Over 200 students from Caernarfonshire attended Oxford between 1540 and 1642. For some it was a golden age but for the majority it offered nothing. Gwynfor Evans observes, 'The noblemen, who had been the leaders of Wales in the past, were still the country's natural leaders in the time of the Tudors and afterwards. It was these who betrayed the nation.' As R T Jenkins recognised this 'was the design of Henry VIII and Elizabeth: to create a new landowning class in Wales, to bind them tightly to the throne and to turn them into Englishmen'. Within a couple of generations the dynastic leaders of Wales, the Uchelwyr, abandoned their countrymen in pursuit of individual power and wealth. Cynically demanding tribal loyalty when it suited them the Uchelwyr couldn't wait to transform themselves into English Country Gentlemen.

Union With England

When Henry VIII's parliament passed 'The Act of Union' in 1536 Wales was incorporated into England. The peculiarities of English rule over Wales were extirpated and English law universally applied. No more Marches, no more Welsh civil law and no official recognition of the Welsh language. Unlike the Acts of Union applied to Scotland (1707) and Ireland (1801) in 1536 the supposed partner had no say in the matter. The parliaments of Scotland and Ireland may have been bribed and coerced into accepting England's overtures but Wales was simply not asked. Politically it was a disaster but socially and economically Union opened doors for the rich and ambitious. The abolition of gavelkind enabled the Uchelwyr, to pass their entire land and wealth to the eldest son rather than follow traditional Welsh practice of dividing the inheritance equally amongst all offspring. This both encouraged and facilitated Estate building. Outstanding amongst the rising class of Welsh gentlemen were the Creuddyn's premier family, the Mostyns of Gloddaeth.

From ap Hywel to Aping the English

Thomas ap Richard ap Hywel (1483-1558) was the master-in-waiting at Gloddaeth Hall when Union was enacted. For a thousand years the 'ap' or 'son of' form of naming had prevailed in Wales emphasising the

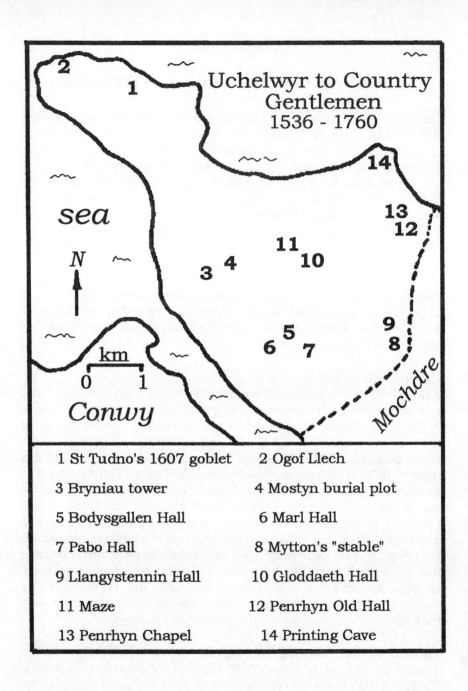

Uchelwyr to Country
Gentlemen
1536 - 1760

sea

N

km
0   1

Conwy

Mochdre

1 St Tudno's 1607 goblet   2 Ogof Llech

3 Bryniau tower   4 Mostyn burial plot

5 Bodysgallen Hall   6 Marl Hall

7 Pabo Hall   8 Mytton's "stable"

9 Llangystennin Hall   10 Gloddaeth Hall

11 Maze   12 Penrhyn Old Hall

13 Penrhyn Chapel   14 Printing Cave

dynastic links binding traditional society. Almost immediately on inheriting the Gloddaeth Estate on the death of his father in 1539, Thomas ap Richard ap Hywel anglicised his name to Thomas Mostyn. The abolition of gavelkind enabled Thomas to receive an undivided inheritance but in a remarkable act of prescience his father had already guaranteed primogeniture by conveying Mostyn estates to trustees with beneficial use reserved for his own lifetime. The Mostyns knew there was no profit in reviving dreams of national liberation but there was plenty of money to made from accommodating to English demands and cosying up to the Crown.

Thomas Mostyn married Sian (1503-1572), the daughter of Sir William Griffith of Penrhyn uniting one of the leading houses of north-east Wales, the Mostyns, with the greatest family in Gwynedd. This was no simple love match for the two dynasties had previously signed a formal contract agreeing that should either party die before the marriage was consummated then Richard ap Hywel would supply another son for the ceremony and Sir William would offer an alternative daughter! Thomas and Sian subsequently raised thirteen children at Gloddaeth where visitors were struck, as they still are, by the family's flamboyant expression of loyalty, for over the dais in the Great Hall they installed the Royal arms of the Tudors adorned with the motto, 'God Save Our Noble Queene Elizabeth and sende Hir longe to Reigne, 1584'.

Thomas Mostyn served the Crown as a Justice of the Peace in Flintshire and as Sheriff of Anglesey, 1553-4. Curiously he was never appointed Sheriff of Caernarfonshire although two of his sons were, Richard in 1572 and William in 1567 and 1568.

Richard of Bodysgallen

As Thomas's older son William (1520-1576) was likely to inherit Gloddaeth his second son, Richard, was granted Gloddaeth land in Bodysgallen township on which he erected Bodysgallen Hall. There may have been an existing watchtower at Bodysgallen, erected to provide lookout facilities on the eastern side of the river for a newly erected Conwy Castle but the Hall has been so drastically remodelled over the years that nothing pre-seventeenth century appears to have survived.

Richard and William spent years disputing rival property rights over land in the Creuddyn until the matter was resolved by the courts. The main issue concerned competing claims to the Bishop of Bangor's Manor of Gogarth. Since the Bishops had abandoned their Palace in favour of full time residence at Bangor they had leased out the Manor of Gogarth. Unfortunately successive Bishops independently issued multiple and

Bodysgallen

Gloddaeth

mutually incompatible leases. As the brothers argued over their respective claims 'unkindnes grue' and eventually William sued Richard before Bishop Rowlands, sitting at Worcester on 22nd May 1573. Concluding an unsatisfactory settlement Bishop Rowlands remarked on the obvious duplicity of both parties and observed that the Mostyn family 'were cunning and would lightly counterfeit'. Despite Rowlands perceptive remark, after returning from military service in Ireland and in the Low Countries, in 1584 Richard was appointed to the Revenue Commission.

Richard's daughter, and sole heir, Margaret Mostyn married Hugh Wynn (d.1614), a cousin of John Wynn of Gwydir and so alienated Bodysgallen from Mostyn ownership. Of course the marriage also introduced the powerful political influence of the Wynns into the Creuddyn. It was Margaret and Hugh's son, Robert Wynn who erected the earliest surviving, three storey hall at Bodysgallen, dateable by a panel above the ground-floor window in the south gable marked 1620/R.W.K. (for Robert Wynn and Katherine, his wife).

Meanwhile, Back at Gloddaeth

When William Mostyn died he had become an extremely wealthy man with an annual income of about £4,700, when the average English Peer of the Realm would have been pleased to receive a third of that amount. In 1576 Gloddaeth passed to Thomas, William's son. Thomas Mostyn (1538-1618) was a determined estate builder, even excluding tenanted land, he expanded the Gloddaeth demesne to 494 acres creating a Creuddyn estate that returned an annual income of £567 8s 8d. Of course Thomas's empire extended well beyond the Creuddyn to include Mostyn and much else besides. He spent most of his early life at Gloddaeth Hall to which he added the dovecote, that survives as an exquisite edifice and a metaphor for the age. Whilst tenants were denied their own dovecotes Gloddaeth's free-flying pigeons fed off the crops in their fields. Young birds (squabs) supplied meat that the Church allowed to be consumed even on the three 'fish days' of the week. The older birds were kept for their eggs and their droppings, which not only improved the fertility of the soil but in the 16th and 17th centuries supplied saltpetre for making gunpowder.

Thomas Mostyn's career reflects the successful advance of the family into English society. He held many official positions including Member of Parliament and was knighted in 1599 on payment of a £1,095 fee. In later life Sir Thomas Mostyn took up residence at Mostyn Hall and appointed Andrew Mostyn as Steward to run the Gloddaeth estate.

Andrew also ran personal errands for his master, who continued to refer to him as 'my servant' but was generous enough to bequeath him forty shillings in his will.

Pughs of Penrhyn

Since first arriving in the Creuddyn in 1457 the Mostyns had made rapid progress socially, politically and economically but in 1536 the Penrhyn Hall dynasty were socially and politically if not economically their equal. However just as events were moving in a direction favourable to the fortunes of the Mostyns they were turning against the interests of the family at Penrhyn. Yet the lineage of the family was as distinguished as that of the Mostyns and their hall as impressive as Gloddaeth. Tudor antiquary John Leland noted its age and location in his 'Itinerary' (1536-9), 'Place Penrine an auncient stone house by est noth est (east-north-east) on the shore'. The Penrhyn family claimed descent from the brother of Ednyfed Fychan and the incumbent in 1536 was Robert ap Hugh. Under the early Tudors the house of Penrhyn prospered. The Patent rolls of Edward IV record Robert ap Hugh of Penrhyn as owner of the eponymous township, Lord of Trewarth township and lessee of both the Conwy and Talycafn ferries. In 1551 Robert ap Hugh was High Constable of the Creuddyn, in 1559 M.P. for Denbighshire, in 1560 High Sheriff of Caernarvonshire and in 1562 High Sheriff of Denbighshire. He was the very epitome of an aspiring Tudor gentleman but when he died in 1567 the family's fortunes took a dramatic turn for the worse.

A Reformation Too Far

Tudor reshaping of the constitutional, legal and economic framework of Wales hadn't exhausted their reforming zeal. Henry VIII's dramatic break with Rome set in train a fundamental reformation of the Church that under Elizabeth I (1533-1603) sent shock waves across Britain. At Elizabeth's 1558 coronation she had taken the ancient oath to preserve the Church and had attended Mass yet soon the Mass was replaced by a form of Common Prayer and the Queen herself was appointed head of the new Church. Because the Bishops refused to conform they were deprived of their sees and imprisoned. Similarly many priests were banished or incarcerated. Students were no longer permitted to train for the priesthood and Catholic recusants who refused to attend reformed services were subject to ever increasing penalties and harsher punishments. To preserve the cause within Elizabeth's realm in 1568 the Catholic Church founded a seminary at Douai (later transferred to Rheims) to train missionary priests. In response to Elizabeth's repression in 1570 Pope Pius V issued the papal bull 'Regnans in Excelsis' excommunicating her. It was tantamount to licensing the Queen's assassination, Catholics within her realm were at a stroke transformed into potential traitors and proselytisers made liable to be hunted down and executed. Unfortunately for the fortunes of Penrhyn, Robert ap Hugh's estate was in the hands of his step-grandson, Robert Pugh, an unreformed adherent to the Old Faith, a fundamentalist Catholic recusant.

Before the reformation gathered pace the Pughs celebrated mass in the private chapel at Penrhyn, that survives today in a sadly neglected state in a field alongside the Old Hall. A 'Valor Ecclesiasticus' of 1535, a Record of Caernarfon entry for 1538 and a 1548 grant recorded in the Calendar of Patent Rolls all refer to 'Capella Beatae Mariae de Penrhyn' and it seems services had been celebrated at Penrhyn since at least the previous century. In the early sixteenth century a perpetual curate, John Fychan, was maintained at Penrhyn with half the tithes of Llandudno granted to him each year. It was then customary for the rector of St Tudno's Church to celebrate three masses a year in Penrhyn Chapel, at Christmas, Easter and Pentecost. The Easter Communion service was frequently well attended by parishioners from St Tudno's.

Penrhyn's Response to Repression

After 1570 Robert Pugh was forced to be more circumspect about celebrating the old mass and is thought to have fitted up a large cave on the Little Orme to serve as a chapel, complete with wooden panelling and an altar. Pugh didn't simply keep his faith to himself but actively encouraged and facilitated the celebration of Catholicism throughout north Wales. The Creuddyn was regarded by the authorities as a notorious hotbed of recusancy and Penrhyn Hall was the powerhouse behind this principled stand against the religious conformity demanded by the Tudor State.

Pugh was at the heart of a secret Catholic network dedicated to keeping alive the old faith. Catholic priests lived a clandestine existence, travelling in secret between the homes of sympathetic gentry willing to shelter them and arrange venues for the celebration of the Mass. In 1582 the Reverend John Bennett, a Catholic priest born at Holywell, and almost certainly on his way to Penrhyn Hall, was arrested by Sir Thomas Mostyn as he passed Gloddaeth. Bennett was sentenced to death but after a period of imprisonment at Ludlow Castle in September 1585 his sentence was commuted to perpetual exile. Like Pugh, Bennett was another key player in the underground network and before his arrest he had inspired a third local man, William Davies to travel to Rheims to train as a missionary priest. Davies was born at Groes yn eirias, near the bridge carrying the Abergele Road over the Eirias dingle. He took a degree at Oxford in 1578 and following Bennett's advice entered the seminary at Rheims on 6th April 1582. Ordained in April 1585, on 6th June William Davies returned to north Wales on the most daring of missions, a venture hosted by Robert Pugh that was to cost Davies his life.

Conspiracy at Rhiwledyn

With the assistance, inspiration and technical help of other members of the underground network whilst Davies was training in Rheims Robert Pugh had installed a printing press in the cave at Rhiwledyn, the Little Orme. With the State doing all it could to extinguish their religion the faithful hatched a bold scheme to steal a march on Elizabeth by printing Catholic tracts, not as before in Latin, a language understood only by an educated elite, but in the language of everyman, Welsh. William Davies brought with him from France the manuscript of 'Y Drych Cristianogawl' (The Christian Mirror) a tract written in Milan by Gruffydd Roberts the exiled Archdeacon of Anglesey.

Printing copies of the book on a wooden hand press was an extremely skilled job and after running off several trial booklets work began in earnest in June 1586. Surviving copies of 'Y Drych Cristianogawl' show Pugh, Davies and colleagues produced a small format book of 180 pages, measuring 5½ inches by 4 inches and printed in black Gothic type. It contains four chapters, the first is an appeal to Christians to form a habit of mental prayer and meditation on religious subjects. The second calls on readers to love God in gratitude for his worldly gifts of food, shelter, health and more. The third chapter sets out the supreme motive for loving God, namely the Incarnation and Redemption. The book finally closes with an appeal to Christians to love God for the happiness he has prepared for us in Heaven. The author had no doubt who was to blame for the ordinary people turning from God to Mammon, for it was the Welsh gentry 'who set an example to the poor commons to be without faith or conscience.' 'Y Drych Cristianogawl' was a remarkable achievement, completed under the most desperate circumstances. It was the first book ever printed on Welsh soil and it proved hugely influential but it was not received with universal acclaim.

Opportunism and Integrity

The authorities in north Wales were reluctant to suppress recusancy. The

Pughs' position was widely known and generally tolerated and when, in October 1582, a Writ of Outlawry was issued against Robert Pugh and his wife no apparent action was taken to enforce it. In 1584 the Bishop of St Asaph reported the pair to the Justices of the Great Sessions but again there was little response. The Pughs were not immediately apprehended for three reasons. Firstly, recusancy was more tolerated the further from London it was practised. Secondly in operating the Tudor system the Uchelwyr retained sufficient clan loyalty to err on the side of leniency. Thirdly, the gentry were mindful that a future monarch might return the realm to Catholicism and so it was wise to keep one's options open.

The Pughs' near neighbours at Gloddaeth were certainly reluctant to intervene. Contemporary reports describe Sir Thomas Mostyn as 'a man not very rigid against Catholics but one that complied with the times'. It appears that he only arrested Father John Bennett after he publicly declared his involvement in promoting recusancy in front of Mostyn's servant in a manner impossible to ignore. In 1586 the Star Chamber tightened the screw with a decree clamping down on clandestine presses. The Earl of Pembroke was charged to implement the measure in Wales and a letter included in the State Papers of Elizabeth I and dated 16th April 1587 informed him that a recusant press was operating in a cave at Rhiwledyn.

Sir Thomas Mostyn was instructed to act immediately and arrest all involved. Sir Thomas promptly laid siege to the cave but using the lateness of the hour as excuse for delay he decided to wait until morning. Overnight, under the cloak of darkness, the entire printing party made their escape by sea.

Nothing further was heard of Davies or Pugh until 15th March 1592 when they were apprehended at Holyhead whilst making arrangements for a party of students to embark for training at a new seminary at Valladolid in Spain. Pugh managed to escape from his captors and continued to lead a fugitive life, sheltered by sympathisers including the Houghtons at Lea Hall near Preston and Lord Montagu at Cowdray, Midhurst. The Caernarfonshire Lay Subsidy Account for 1598 records Robert's son, William, in possession of the Penrhyn Estate but we know that Robert was still alive and returned to north Wales from time to time. He was always welcome in the Creuddyn, which remained a recusant stronghold for many generations. An arrest warrant records that in 1603 Robert Pugh was warmly received at the home, near Betws y coed, of Justice of the Peace, Cadwalader Wynn. According to a cywydd (poem) composed by Gwilym Puw in 1676, Robert lived on into the reign of James I when he was finally permitted to return and spent his final years at home in the Creuddyn.

Martyrdom of William Davies

Davies was less fortunate. Tried at Beaumaris the authorities repeatedly attempted to persuade William Davies to at least give the appearance of conforming to the reformed religion but he resolutely stuck to his principles and rejected all offers of compromise. After sixteen months imprisonment on 27th July 1593 he was taken from Beaumaris gaol, tied to a hurdle and dragged to a place of public execution, where he was hanged, drawn and quartered. In a gruesome postscript to the story it was reported that one of Davies's bloody hands was secretly conveyed to Penrhyn Hall where it was preserved as a saintly relic. It may be apocryphal but it is recorded that after the departure of James Caetmore Pugh, the last of the dynasty, in 1760 an old trunk was discovered at Penrhyn Hall that when opened was found to contain a withered hand.

Tudor Law and Order

The Elizabethan purges destroyed the fortunes of the Pughs and strained the loyalty of fellow members of the gentry. The Mostyns publicly obeyed the letter of the law although they installed a priest-hole at Gloddaeth where they also took risks to preserve a pre-reformation life-size carved oak Christ figure. This rare pre-crucifixion representation of Christ seated on a rock, bound and wearing a crown of thorns probably dates to 1518 and originates from Rhuddlan Priory. (the 'Mostyn Christ' can be viewed at Bangor Cathedral, where it has been on permanent loan since 1953).

Sir Richard Bulkeley, whose daughter Jane married Robert Pugh and was jointly charged with him of recusancy was himself initially solidly Catholic. In 1574 his name was included in a list drawn up by supporters of Mary Queen of Scots along with a note that, 'All the Bulkeleys are Catholics' but as the repressive noose tightened Sir Richard adopted an increasingly protestant approach. By 1590 he had risen high in royal favour and was entrusted by the Privy Council to inform them of 'bad disposed Persons, Seminary Priests and such others'.

As the Tudors intended the Uchelwyr were unable to resist the lure of preferment. An essential requirement was appointment as a Justice of the Peace, a post that in the Tudor period guaranteed status, power and commercial advantage. In an age when most aspects of local administration, from bridge building to the punishment of petty crime and administration of the poor law were directed by the Justices, securing appointment as a J.P. was a prerequisite to effective estate

Y DRYCH CRISTIA NOGÁWL:

YN YR HWN Y DICHON POB CRISTIAWN
GANFOD GWREÎDHIN A DECHREVAD
pob daioni fprydawl:

SEF GWYBOD MODH I WÁSANA
ethu Duw, drwy ei garu ai ofni yn fwy
na dim, ag i daflu ymaith beth byn-
nag a r a fo rwyftr i hynny.

Y RHANN GYNTAF
yn peri gwafanaethu Duw
drwy ei garu.

Conuertimini ad me, & conuertar ad vos,
ait Dominus exercituum. 3. Malach. 7.

Dymchwelwch chwi atow fi, a mineu a
dhymchwelaf atow chwitheu, með
Arglwyð y lluoeð.

Rhotomagi apud hæredes
Iathroi Fauonis.

1585

building. It was no coincidence that the Creuddyn's most accomplished estate builder, Sir Thomas Mostyn not only held J.P. appointments in three counties but also served as Sheriff of Caernarfonshire, Flintshire and Anglesey and Muster-Master and Custodian of Crown Arms and Armour in Flintshire. As holder of so many official posts and the largest landowner from the Conwy to the Dee he was naturally expected to act as local shipping increasing fell victim to Barbary pirates, in the early part of the seventeenth century. His response was to erect an early warning system, consisting of a chain of four lookout towers situated, respectively at, Bryniau Hill, Llandrillo yn rhos, Abergele and Whitford. The Llandrillo post comprised the addition of a small raised and castellated section to the already existing church tower. The other three posts were circular, free-standing, stone towers erected on elevated land and sited to enable them to signal to each other by means of lighted beacons if pirate ships were spotted along their respective section of the coast. Construction probably took place sometime in the reign of James I after the Elizabethan Navy had become depleted and the commercial fleet grown increasingly vulnerable to attack. G M Trevelyan observes 'the Royal Navy did almost nothing to protect them even in the Channel. Between 1609 and 1616 Turkish pirates from Algiers guided by English renegades, took 466 of our merchant vessels; in 1625 they carried off 1,000 of our seamen as slaves and took twenty-seven vessels in ten days.' The dangers of seventeenth century piracy even reached the ears of the parishioners of Llanbedrycennin where vestry documents record a decision to send monies 'towards the redemption of the poor captives that have been lately taken by the Turkishe Pirates'.

Creuddyn Crimewatch

Safeguarding shipping from 'Turkishe Pirates' was an exceptional responsibility of Tudor magistrates who routinely dealt with more familiar crimes and misdemeanours. The County Court session presided over by Richard Bulkeley and fellow J.P.s and held on 6th October 1541 at Caernarfon judged a couple of typical Creuddyn cases. It was claimed that 'Thomas ap David ap Edward lately of Bodysgallen (township) . . . yeoman, on the fourth day of September . . . with force and arms etc at Bodysgallen . . . made an assault upon a certain Jonet ferch (daughter of) Hywel ap Benet and then and there did beat and maltreat the same Jonet against the peace of the lord the king.' Thomas was judged guilty of assault and fined accordingly.

It seems Thomas had an accomplice for the Quarter Session records also note that 'Margaret ferch Hugh ap Gruffydd lately of Bodysgallen . .

. housewife, on the said day, year and place with force and arms etc. made an assault upon the aforesaid Jonet . . . and did beat and maltreat the same Jonet against the peace of the lord the king.'

Later in the Session judgement was given against and a fine imposed upon 'Gruffydd ap David lately of Kyngrrayder', a yeoman from one of the three Great Orme townships after he was found to have assaulted Henry ap Llywelyn ap Hulta at Gloddaeth township.

A decade later a trio of interesting indictments were issued by the Caernarfonshire J.P.s. In the first case, heard on 20th December 1551, it was claimed that 'Richard ap John ap Sciencyn of Trewarth, yeoman, at Trewarth forcibly entered upon a parcel of land belonging to Robert ap Hugh gentleman, and struck Elin ferch Sir Rhys Fychan, widow, who had been sent to plough the said land, and also struck her oxen'!

On 25th December, 1551, an indictment held that 'Rheinallt ap Robert ap William of Trewarth, gentleman, on the feast of Christ's Nativity at Trewarth in the parish of Llangystennin stole 20d. in cash of good and lawful English money belonging to Robert ap Hugh, gentleman.'

The third indictment, heard on 13th June, 1552 paints a picture of a lively dispute that occurred at the Little Orme. 'Rheinallt ap Rheinallt ap Ken' of Rueledyng, yeoman (and) Alice ferch Robert, his wife of the same, housewife (and) Margaret ferch David ap John, widow (and) Thomas ap Richard ap Rhys, yeoman (and) Hugh ap Richard ap Hywel ap Ieuan, yeoman (and) Margaret ferch Hugh, housewife (and) David ap Richard ap Rhys, yeoman, all of the same, at Rueledyng with swords, staves, crossbows, spear and other defensive weapons assembled in a warlike manner in one rout and riot to the great affray and disturbance of the lieges of the lord the king and made an assault upon Gruffydd ap Richard Lewis.'

Hiccup at Gloddaeth

When Sir Thomas Mostyn died in 1618 the ascendancy of Gloddaeth seemed assured. The family had skilfully steered a profitable path through the exigencies of the reformation in contrast to the Pughs whose fortunes continued to decline. For a couple of generations all appeared well but Colonel Sir Roger Mostyn (1623-1690), Sir Thomas's Great-Grandson and heir, placed centuries of estate building in jeopardy when he backed the wrong side in the Civil War.

The roots of the war stretched back into matters left unresolved by Tudor reformers. No sustainable balance had been struck between Catholics and Puritans, between Church and the State and between monarch and merchants. Added to the powder keg of societal conflict was a spark of human bloody-mindedness. Charles I (1600-49) was temperamentally unsuited to the work of reconciliation and compromise necessary to carry forward essential reforms of Church and State. Charles was financially profligate but too arrogant to seek the support of parliament necessary to properly raise taxes. Instead he raised money improperly, squeezing cash from his subjects until they finally began to squeak.

As part of his money-making schemes in 1627 Charles privatised the Conwy ferry and the following year sold off Conwy Castle for £100 but it was his incessant demands for 'Ship Money' that upset most people. Traditionally 'Ship Money' was a tax levied only on coastal areas to finance their defence and protect their maritime trade. In 1635 Charles began demanding Ship Money from inland areas purely to provide himself with extra funds. It was imaginative but deeply resented and damaged the public's perception of the monarchy although the Creuddyn remained loyal to the King.

Colonel Roger Mostyn's War

On 22nd August 1642 the Royal Standard of King Charles I was raised at Nottingham signalling the start of a Civil War. Colonel Roger Mostyn's (1623-90) father had died just four days before but he was forced to miss the funeral in order to organise the defence of Flint Castle on behalf of the Royalists cause. Selling off most of the family's collection of almost a hundredweight of gold and silver plate to finance his campaign Colonel Mostyn raised a troop of 1,500 soldiers in just 12 hours. Mostyn's troop proved ill-disciplined and on 2nd February 1643 infamously rampaged around Chester and looted the home of the Commander of the Parliamentary forces. Discipline was eventually restored and in November of the same year Mostyn's troopers helped recapture Hawarden Castle. After suffering several reverses by 1644 Mostyn's force had been reduced to 300 men. At the end of May 1646 Colonel Roger was at Gloddaeth preparing to defend his Estate from despoliation by Thomas Mytton's (1608-56) Parliamentary troops who were advancing to attack Conwy. During the ensuing siege Mytton used Llangystennin Church to stable his cavalry. Canons mounted at Cae Battery, Llandudno Junction battered the castle walls, and a 7 foot long specimen with a 5½ inch bore employed in the siege was subsequently retrieved and is now on show at Gloddaeth.

In November 1646 Conwy Castle finally surrendered to the Parliamentary forces. Mostyn's Royalist fortunes continued to decline until in January 1649 the King was arraigned by Parliament and condemned as a tyrant and traitor. On the 30th January 1649 Charles was beheaded at Whitehall and although the war dragged on until 1651 Parliament was eventually victorious. Mostyn returned home and attempted to retrieve what he could of his estates. His involvement in the war was estimated to have cost him £60,000 in equipping soldiers and fortifying Flint Castle plus a huge punitive fine imposed after the war by Cromwell's protectorate.

Colonel Hugh Wynne of Bodysgallen

The grave memorial of Wynne's daughter in Llanrhos Church records that Roger Mostyn's cousin, Colonel Hugh Wynne of Bodysgallen (1620-74) 'at his own expense raised a Regiment of foot for the service of King Charles (and) was a great sufferer for the Royal Cause'. Wynne was frequently called to defend Flint Castle on behalf of the Governor, his cousin Colonel Mostyn. In 1643 he took his regiment to Chester and defended the City throughout the long siege. During negotiations for the City's surrender he acted as one of two named hostages. On 3rd February 1646 he accompanied his men on their honourable march back to their homes in north Wales, with each man bearing arms and permitted twelve cartridges as a defence against possible ambush. Colonel Wynne continued the struggle in defence of Denbigh until he was captured in 1650 and fined £63.

Captain Robert Pugh of Penrhyn

Having been persecuted by the Crown for generations the Pughs enduring faith assured the Royalists of their support against Parliamentary Puritans. In October 1645 Captain Robert Pugh (1599-1659) marched with 100 men to join the Royalist forces at Denbigh, having contributed £10 for their maintenance and the provision of colours and drums. Robert's younger brother, Captain Gwilym Pugh served under the Marquis of Worcester and was captured at Raglan Castle. After the war Robert Pugh, who is thought to have secretly trained as a Jesuit priest in his youth, became Chaplain to Henrietta Maria (1609-69), wife of the executed monarch.

Archbishop John Williams at Gloddaeth

Archbishop John Williams (1582-1650), was born in Conwy, died at Gloddaeth and was probably the most important and controversial local character of the Civil War. Educated at Cambridge he impressed James I with one of his sermons and was appointed King's Chaplain in 1617 and Bishop of Lincoln in 1621. Charles I was less impressed and in 1625

Williams lost his position as Keeper of the Great Seal, in 1637 he was heavily fined by the Star Chamber and in 1639 he was condemned to the Tower of London. Rehabilitated in 1641 he joined the House of Lords and was appointed Archbishop of York. Chased out of York by Roundheads he returned to his native Conwy where he set about reinforcing the town's neglected defences at his own expense, on behalf of the king. When Charles received news of this demonstrable loyalty he wrote a letter, dated 1st August 1643, guaranteeing repayment of Williams' costs and appointing him Governor of Conwy. Unfortunately Williams found Charles was not as good as his word when control of Conwy was subsequently granted to Sir John Owen. As relations soured in May 1645 Sir John Owen unceremoniously turned him out of the castle. Affronted at this indignity and offended by Owen's practice of raiding the farms of friend and foe alike to obtain military provisions Williams decided to defect to the Parliamentary side.

Taking temporary refuge at Gloddaeth as a guest of Lady Mostyn, John Williams wrote advising friends and family in Conwy to evacuate the town. After contacting the advancing Parliamentary forces in early August 1646 Williams attended a meeting organised by Mytton to plan the capture of Conwy. Williams advised his former enemy how best to destroy the very defences he had previously reinforced. Fighting commenced on 9th August and Williams was directly involved in the action, receiving a serious wound in the neck. By then a tried and trusted member of the Parliamentary cause Williams was one of the trio of Commissioners appointed by Mytton to negotiate Sir John Owen's November surrender.

Local Royalists deeply resented Archbishop Williams' betrayal but after the execution of King Charles he sought forgiveness through prayer. He was invited back to Gloddaeth Hall by Lady Mary Mostyn, where he died on 25th March 1650.

Gogarth's Regicidal Lord of the Manor

Fighting ended in 1651 but retribution continued. Besides being stripped of their offices and heavily fined the Mostyns were deprived of the Manor of Gogarth, which was granted to Colonel John Jones, a zealous Puritan officer who in 1647 Archbishop John Williams had called, 'The most universally hated man in north Wales.' Unlike Williams, Colonel Jones was a man of ruthless consistency, a 'Fifth Monarchy' man. The new Lord of the Manor of Gogarth was a fundamentalist who regarded the Civil War and the beheading of the monarch as necessary preludes to the physical return of Christ. The Fifth Monarchy men drew inspiration from prophecies contained in the books of 'Daniel' and 'Revelation'. Claiming that the kingdoms of Babylon, Persia, Greece had, as predicted by the bible, been violently overthrown it was their historic mission to complete the destruction of the Church of Rome and usher in the Kingdom of God on Earth.

During the Civil War Colonel John Jones fought against Sir John Owen in north Wales. He was a judge at Charles's trial and he signed the King's death warrant. Doubting Cromwell's commitment to the Godly Kingdom, in 1653 he opposed the imposition of the Protectorate although in 1656 he married Cromwell's widowed sister. A Fifth Monarchist plot to overthrow the Protectorate failed in 1657 and although the restoration of Charles II guaranteed amnesty to former Parliamentary soldiers it excepted the regicides.

Jones made no attempt to escape abroad. He was arrested in June 1660 and at his trial in October he proudly claimed responsibility for killing the king. On the 17th October 1660 John Jones was dragged to Charing Cross where he was publicly hanged, drawn and quartered. Witnesses were deeply moved by Jones's conduct as death approached. The newsbook of 'Mercurius Publicus' observed that he 'lifted up his hands as he was drawn upon the hurdle and at the place of execution to gain the people's prayers.' Diarist John Evelyn arrived too late for the main event but captured the immediate aftermath, 'The traitors executed were Scroop, Cook and Jones. I did not see their execution, but met their quarters mangled and cut and reeking as they were brought from the gallows in baskets.'

Tolerance, Recusancy and Nonconformity

The Civil War destroyed the vitality of Catholicism in Wales but fertilised a range of protestant non-conformities. Fearing the seditious potential of groups demanding more godly rule or organising alliances with believers abroad the authorities attempted to clamp down on religious radicalism. The restoration of Charles II was accompanied by the enactment of the Clarendom Code which severely restricted religious dissent. Nonconformity made no further inroads into the Creuddyn until almost the opening of the nineteenth century but in the late seventeenth century the authorities remained wary of the Pughs' continuing support for the Catholic cause.

Just before Christmas 1687 the magistrates ordered the Constable and his assistants to search Penrhyn Hall, suspecting the family of harbouring Irish rebels intent on opposing the landing of William of Orange. The Constable's party found only sufficient weapons to arm a single foot soldier but vented their frustration by vandalising Penrhyn's private chapel. In 1688 Robert Pugh volunteered to raise a local levy to support James II against an Orange invasion and was subsequently killed fighting for the Catholic cause in Ireland. Although Catholicism was less feared after the 1689 Act of Toleration, as late as 1696 the Constable is recorded as having again defaced the Pughs' chapel so it is quite possible the family continued to suffer low level harassment for their religious beliefs.

In 1681 William Lloyd (1627-1717), Bishop of St Asaph, ordered the compilation of a Notitiae recording information on parishioners in his diocese. This revealed there were then 4 declared recusants in the parish of Llangystennin, Blanch Parry, widow, Dorothy Williams her daughter, Dorothy Pue, the wife of William Salisbury and Catherine Salisbury, his daughter. Furthermore, Owen Evans, Mary Jane Griffiths, David Williams, Elizabeth Owen and Jane Richard all refused to send their children 'to be catechised'. Notitiae returns for 1686 provide some perspective on the numbers of those refusing to accept the authority of the Anglican Church by recording that Llangystennin Parish comprised a total of 265 individuals living in 70 family groups that included 87 children under the age of sixteen.

Iconography in the Creuddyn

Besides reshaping the religious behaviour of the people the ideological zealots of the sixteenth and seventeenth centuries stripped the altars and refashioned the churches. Virtually nothing of the decorative medieval fittings of the Creuddyn's ancient churches escaped the destructive attention of the Puritans. Astonishingly five of Llangystennin's painted windows of about 1500 survive, possibly because they were temporarily removed for safekeeping by an assiduous parishioner anticipating Mytton's sacriligeous use of the building.

The post-medieval, reformed Church of England generally cast off its old Catholic imagery in adopting a stripped-down aesthetic evident in the Creuddyn's surviving seventeenth century church plate. The simplicity of St Tudno's silver goblet of 1607 suggests it was originally designed as a secular piece donated to the church for communion use, perhaps replacing a pre-reformation chalice. The Llanrhos chalice reveals, or perhaps conceals, an altogether more complex and intriguing story for the bottom half is Catholic in design whilst the top is Anglican! Although the cup is inscribed, 'The gift of Sir Roger and Dame Lumley Mostyn, his wife, to the church of eglwys Rhose, 1673' it has undoubtedly been fitted to a stem and base produced earlier in the same century.

Hierarchy of Eighteenth Century Gentry Houses

After centuries of fighting, lawlessness and religious upheaval 1700 ushered in an age of comparative peace and prosperity in the Creuddyn. By 1700, local gentry houses had settled into an enduring order of seniority. Gloddaeth formed the pinnacle, followed by, in declining rank order, Bodysgallen, Penrhyn, Marl and Llangystennin. The last mentioned hall was erected around 1638 and occupied in the 17th and 18th centuries by the Lloyd family. A floor slab in the church records the burial of Robert Lloyd of Hendrewaelod (and Llangystennin) on 25th July 1691 whilst a grave plot contains the bodies of several generations, from 'John Lloyd of Llangystennin . . . who was buried the 25th July 1701 in the 82nd year of his age' to 'Catherine Lloyd . . . great-great-grandaughter of the above . . . who departed this life on the 9th day of March 1799'. The Lloyds never wielded much power in the Creuddyn, were not of the same social rank as the Mostyns and at the end of the eighteenth century antiquarian Hyde Hall noted further slippage of the Estate's status, 'Llangystenin Hall, once the residence of the family of a country squire; but now in the occupation of a tenant'.

Marl Hall had greater claim to Manor House status but was seldom the principal seat of a gentry family and was adversely affected by repeated changes of ownership and two devastating fires. It began well as the new Hall of aspiring Elizabethan gentleman William Holland, a burgess and churchwarden of Conwy and son of a barrister. William also owned property at Beaumaris and was duly appointed Justice of the Peace but in 1623 fell out with Thomas Mostyn over their relative Quarter-Sessions jurisdiction and then financial problems compelled him, in May 1624, to mortgage the Estate to Archbishop John Williams. The family stayed in residence but didn't pay the rent and as Williams had huge fines to pay he sold the property to Sir John Wynn. Still no rent was forthcoming so in July 1641 Margaret, William's daughter and the sole surviving member of the family, was turned out of Marl by the Under-Sheriff. A few weeks later she was dead and was buried along with her little daughter in Conwy churchyard.

Archbishop John Williams reacquired Marl but it appears that during the Civil War Colonel Mytton's troopers burnt down the Hall. Williams died in 1650 and it was his heir, Sir Griffith Williams who in 1661 rebuilt Marl, possibly to celebrate his appointment as a baronet. The Williams family were immensely wealthy, owning lands that comprised a third of Caernarfonshire and although Marl included the lucrative licence to operate the Conwy ferry it was essentially peripheral to the family's operations. In any case in about 1733 Marl was again devastated by fire and left derelict. In 1809 Hyde Hall observed 'Marl is a respectable looking mansion in the midst of a fine wood and commanding a noble view of Conway Castle, but the interior of it, with the exception of one wing, has been suffered to remain in a delapidated state since its destruction by fire.' It would never again regain its former status.

The ancient Penrhyn Hall had once been the equal of Gloddaeth but by 1700 had been dragged down by the punitive effects of the reformation. The Pugh family's faith excluded them from political office and increasingly isolated them from their neighbours. The Hall and Estate became increasingly neglected and when, in the late 1750's, James Coetmore Pugh inherited Penrhyn he was quite happy to sell. In any case he was the last of the line and when he died in 1769 one of the Creuddyn's most historic families was extinguished.

Developments at Bodysgallen

In 1700 Bodysgallen was in the hands of Robert Wynn (b.1655) of Berthddu and Plas Mawr, maintaining its function as a magnificent secondary mansion house to a family whose political influence ranged far and wide. Fortunately for the Creuddyn the Houses of Bodysgallen and Gloddaeth, linked by family ties since the sixteenth century, generally enjoyed good relations. Robert Wynn (1520-98), builder of Plas Mawr, chose Sir Roger Mostyn (d.1642), for example, to act as his executor. Occasionally the families didn't see eye to eye and after Robert's death Sir Roger had to face fierce criticism from the Wynns that he had mismanaged their inheritance.

Between 1700 and 1730 Richard Mostyn's additions to the 1620 Hall tripled the size of Bodysgallen, improving accommodation and adding a new kitchen and a servants' hall. The grounds were developed to emphasise to visitors the status and enlightened renaissance sensitivies of the Wynns, with a formal sunken Dutch garden installed south of the house. South-west of the Hall an impressive grass terrace, over 100 metres long, was laid out to take advantage of the view over Conwy and the river estuary. Antiquarian travellers, Pennant who visited in 1782 and Fenton in 1810, were both suitably impressed. Fenton observed not only the 'fine grassy terrace' but also a curiosity that has since disappeared. At one end of the terrace he spied a covered seat 'formed out of an old bed of Oak, inlaid with other wood, in a compartment of which I observe the date of 1581, with the initials, R.W.'

A walled, two acre, kitchen garden was later added and vines planted and by 1755 wines were being produced at Bodysgallen.

Llangystennin
Hall

Penrhyn
Old
Hall

Marl
Hall

Golden Age of Gloddaeth

The Civil War cost Colonel Sir Roger Mostyn dear and in 1674 he wrote to a neighbour, Piers Pennant, pleading for prompt payment of a £4 debt 'for I want the money to make up £20 to send my son to Oxford next week'. Curiously he still felt able to enjoy the leisured lifestyle of a renaissance gentleman. As George Hiller observes, 'Sir Roger was a great sportsman and was always giving gifts of horses and hounds'. Fortunately the coffers were soon replenished from the profits of the family's coalmines at Mostyn although there was a temporary setback in February 1675 when a miner's candle ignited fire damp, blowing apart the pit and blasting the miner's tattered body 100 feet into the air.

Late seventeenth century gentleman no longer hunted deer or went hawking for sport as the truly fashionable preferred shooting game birds for pleasure. Colonel Sir Roger enjoyed shooting at Gloddaeth although the ruined pheasantry belongs to a later era. The dovecote with its crow-stepped gables and similarly styled water tower were either his work or that of his son, Sir Thomas (1651-1700), who incidentally exemplified the time-honoured Mostyn pattern of alternately naming the head of the family either Thomas or Roger. Sir Thomas and his wife Bridget were certainly responsible for erection of the eastern wing of Gloddaeth that doubled the accommodation provided by the original Hall. A decorative plaster panel above a doorway to a small lobby in this wing incorporates the monogram TBM 1673, for Thomas and Bridget Mostyn. Thomas and Bridget also laid out ornamental terraces at Gloddaeth and a doorway from the present main terrace to the former rose garden bears the date and initials T.B.M. 1680.

Ogof Llech

Thomas was also the likely creator of Ogof Llech, that enduring and most intriguing of Llandudno's mysteries that can still be visited today, though the route is extremely dangerous. I can't better the description proffered, in 1875, by Reverend Owen Jones, 'On the northern side of Pen Gogarth, almost under the lighthouse, there is a sort of cave, called Ogof Llech by the natives. Its shape is a half octagon, and at the entrance there are two columns of masonry, one on each side of the opening. The back of the cave and the benches are of similar construction. Some years ago there was a carved stone table in the middle, but now only the pedestal remains. At the side of the entrance there was also a stone water trough constantly filled with the purest sweet water, which was conveyed to it along a channel ingenuously carved in the rock; the same water filled a basin skilfully carved in the rock below the cave . . . Some consider this to

148

have been the old primitive cave of St Tudno . . . Others consider it to have been a sort of pleasure house built by the ancestors of the old Mostyn family, who would visit here for refreshment when hunting on the mountain.' A Cywydd entitled 'Ode to the Llech in Llandudno' composed in 1693 by Sion Dafydd Las and translated literally by Spinther James in 1913, adds poetic detail;

There is one cave in an abyss
Of fine stone, hard by the wave;
An old building founded by God, of good substance,
It was ever a cell in the cliff's base . . .
. . . This was fitted up with skill and taste
For Mostyn's heir, a man of wit'
. . . the new abode of hewn stone
To fishing he devotes himself
Free from care and full of bliss.
Thence to the shore – to his abode.
The cheerful cave daintily equipped . . .
. . . stones in its mighty round walls
Serving as tables and pleasant seats
And a round table of hewn-stone.
In the grotto is all supreme
A spring of water cold and clear.

Sion Dafydd Las (d.1690) was one of Wales last itinerant poets, and the Cywydd was likely a commission from Sir Thomas, a great sponsor of the arts. Ogof Llech was said to have sheltered St Tudno and so at a time when it amused renaissance gentlemen to create romantic grottoes and follies it would have appealed to Sir Thomas to convert the natural shelter into a cross between a chapel and a summerhouse. As a sportsman Ogof Llech permitted Sir Thomas to enjoy modest hospitality whilst shooting on the Great Orme or fishing off the headland but it would perhaps more importantly show his companions that he was a fashionable gentleman. Society diarist John Evelyn (1620-1705) returned from visiting top Italian renaissance gardens an ardent advocate of rugged naturalistic features. He urged upon gentlemen 'the introduction of Caves, Grotts, Mounts and itrregular ornaments (which) do contribute to contemplative and philosophical Enthusiasms . . . (and) influence the soule and spirits of man, and prepare them for converse with good Angells.'

Thomas was particularly interested in Welsh literature, he collected manuscripts and expanded the Gloddaeth library collection, but he was also a shrewd businessman. His marriage to Bridget added 6,000 acres of Cheshire to the Mostyn estates but unfortunately came with a less welcome inheritance, a land steward named William Chantrell. Sir Thomas suspected Chantrell's probity and invited him to deliver copies of his accounts to Gloddaeth for inspection. Officially Chantrell's remuneration consisted of £8 a year salary, together with stabling for his horse, food for himself and his master's cast off clothing. Despite the steward's books proving almost indecipherable, including one apparently soaked in seawater, Sir Thomas found Chantrell had creatively increased his remuneration by £550.

Drawing up a draft will in 1680 Sir Thomas demonstrated a similarly calculating approach. Mindful of his wife's Catholic religion and the fact that for adherents it brought exclusion from public office he noted the 'danger my children would be in of falling into Popish hands by my death . . . ' and he went on to request that the 'Dean of Bangor appoint and nominate trustees as the guardians of my children during their minority to be by them . . . educated, brought up and instructed in the true Protestant religion as it is now established by law in the Church of England . . . and keep them from the company and converse of their Popish relations or such others as may seduce them to Popery'.

Sir Roger Mostyn's Amazing Parkland

Thomas's son, Sir Roger Mostyn (1673-1739) continued to develop Gloddaeth, implementing an extensive and imaginative tree-planting scheme. A network of walks and rides were created and although now much neglected a number of the original trees survive, mature specimens of yew, lime and oak. In 1792 Pennant noted that 'Part of the plain below the house was planted . . . with forest trees , and laid out . . . in straight walks, intersecting each other, or radiating from a centre, distinguished by a statue'. The over life-sized lead statue (of Hercules) remains in situ and the patterns of radiating walks can still be seen on the ground. Hercules stands on a sandstone plinth bearing the initials of the famous early eighteenth century sculptor, John van Nost, who died in 1729. Pennant remarked that 'The upper walks, having fortunately a steep and stubborn rock for their basis, checked the propensity to rectitude' but failed to mention a unique feature mapped in 1742 by Thomas Badeslade (1690-c.1750) a land surveyor employed by the Mostyns. Badeslade's map of the Gloddaeth Estate depicts a huge maze, set on a plateau at the top of the slope that rises from behind the Hall. Nothing can be detected today but Llandudno guidebooks of 1849 and 1856 remark on its existence and plead for its restoration. John Hicklin (1856) observed, 'At the entrance of Gaer Wood, on top of a rock near the hall, are discoverable the outlines of a Maze, much larger than the one at Hampton Court; and hopes are entertained that the Noble Lord may be induced to restore this labyrinth, for the amusement and exercise of the inhabitants and visitors of Llandudno'. Although, in 1860, the Mostyn agent, George Felton, drew up a detailed plan of the maze it was never restored.

Power in the Land

Just as representatives of the local Uchelwyr entered the eighteenth century as country gentlemen with impressive mansions set in manicured parkland and surrounded by extensive estates so a class of yeomen emerged in the Creuddyn, living in detached farmhouses amidst acres of agricultural land. The majority of farmers leased land from the Mostyns, some leased farms from the Bishop of Bangor and a few rented from minor landlords. By 1700 leases were commercial contracts largely shorn of the usual pre-capitalist cocktail of military, labour and produce obligations. Farmers paid rent to landlords but were no longer obliged to work the gentry's land or pay formal homage but an informal set of expectations survived. Enfranchised tenants were expected to vote for their landlords, or their landlord's nominee at election time, to bow and scrape in their presence and to worship in the Established Church of England, on pain of eviction.

Like estate building, establishing a permanent farmholding was a fluid process. An ambitious agricultural labourer might begin by simply working on other farmer's land and saving his wages until he could afford to rent a smallholding. If he proved an efficient and ambitious farmer his landlord might transfer fields from an inefficient holding to his stewardship and so increase the size of his farm. So labourers could over the generations rise to run farms but by 1700 there was limited opportunity to rise above the level of yeoman-farmer as the majority of the land was retained by either the Mostyns or the Church. The Mostyns were in the ascendant and as their power increased the Church's declined. Three factors had caused this situation, firstly the Reformation forced the privatisation of much Church land. Secondly the withdrawal of the Bishop of Bangor after Glyndwr's attack on his Palace at Gogarth had reduced his commitment to the Creuddyn and day-to-day oversight of his Estate. Thirdly, and linked to the former factors, the rise of the Mostyns, with their acquisitive instincts reduced both the absolute and relative influence of the Church. In 1680 the Bishop discovered from a

151

survey of his Creuddyn property that the Mostyns' illegal enclosure of land was so extensive that the boundaries of Church land have been 'so utterly broke up and destroyed that it is impossible to find them out.'

Yeoman Farmers

The late seventeenth century was a period in which many Creuddyn farms and smallholdings came into existence but most have long since disappeared. Rare survivals from this period are Penybryn ucha and isa, on the Great Orme; Bryn Gosol and Bryniau at Llanrhos; Holland, Fferm, Cwm Howard and Bodafon in Llandudno; and Tŷ Ucha on the Little Orme. The history of the last three examples offers some insight into the history of local yeoman farmers.

Tŷ Ucha was the largest farm in Rhiwledyn township, amounting to about 80 acres at a time the Penrhyn Estate comprised 300 acres. It originated from numerous acquisitions by purchase and inheritance by the Mostyns in the 15th and 16th centuries. Between the years 1655 to 1669 the process of amalgamation was accelerated to create commercially viable farms although Tŷ Ucha doesn't appear in rental lists as a unified holding until 1717. From 1717 until 1742 Tŷ Ucha was farmed by Richard Hughes and the earliest surviving buildings on the site, especially the cartshed, loft and cowshed, date from the that period.

Cwm Howard Farmhouse now sits awkwardly on a 1½ acre plot amidst a large Local Authority housing estate but in 1700 the farmhouse was already 150 years old and the landholding extensive (c.80 acres). Marked on Lewis Morris's 1748 map as Cwm Hewert the name has appeared in many guises over the years. On the east side of the chancel in Llanrhos Church a stone slab commemorates the death of John Parry of Coummaward in 1688. It's not clear exactly when Cwm Howard was acquired by the Mostyns but it appears on the 1808 rent roll in the occupation of Charles Edwards at an annual rental of £55. The major part of the existing farmhouse is Elizabethan with many original timbers, whilst the smaller, eastern extension appears to have been constructed around 1700 to provide extra accommodation and a bakehouse.

Reference to Bodavon (Bodafon) lands appear in a March 1539 lease granting the entire township to Dame Jane Griffith and her eldest son William Griffith by John Byrd, Bishop of Bangor. After several separate dispersals and acquisitions of land, by 1656 the township was in the hands of the Mostyns. An indenture of 1664 records the existence of a farmhouse, Bodvavon, on the land, occupied by a Robert Thomas. At that time some of the fields around the house were let to others but by 1661 the land had been consolidated and the entire holding of about 80 acres was leased to Robert Thomas at an annual rental of £25. In 1672 the tenancy of Bodafon Farm was transferred to a Henry Kenricke, and a 21 year lease agreed at the same rent enjoyed previously by John Thomas. On termination of the lease in 1693 the tenancy passed to Piers Meredith and in 1719 to William Evans who farmed the land until his death in 1746. Bodafon farmhouse is now known as Bodafon Hall, with the original name transferred to the property across the road that was converted from agricultural buildings in 1876. Nothing of the earliest house remains although the front section of the old Bodafon farmhouse dates from the eighteenth century, probably sometime during the occupation of William Evans.

Below this class of semi-independent farmers were hundreds of labourers and cottagers attempting to survive on miniscule incomes eked out by produce from their holdings of little or no land. At the end of the seventeenth century almost the entire population of the Creuddyn was involved in agriculture. It was a golden age for farming with good harvests and rising wages for labourers although a new local enterprise held out the prospect of even more rewarding employment.

Venturing Underground

In April 1692 Sir Thomas Mostyn restarted copper mining on the Great Orme at Maes y fachrell. Three years later Sir Thomas's son, Sir Roger Mostyn leased the right to mine for copper for 21 years on his lands at the south-eastern end of 'Llandudno Mountain' to five London merchants, John Cooper, Joseph Cope, Leonard Fletcher, Thomas Fryer and John Perry calling themselves the 'Welsh Copper Company'. In 1738 the Bishop of Bangor issued a 21-year mining lease to Richard Manley of Chester and William Manley of London but none of these ventures was successful. As miners burrowed down into the Great Orme they discovered viable deposits of copper ore but found it impossible to prevent the works from flooding. In 1748 Lewis Morris observed 'there was formerly a great copper mine at Llandudno . . . which now lies under water'. The challenge was to get rid of the water.

Chapter Ten

Reopening the Copper Mines, 1761

In the eighteenth century great landowners, like the Mostyns, began to realise that industry might prove even more profitable than agriculture. Copper was in particular demand, as overseas supplies dwindled and smelting techniques improved its value increased enough to persuade a syndicate of Holywell businessmen that it was worth re-opening the Great Orme mines.

New Mine

In 1761 Sir Roger Mostyn granted a mining lease to this partnership of Francis Smedley, Anthony and Henry Steeple authorising them to extract copper from land at Penymynydd, Pyllau, Tynycoed and Maesyfachrell. The enterprise became known as the 'New Mine' and the lease guaranteed the Mostyns one-seventh of the ore as a royalty. When it expired it was replaced with a more sophisticated contract agreed, jointly, with John Lloyd of Wigfair MP, William Bridge of Amlwch and Reverend John Ellis, vicar of Bangor. This specifically permitted the erection of buildings, engines, stamps and even a quay for shipping ore, timber and coal but also demanded a certain level of efficiency in operating the works. To ensure the return of sufficient royalties the lease required that at least six miners were employed for nine months of each year. The second trio unwittingly sublet the mine to a bunch of unskilled adventurers. Realising what they had done they wrote giving notice, 'to those novices who have presumed to take upon themselves the direction of Llandudno Mine; that if they do not appoint a proper agent, one of sufficient skill and judgement who has had much experience in copper mines . . . we shall forthwith apply to the court of Chancery for leave to make such an appointment.'

Fortunately a skilled agent, George Edwards was appointed, and served faithfully until his death in 1813 at the age of 84. Edwards was succeeded by William Jones who began the expansion of the works but died in 1827. Thomas Jones was then appointed and served as the New Mine's last agent. Throughout the period John Lloyd maintained his position as a director of company but was supported by different partners with Elizabeth Lester, Tŷ Coch, the only Llandudno investor, holding 10% of the stock.

Despite employing various de-watering devices flooding remained a

The Great Orme Mine Works, circa 1845

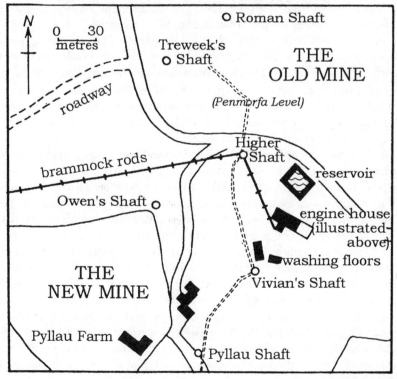

N

0 ___ 30
metres

○ Roman Shaft

Treweek's
○ Shaft

THE
OLD MINE

roadway

(Penmorfa Level)

Higher
Shaft

brammock rods

reservoir

Owen's Shaft ○

engine house
(illustrated
above)

washing floors

THE
NEW MINE

Vivian's Shaft

Pyllau Farm

○ Pyllau Shaft

serious problem. Limited drainage was provided by a tunnel, or level, that emerged near Pyllau Farm and this was supplemented in 1812 by horse-driven pumps supplied by Rigby's Ironworks, Hawarden . In 1827 Thomas Jones constructed an ingenuous but unfortunately inefficient flop-jack water-powered engine, nicknamed 'Tom and Jerry' after a contemporary Pierce Egan cartoon series. Water-power came from the Gogarth spring and the engine was linked to pumps at the mine by a series of 'brammock rods' whose course can still be traced on the Great Orme. Unfortunately this device proved very inefficient and was replaced within a few years by a water-pressure engine.

Old Mine

In 1774 the Bishop of Bangor leased land for mining to John Bagnall of Berkshire but soon the main works on the Bishop's land were being managed by a Macclesfield partnership whose accounts reveal that between 1793 and 1801 it was paying the Bishop royalties of 1/8th of the ore extracted. This group's earliest surviving lease, dated June 1801, bears the names of partners, Robert Hodgson, Abraham Mills and Edward Hawkins operating as the 'Llandudno Mine Company' but the works were more familiarly known as the 'Old Mine'. The Bishop appointed Samuel Worthington, who had been involved in the development of the Penrhyn slate quarries, to act as his agent on the this contract. In 1824 Worthington took over the mine himself, paying the Bishop the prevailing royalty rate. The lease was renewed in 1837 for the lives of Worthington's sons Archibald and William, with Cornishmen Jonathan Rawlings employed as their mine agent.

As the mine went deeper flooding inevitably increased and so in 1835 a Cornish steam engine was installed, primarily for pumping out water but also for winding on two shafts and for operating an ore crusher. A more ambitious project was also begun, in conjunction with the New Mine, to dramatically lower the whole water-table by draining water down to sea-level. The plan was jointly devised by Thomas Jones of the New Mine and Captain George Davey of the Old Mine. They intended to tunnel on a slight incline, half a mile into the mountain from Penmorfa until they met the lowest level of their mine works. The theory was that once a connection was made water could simply flow out to a washing pool at West Shore where it could be exploited for dressing ore before debouching into the sea. Work began in February 1834 and for the next eight years 12 miners worked round the clock until in October 1842 three holes were drilled through releasing water that drained a depth of 400 feet of workings.

Tŷ Gwyn Mine

The Tŷ Gwyn Mine, named after the nearby farmhouse, opened in 1835 after the chance exposure of copper ore when a cow dislodged turf at Y Fach (Happy Valley). Edward Jones, who farmed Tŷ Gwyn, had insufficient capital to exploit the find so he retained only 2 of 126 shares of an enterprise incorporated to mine the area. William Jones, Bodhyfryd, with 23 shares appears to have been the only other local investor. Tunnels, or adits, running back into the mountain from the area now occupied by the pier, were developed as miners at Tŷ Gwyn followed the veins of ore. Some of the works ran below sea level and flooding was a problem that even the installation of a 90 horse power Cornish pumping engine in 1836 (sited just west of the present Empire Hotel) couldn't completely cure. To provide clean water for the engine's boilers a reservoir, known as Llyn Mawr, was constructed at Tŷ Coch. In 1841 a massive 200 horse power Cornish pumping engine was installed just west of the Empire Hotel but it proved difficult to operate and was assisted by a small portable steam engine. To capture the power of water pumped from the Tŷ Gwyn as it flowed on its way into the sea a 15 foot diameter waterwheel was erected on the site of the Min y Don Hotel and used to operate an ore crusher.

Attractive Employment

From 1761 until 1800 the mines employed few people. Thomas Pennant in 1778 referred to 'several copper works, which at times are worked to advantage'. At that stage the miners tended to be local men with only expert mining engineers and investors coming from outside the Creuddyn. As the demand for copper continued to increase the mines expanded attracting workers, especially from the old north Wales metalliferous mining areas of Flintshire and Anglesey. The 1761 population of Llandudno was around 200, by 1801 it had expanded to about 300 but in 1851 it had leapt to 1,137.

Mine Organisation

The Llandudno works didn't operate like factories, there was less hierarchy and more individual autonomy. The miner wasn't directly employed but formed a small team of about half-a-dozen men who appointed a representative from amongst themselves to negotiate a rate of remuneration for working a particular pitch in the mine. This was known as a 'bargain'. The team was generally referred to by the name of their representative i.e. John Jones and partners. Each team worked independently on extracting ore from their allotted section of the mine.

After crushing sorting, weighing and bagging up the dressed ore, accounts were prepared and eventually disbursements were made to team leaders. Sometimes teams agreed to work as 'tributers', who were paid in kind, receiving a proportion, typically 1/3 rd of the ore they excavated, which they sold themselves. Tributers kept a record of the number of tubs they filled before they sent them to the surface and in recent years a tributer's tally was found in situ 80 feet below the surface in Treweek's Shaft. The tally consisted of a six by one inch strip of clay with twenty holes having been indented on the left side and a further three on the right with a small peg remaining in the last one. Presumably this team had already despatched 23 tubs for winding to the surface before their work was interrupted.

Men engaged in service work, such as those operating the winding gear, were generally paid by the shift, which for miners at Llandudno meant six hours. Only a few mineworkers with particular skills, like blacksmiths and boilermen received regular weekly wages. Even when business was booming and Llandudno's mines employed hundreds of people only 14 individuals were on the New Mine payroll. Most miners were therefore more or less self-employed.

By the early 1840's the average Llandudno miner cleared about 14 shillings (70p) a week, after deductions. Mine captains and mine agents received five or six times the remuneration of ordinary miners, around £50 a quarter, plus a share of the profits. 'Captains' were technical experts, senior mine engineers, in contrast to 'Agents', whose responsibilities and expertise were more on the commercial side, their role was to act as a mine's General Manager. Financially the mines operated a 'cost-book' system that involved initially selling shares to launch the mining company then distributing profits quarterly. Raising capital for further investment depended on successfully appealing to existing stock holders for cash, this was rarely effective. Consequently the Great Orme mines lacked sophisticated mining equipment and had insufficient funds to ride out reverses in market conditions. Nevertheless C J Williams estimates that nineteenth century mining produced about 50,000 tons of ore yielding 2-3,000 tons of copper.

Going Underground
Miners entered the works by climbing down wooden or chain ladders. In some parts rungs, or stemples, were permanently wedged across shafts to facilitate access. Initially miners carried sacks of excavated rock to the surface on their backs but as shafts sunk lower windlasses were fitted to wind up ore in buckets or tubs. By 1800 horse powered winding engines,

also known as gins or whimseys were used to raise the ore. Because of the distance of the nearest, Flintshire, coalfields from Llandudno the expense of importing the fuel discouraged the early installation of steam engines until flooding left little alternative. Winding engines were never used at Llandudno to raise or lower men down the shafts, even when workings reached a depth of 500 feet.

The works radiated from about eight main shafts, named variously after their location like Pylllau and Tynyfron or after mine captains, such as Vivian's and Treweek's. From these vertical shafts radiating levels were cut following the veins of ore. To drive these levels gunpowder was used to fracture the rock but preparation for blasting was a laborious and dangerous process, particularly as the safety fuse wasn't invented until the latter years of mining at Llandudno. Shot holes were made by hand with one miner holding a drill against the rock and slowly rotating it whilst another struck it with a hammer. Drilling downwards at a slight angle allowed water to be poured in to minimise dust. Once the hole about 18 inches deep was drilled it was cleaned out with a scraper and allowed to dry. A few inches of gunpowder were then poured in from a powder horn and gently tamped down. A plug of clay was inserted and rammed down with a wooden stick. A long, thin metal pricker was then pushed down one side of the hole until it reached the gunpowder. After this was withdrawn, a straw fuse filled with gunpowder, was inserted into the hole. Following a shouted warning, the fuse was ignited by the flame of a candle. Once the Penmorfa and Tŷ Gwyn adits were completed miners could access much of the works by walking in on the level rather than descending long ladders and children employed in the mines often entered that way. Rails were laid in these two levels to allow the ore to be trammed out of the works direct to the dressing floors.

To ventilate the mine and clear the smoke and fumes a circulation of air had to be ensured. Where natural draughts proved inadequate a network of baffle boards and sacking were installed to divert and channel air circulation. The ore was usually extracted from below and as the miners worked their way upwards they erected wooden working platforms to support themselves. The areas from which ore was removed were known as stopes and in some places large underground caverns, as much as 30 feet wide and 100 feet high were created. In other parts discarded, ore-less rocks were packed together filling disused galleries and in some places mysterious depositions remain. Noone knows why mummified cats, clay pipes and berries have all been found carefully laid out in abandoned corners. It's thought the miners intended to leave offerings to appease the spirits of the mine, some miners believed they shared the works with elusive little folk, 'the Knockers' but it's difficult to know if these deposits were merely customary or reflect more deeply held and enduring beliefs.

Despite the dangers miners generally wore soft felt, or leather, hats with wide brims to shield them from dripping water. Affixed to the front of the brim was generally a tallow candle for illumination. An old fustian jacket, a flannel shirt, corduroy or coarse linen trousers and clogs completed the miner's outfit. Working in a cramped passage a miner would often discard much of his apparel to keep cool and for ease of movement. Makeshift lanterns were sometimes used to provide more light and a lantern with a birch-bark reflector has been found in the Old Mine. Miners were generally loathe to use too many candles as deductions were made to cover the cost, along with charges for gunpowder, fuses and tools.

Few details survive of men crippled or killed in the works but there are at least three recorded fatalities. Thomas Evans died in 1770, John Davies in 1813 and John Smith in 1848. Davies of Bryn Glas, died aged 35, when a roof collapsed. John Smith of Siop Isaf was 38 when he was killed in the mine and was buried in St George's churchyard. Other recorded disasters include the flooding of the Tŷ Gwyn mine, in 1844 when the pumps broke down and again in 1850 when seawater broke into the works and fleeing miners abandoned their tools in their haste to escape. In 1856 a boiler at the Old Mine exploded but apparently without any fatalities.

Dressing and Smelting the Ore

Smelting wasn't done at Llandudno because the process consumed so much fuel it was cheaper to take ore to the coal than vice versa. Before the ore was despatched it was brought down the mountain, crushed into fragments and the waste rock removed. The Minydon waterwheel powered massive enormous wooden hammers that pounded the rock into fragments that were then washed and sorted at a dressing floor in the area now occupied by Tŷ Isa Road. Ore taken out along the Penmorfa adit tramway was crushed manually by teams of 'Copper Ladies' wielding heavy hammers. Children assisted with sorting and dressing the ore. Water draining down the Penmorfa adit formed a pond that was used for washing the ore. Once the ore was bagged up it was loaded onto flat bottomed boats and despatched to smelters from the shore nearest the dressing floor. If wind or tide conditions proved adverse either shore could be used for a launch.

Bagged ore was carried by ship to Liverpool or Ravenshead until their

160

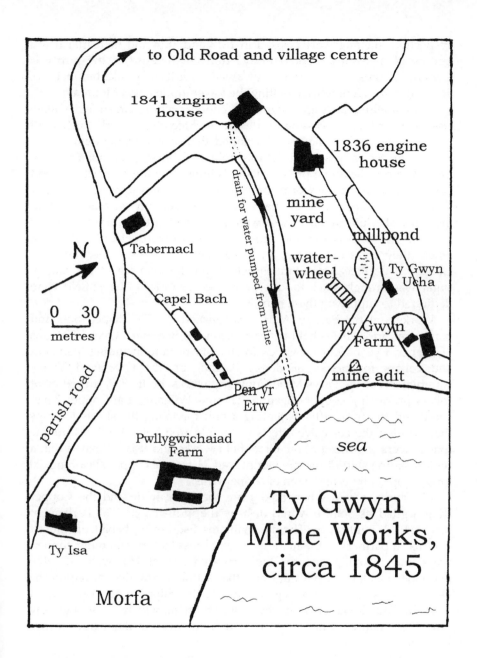

to Old Road and village centre

1841 engine house

1836 engine house

drain for water pumped from mine

mine yard

millpond

Tabernacl

N

water-wheel

Ty Gwyn Ucha

Capel Bach

0   30
metres

Ty Gwyn Farm

parish road

Pen yr Erw

mine adit

Pwllygwichaiad Farm

sea

Ty Gwyn Mine Works, circa 1845

Ty Isa

Morfa

respective smelting works closed in 1813 and 1814 and thereafter it was processed at Swansea and latterly Amlwch. Because of the purity of Llandudno ores Amlwch not only valued it for its own sake but included it as a fluxing agent when smelting the lower grade Parys Mountain ore.

After smelting at Anglesey most of copper went to Greenfield Valley, Holywell for final processing. In the late eighteenth and early nineteenth centuries two linked markets developed that increased the demand for copper; protective plating for ship's hulls and brass goods for the slave trade. Copper sheathing protected ship's hulls from the destructive wood boring action of marine worms prevalent in tropical waters. Some copper sheeting was supplied to the navy but a vast quantity was used to clad the hulls of 'Guineamen'. These were ships plying the Golden Triangle; carrying finished copper and brassware from Liverpool to West Africa where they were exchanged for black slaves who were then taken to labour on Caribbean plantations before, on the final leg of the sailing, sugar was brought back to Liverpool. Two factories at Greenfield were dedicated to supplying these markets.

Workers at the Battery Works, established in 1776 shaped pots and pans from brass sheets held beneath heavy tilt hammers. Over 1,000 tons of copper a year went for goods for the slave trade including 'padlocks and collars for blacks or dogs'. Further up the Greenfield Valley waterwheels at the Parys Mine Company works, built 1787, turned giant rollers producing copper sheeting. Thomas Williams, the Copper King, controlled the trade after patenting a bolt for fixing the sheets to ships that avoided the corrosive effects of the old iron bolts. Williams unique fixings were produced at the Greenfield works and it is estimated that a typical sailing ship of the time employed 11 tons of copper sheathing, 20 tons of copper bolts and a ton of copper nails!

Llandudno's mines benefited from the slave trade and the Copper King argued its demise would destroy the industry. In 1788 Parliament received, 'A petition by Thomas Williams Esquire on behalf of himself and his co partners in the manufacture of brass battery and other copper, brass and mixed goods for the African trade at Holywell . . . the petitioner has lately been informed that a Bill is now depending on the House for the purpose of regulating . . . the shipping and carrying of slaves in British vessels from the coast of Africa, which . . . will greatly hurt, if not entirely ruin, the British trade to Africa in the manufactures aforesaid.'

At least two of the forty ships transporting copper between Amlwch and Greenfield, the 'Prince of Wales' and the 'Polly to Bonny', also carried African slaves to the Caribbean. Glan Conwy gentleman, Hugh

Chambres-Jones ran regular slaving ships from Liverpool and it is clear that the copper trade was a dirty and dangerous business, and not just for the miners.

Chapter Eleven

Heart of the Village, 1800 . . .

Nineteenth century Llandudno was bursting at the seams. After the reopening of the copper mines the old dispersed community living on farms and smallholdings scattered across the parish began to congregate along Cwlach Street. Mine owners and speculative builders infilled established dwellings and erected houses and shops to cope with the increasing demand for accommodation. As the nineteenth century advanced Llandudno was no longer just another of the Creuddyn's three sleepy parishes but a community drawing incomers from across north Wales and beyond.

Meet the Villagers

Thomas Rowlands, one of the old miners and village residents chronicled the lives of his friends and neighbours before he died so we can still metaphorically stroll in his company through mid-nineteenth century Llandudno. As we metaphorically continue our journey I have included, where possible, details of the earliest known reference to buildings mentioned.

The King's Head (see village map) is a good place to start for this was the nearest thing to a hotel the old village possessed. Erected in the reign of George III (1760-1820), here we'd find locals chatting to the landlord 'old, lame William Owen'. John Williams of Bodafon tells us, 'He is called the King and his delight is in directing his subjects to objects of interest; but he never dictates. He possesses a fund of local information, and is very communicative. His table, for quality and quantity, is usually in keeping with his dignity; and the tax which he levies is so moderate, that his subjects pay it unhesitatingly being satisfied that they have received value, thereby doing away with the necessity of being obliged to employ a tax collector, a being so obnoxious to the community in general. Long may he reign!'

William Owen's reign ended when his daughter, Anne, married Isaiah Davies, who was born on a farm on the Little Orme. Isaiah Davies then took over as the young landlord of the King's Head. 'This was the rendezvous of the miners. They drew their money quarterly; the money would be brought from Conwy in a conveyance to the commencement of the hill, and on very successful quarter days the money would be taken in a wheelbarrow up to the King's Head. After the sharing a miner would pin up a £1 note on the chimney-piece of the parlour of the King's Head

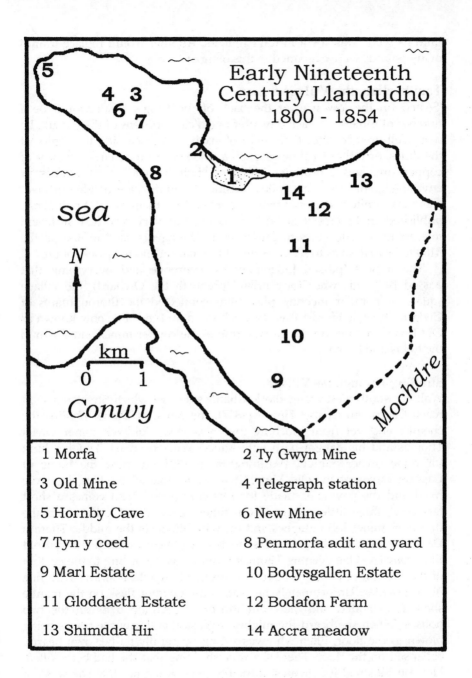

Early Nineteenth
Century Llandudno
1800 - 1854

5
4 3
6 7
2
1
sea
8
14
12
13
11
N
10
km
0 1
9
Conwy
Mochdre

1 Morfa   2 Ty Gwyn Mine

3 Old Mine   4 Telegraph station

5 Hornby Cave   6 New Mine

7 Tyn y coed   8 Penmorfa adit and yard

9 Marl Estate   10 Bodysgallen Estate

11 Gloddaeth Estate   12 Bodafon Farm

13 Shimdda Hir   14 Accra meadow

until its value was spent in refreshments. Another would replace it until many pounds were expended in this manner.'

Tanyberllan, the Village Square

'Seated on the low wall at the back of the King's Head would be a number of miners . . . each day after one o'clock dozens of them could be seen well-dressed after their stem of six hours, discussing the topics of the times, or rather local news, such as the state of the markets, prices of copper ore, and repeating old tales. Their knowledge of politics or anything going on a few miles outside the immediate neighbourhood, was very limited, the only newspaper read by them being *Yr Amserau*, published in Liverpool at 3d per. week, but very few had sufficient interest in outside news to purchase it. The agents used to take in the *Mining Journal*, so as to see the state of the market and the prices of ore.'

The miners 'passed judgement on everyone and everything that passed by!' This was 'Tanyberllan' (Beneath the Orchard), the village square, a popular meeting place that connected the thoroughfares of Cwlach Street, Y Ffordd Plas, Tŷ Coch Road and the lane, now known as Old Road, that ran up the Great Orme to the copper mines and down to the fields and beach.

Strolling Through the Village

Walking south-west along the left-hand side of Cwlach Street we soon reach Caersalem Chapel House (1837), the home of Daniel Phillips the chemist and vet from Mochdre and next door Amlwch miner Owen Thomas and his Bangor-born wife Elinor. We soon reach Tŷ Glas, built for mine owner Samuel Worthington in 1824 but now the home of Captain Davey of the Old Mine. 'It was here that all the bargains were fixed and the payments made for this enterprise.' Next comes a short terrace of three little cottages (sometimes called Troed y Rhiw), in the first lives miner John Hughes and his wife Elinor, in the middle Thomas Davies, y burym who sold yeast to his neighbours and in the last old Ellen Davies. 'One evening Thomas Davies was, according to the custom of those days, prior to the advent of fuses, filling wheat straws with fine black powder. Unfortunately he placed the powder flask on the mantle shelf. It exploded and blew out the brick partition between the two houses. When she heard the mighty explosion and saw the bricks being blown to the floor, Ellen who was sitting peacefully by her own hearth, collapsed on the floor. There she was, shouting that she had been killed. Her son Ellis had the greatest difficulty persuading her that she was not dead.'

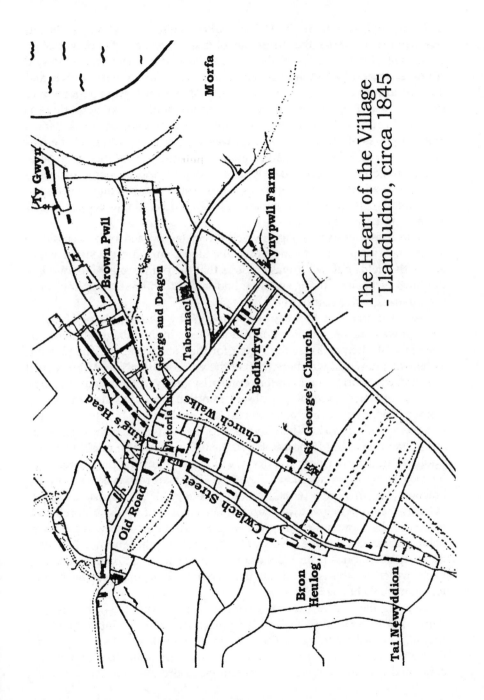

The Heart of the Village
- Llandudno, circa 1845

Morfa

Ty Gwyn

Brown Pwll

George and Dragon

Tabernacl

Tynypwll Farm

Bodhyfryd

King's Head

Victoria Inn

Church Walks

St George's Church

Old Road

Cwlach Street

Bron Heulog

Tai Newyddion

Pendyffryn was home to a stern-looking man, Owen Owens and his wife Gwen. 'He was the constable of the place and the only person responsible for the peace of the village.' Next door, Ty'nymaes housed Amlwch miner Robert and Jenny Parry. He 'was a very active and industrious old man. I don't think Robert Parry ever wasted a moment of time. He was like the ant, thrifty and industrious.' Next door them is Tygwyrdd, home to William and Ann Parry, neighbours to Scotsman Duncan James at Penyfron. Duncan was very tall and 'although he was only able to hold limited conversations with the inhabitants because of his language he appeared to be perfectly happy, and prepared to live in peace with all. Under the same roof lived Isaac and Hannah Owen' and in a small cottage tucked behind Tŷ Gwyrdd resided copper miner Thomas and Mary Ffoulkes.

Only a few houses along Cwlach Street faced each other across the street, most were sited facing down the slope, enjoying extensive views across the fields below. 'It was obvious that the old people were aware of the laws of healthy living, as they had, almost without exception, built their houses with a southern aspect.'

Next we arrive at Frondeg, built in 1833 by Thomas Parry of Valley View, it was one of the most important houses in the village as it was the residence of Thomas Jones the Agent for the New Mine, or 'The Steward as he was known. It was here that all the work for the New Mine was let out, and where the miners of that enterprise received their quarterly pay. He was, at times, exceedingly absent minded. Once, having business in Conwy, and there being a likelihood of rain he took his umbrella and proceeded on his way. When he reached the bridge the atmosphere had cleared and he asked Robert Roberts, the toll keeper, if he might leave the umbrella in a corner near the door . . . On his return he picked up what he took to be his umbrella . . . A short distance from what is now the junction he met up with his old friend, Mr Williams, Bodafon. ..Unfortunately it began to rain and Mr Williams put up his umbrella, Mr Jones did the same but to his great chagrin, what he raised was the brush belonging to the bridge sweeper'! Thomas's brother-in-law, Flintshire miner Reuben Jones from Llanhasa lived in the adjacent cottage, Frondeg Bach, which he shared with labourer Thomas Rowlands whose mother, Jane ran a bakehouse from there.

Nearing the end of the street we notice Tanyfron (1754) the home of Amlwch miner Hugh Parry and Betty his wife, an 'old couple, quiet and frugal'. The last building on Cwlach Street, a small sweet shop, was run by Catrin Parry. 'The front window was about three foot square and contained a grand display of differently-coloured sweets . . . However urgent one's business it was too great a temptation to pass without staring at the mint cakes and different coloured sticks. The sugar candies and the cakes made to represent different animals, the pig, the dog, the dove, the ox and the donkey, composed of flour, sugar and water with eyes of currants. It was too great a challenge for any student of philosophy to differentiate between the dog and the donkey, and the pig and the ox. Having obtained a halfpenny to spend . . . it is amazing to recollect how long we took to decided what to buy . . . I remember one boy once spending threepence in one week on sweets. And somehow after that, whenever I heard the parable of the Prodigal Son, I immediately thought of this boy.'

Down a Few Steps . . .

To reach the limit of the village centre we descend a few steps to reach a terrace of cottages erected in 1833, 'Tai Newyddion, in front of them were splendid gardens, full of fruit trees, flowers and vegetables'. Walking to the far cottage we stand before the residence of Jenny Davis. 'Next to her William Davies, the shepherd and his wife Margaret, both well known characters. In those days everyone had the right to keep a number of sheep on the mountain and paid a few pence a head to William Davies for shepherding. His wife was renowned for her religious zeal and godliness. Religion and things religious were the objects of her life'.

'Next to them lived Hugh Hughes and his wife Kitty. An old straightbacked manly figure who prided himself on his great strength. He was seen in Penmorfa to grip the handles of a wheelbarrow and to lift it and turn it over his head, an achievement beyond the capabilities of any other Llandudno resident. His wife was as tiny a person as could be found, but despite her miniscule size and her natural simplicity she possessed a kindly sympathetic nature. When passing Tai Newyddion in the late afternoon their son Robert Hughes could be heard reading aloud, and he was an excellent reader. He favoured poetry and to listen to him reading was a feast for the mind.'

'Next to them in the end house lived William and Kitty Williams. William Williams was a shining old Christian and it would be worth walking twenty miles just to hear him utter *Amen*. Not a lifeless, formal *Amen* but one working its way from the depths of his heart and his troubled soul.'

'These houses . . . stood in a glorious spot . . . They, and those who lived in them, were a perfect example of true contentment and a good community.' Retracing our route and 'having climbed the stone steps we find ourselves (once again) in Cwlach Street'.

169

Returning Along Cwlach Street

Returning along the left-hand side of Cwlach Street we notice a slightly elevated terrace of four little cottages, known as 'Queen Street'. 'These were 'small tidy houses owned by Mr George Brookes, Victoria. In the first lived Richard and Sarah Hughes who sold a little flour. She was Mr Brookes's daughter. Next to them lived Owen and Ann Owens, and in the third Enoch and Ellen Hughes. In his leisure time Enoch Hughes made clogs for miners. He was another excellent character. In the fourth and last house lived Thomas Owen the blacksmith and his wife Mary, another of Mr Georges Brooke's daughters. Thomas Owen was the blacksmith of the extensive Tŷ Gwyn Mine. A quiet and unassuming man.'

'A short distance from Queen Street in the same direction we have Tai'nyfron (sometimes 'y Fron'), small houses belonging to Mr Thomas Parry (the mason). In them dwelt William Owen ,Gogarth and his wife and Andreas Jones and his family, the brother of the late Mrs Grace Lloyd, a native of Amlwch . . . At the end of the cottages, standing by itself on a nice piece of land stood Valley View, the residence of Tom Parry . . . Tom was noted for his wit. I remember once, as he stood by his garden wall near Twll Mawr (one of the Tŷ Gwyn mineshafts), a boy tried to drag a donkey forward. The long eared creature had decided not to move and the lad had pulled the bridle over its head and pulled with all its might. The animal had planted his front feet firmly and determinedly. Shortly the donkey began to bray and the boy, in the face of its obstinacy, began to cry. Tom gazed at them intently before remarking to a passer-by, *Which of the two is the ass?* . . . He was an accomplished poet and . . . He sang well, and had also constructed a dulcimer. Those who heard him play this appreciated it far more than if they had listened to the finest orchestra.'

Just past Andreas's cottage and a little higher up we come to Brynhyfyd (1833) the home of miner William Jones and his wife Mally, 'the parents of the Chief Bard, famous throughout Wales, Thomas Tudno Jones. A man who has honoured his birthplace, and although young, has won several of the principal chairs in the National and Royal Eisteddfodau of Wales.' In 1851 William Jones was appointed official census enumerator for Llandudno. Retracing our steps a little we ascend a narrow lane that takes us past the small, traditional, single-storied, two roomed, Cwlach Cottage, the home of Dafydd and Sarah Lloyd. 'Having passed through the wooden gate and alongside the barn we find ourselves standing opposite an old fashioned though substantial house. This is Y Cwlach, where we find Harri Williams and his family . . . I heard him on many occasions praying in a sort of cave in the garden. He prayed for his children and the people and children of Llandudno generally . . . In front of the house is a large garden filled with fruit trees, and the view from this spot defies description.'

'By following the narrow path on the left we climb to Tan'rallt the home of John and Sally Edwards . . . and his large and respectable family'. Returning to the main street, just opposite Pendyffryn, 'are three small houses, Tanynant (1816). The little old lady standing by the wall of the first is Marged Jones, Typobty (the bakehouse). She has a large shell in her hand. At eleven o'clock she can be seen raising it to her mouth and blowing causing a trumpeting noise to resound over the whole neighbourhood. As a direct result several ladies can be seen carrying armfuls of dough to the bakehouse . . . She used to bake once a day, on special occasions twice a day.

The oven, which was considered a good size would bake twelve or thirteen loaves at a time. A notice was required to be given the night before, so as to secure a room in the oven . . . The fuel was wood or bracken and the bread had a most delicious flavour . . . There were not many in Llandudno in those days who knew more English than Margaret Jones, although her entire stock was only four words', yes, no and Good Morning! Next to Typobty was Hugh Hughes and in the third house lived John and Mally Owen and their seven children.

Now we've reached Bodnant (1833), the prominent home of Roger Lester. 'Both he and his son John had enjoyed great success in the mines . . . His outstanding success had enabled him to provide his children with a good education and to bring them up respectfully and honourably.' 'Alongside Bodnant is a small comfortable cottage, the home of Mally Ffoulkes, her sons Richard, Edward, John and William and her only sister Betsy'.

Having returned to Tanyberllan, the village square, at the rear of the King's Head we will continue our exploration of the heart of old Llandudno by strolling a short way up Old Street. As we walk back down to Tanyberllan we will glance across to our left to the area now enclosed by Tŷ Gwyn Road.

Round About Old Road
Turning left up Old Road we pass, on the left, 'a long and very old-fashioned public house' with three dormer windows, called the Miners' Arms, that was erected around 1753 as Tyn'nrhwylfa farmhouse. Old John and Grace ran the farm whilst their son John was the publican. We might visit 'on mine pay night . . . to hear the miners spending hours

apportioning wages to everyone for the preceding three months.' A little further up, but on the opposite side of Old Road we find eighteenth century Hen Dafarn, where miner Robert Jones no longer dispenses beer since his trade disappeared downhill to Tyn'rhwylfa, 'but could relate interesting anecdotes'.

Returning downhill we pass, on the left, Amlwch miner, William Jones's home, Croesonnen (1828), then a semi-detached house called Greenhill (1817) which operated two shops. Ann Jones opened Llandudno's first Post Office here, at 18 Old Road, in October 1838. 'In a small shed by the side of this house the business was transacted by Ann Jones and her daughters, the shed being about 9 feet long and 5 feet wide. Writing letters was considered a luxury then. No envelopes being obtainable, quarto paper was universally used, which was folded in quite an artistic way, and the corners fastened with thin wafers of all colours, which were sold in sixpenny boxes, gum being unknown. All the letters, papers and parcels were carried to and from Llandudno by a stout, hardy, strong man, John Hughes by name, who always used to carry the bags to and from Conwy by the sands. He would arrive here each day about 8 a.m., then walk up to Penygwaith (the mineworks), do a hard day's work and return to Conwy at about 5 p.m.' 'This service had previously been carried out by an old lady, who visited the village twice a week and charged 3d. for each letter and newspaper.' The adjacent shop was run for many years as a grocery by Richard and Elizabeth Jones.

In front of Greenhill is Tynewydd (1817) the home of aged widower William Jones and Siop Tŷ Newydd, run by David Williams and his sister Jane selling drapery and groceries. Turning left into Plas Road we reach Hen Blas, 'the home of Mary Edwards, a quiet and Godly old lady.' 'In the yard of Hen Blas there was a long, low, thatch-roofed building, the only joiner's shop in the village, and all the carpentry required for the villagers was done by Michael Hughes the proprietor and two apprentices'. 'On the lower (right-hand) side of the road was the Tŷ Coch farmhouse where Edward Owen and his sister lived. A little further along the same street was his shop, the only butcher's shop in the place . . . a small room about 10 feet square . . . Two or three hungry men could have consumed the contents of the shop at one sitting . . . Mr Edward Owen used to open this shop occasionally, once or twice a week for a few hours, but every Saturday the shop was opened all day to sell the remnants of what he could not dispose of at Conwy Market the previous Friday.'

Since the reopening of the mines the fields of Hen Blas and Tŷ Coch

Thomas Rowlands, chronicler of
old Llandudno, 1835-1902

had become increasingly occupied by industrial offshoots of the Tŷ Gwyn works and rather mean accommodation. Compared to the Plas Road and Tŷ Coch area, 'Cwlach Street was the aristocratic quarter of the village'. Bryn Gyrnno, in Plas Road was home to Llanrhos labourer William Williams. 'A unique old character, quite unenlightened and deeply ignorant . . . In the same street was Tŷ Siawns, the home of William Hugh and James Thomas, known as the orphans.' Tan yr Ogof terrace at the end of street comprised six cottages including the home of Thomas Kendrick, the man who uncovered the prehistoric remains of Llandudno's first visitors. In front of Tan yr Ogof we can see another terrace of nine cottages both erected, around 1831, and owned by stone mason Joseph Hughes and named King William Street, in honour of the newly crowned monarch. Occupying the first cottage we find Joseph Hughes himself, 'a handsome, smiling man of average height. From the manner in which he extends his hand we immediately perceive that he is in pain and a martyr to rheumatism. His voice is slightly tremulous . . . One of the first enterprises we associate him with was the 1822 contract to provide huge stones from Porthyrheli (a Great Orme quarry) for the construction of the tubular bridge in Conwy.' Other residents of King William Street included Captain William Jones and his wife Margaret, Joseph's daughter, agricultural labourer Hugh Evans, miner Samuel Jones and John and Ann Smith, who ran a small shop from their home.

Llandudno's Chief Emporium
Walking from King William Street along the lane (Ty Coch Road) we pass, on the left, the rear of Mr Pritchard's shop (1832) to arrive back on Old Road. 'William Pritchard's shop was considered the chief emporium . . . It consisted of a narrow door in the middle with a window of small panes, about 5 feet square on each side.. On the left side hand side of the entrance stood a small desk and behind the desk a few tiny shelves upon which could be seen about half-a-dozen small bottles marked *Tincture of Rhubarb, Castor Oil, Paragoric, Oppodildo, Spirits of Nitre* and by itself in one corner a small bottle marked with very red letters; *Laudanum: Poison.* That was the chemists part; Mrs Pritchard . . . was considered as a medical adviser by the villagers and used to administer those on small doses . . . A young miner who was on very affectionate terms with a maiden assistant was caught unawares by Mrs Pritchard, chatting with the assistant in the shop. Mrs Pritchard, in a motherly manner, asked the young man how he was. After some hesitation he answered that he did not feel at all well. Mrs Pritchard asked him for his symptoms and there mixed him a strong dose of physic, which he was compelled to take,

although perfectly well!

By the side of those medicine shelves there were larger ones, containing large pieces of cloths of different colours and value. On the top of those were about a dozen band boxes, which contained all the hats that were on sale here. On the opposite side was the grocery business, Mr Pritchard, as a rule, having charge of this department. Between the counter and the front door you would see a few fire shovels, grid irons, small Dutch ovens, frying pans, saucepans and two or three bellows, that being the ironmongery parties. Small as the building was, they had a little of everything necessary for the requirements of the village; drapery, ironmongery, groceries, millinery, drugs, blasting powder, in fact nearly everything!'

Opposite the shop, on the other side of Old Road is Victoria, 'by far the largest house in Llandudno' and the home of George Brookes, Manager of the Tŷ Gwyn Mine. Victoria is the newest village inn and the only three-storey building in Llandudno. Continuing down Old Road we soon reach the George and Dragon (1829), a small tavern run by Robert and Maria Williams that marks the lowest extent of the village centre.

Special Deliveries

Villagers were spoilt for choice. Besides Ann Smith's King William shop, Owen's butchers, Williams's groceries, Jones's Post Office, and Pritchard's multi-department emporium special deliveries of goods could also be arranged by carriers from Conwy shops or Gyffin mill. 'Shop goods were carted over by John Davies of the Old ferry, an old man, lame of both legs, who used to come from Conwy twice and sometimes three times a week . . . and by the Melin Gyffin cart, which brought over meal on Wednesdays and Saturdays. Before its arrival about noon, small bags of corn could be seen on the low walls each side of Old Road, with the proprietors' addresses on each, which were picked up by Thomas Owen the carrier, and laid in the waggon to be taken to the mill, while in their stead small bags of flour would be placed that had been taken to the mill the previous week, most of the miners purchasing their corn from the neighbouring farmhouses.'

Local Administration

The administration of Llandudno in the 1840's was not hugely different from that created by the Tudors three centuries earlier. Justices of the Peace remained powerful figures whilst much of the mundane business of local civil, as well as church, administration was conducted by the parish. Tax and exercise duties were dealt with by Inland Revenue and

Customs and Excise Officers based in Conwy. Rates and social security were administered by the parish's executive committee, the vestry, until changes in the law forced it in 1837 to combine with 14 other parishes to form, 'Conwy Poor Law Union'. Ultimately the Conwy Union was also forced by central government to open a workhouse to incarcerate paupers but until 1859 Llandudno claimants could remain at home and have their rents paid and receive dole payments from the Union. In the 1840's, for example, two widowed, aged, paupers, Anne Jones (b.1767) and Mary Hughes (b.1766) were maintained in King William Street cottages at the expense of Conwy Union. However if a claimant was deemed to belong to a parish outside Llandudno then they, along with any dependants, were literally carted back to their 'Parish of Settlement'. This happened to the family of Thomas Kendrick (of cave fame) that was unceremoniously dumped back in Ysceifiog after his Flintshire father died in 1835. Llandudno elected representatives to the 'Board of Guardians' who administered the Union and as a J.P. Edward Mostyn Lloyd Mostyn ((1795-1884) was automatically included on the Board as an 'ex officio' Guardian.

Law and order depended on Owen Owens, the Parish Constable who had day to day responsibility for keeping the peace. If unable to ensure the King's Peace he was expected to inform the Justices who would then call in the military to impose order. Drunks or minor miscreants were detained overnight in the parish lock-up, situated near King William Street. This consisted of 'two small, narrow, low rooms . . . the oaken doors were almost obscured by square nails. The place appeared so small that a man could barely turn in them. Mercifully I cannot recall anyone ever having been placed inside.'

When William Jones stole a sheep grazing on the Great Orme in 1820 he was apprehended by the Constable but absconded before he could be confined in the lock-up. Jones had dragged the sheep into nearby cave, bound its legs and left it there, intending to collect it under the cover of darkness. Unfortunately for him the sheep was discovered and a watch put on the cave. He was subsequently apprehended attempting to leave with the sheep incriminatingly draped around his shoulders but escaped. Jones was re-apprehended at Conwy where he was 'very unruly and threatening to kill the Constables'. At Caernarfon County Court he pleaded not guilty but was condemned to death. A sentence immediately commuted to transportation.

In 1839 the Constable received backing from a newly founded, 'Llandudno Association for the Prosecution of Felons' which offered rewards for the successful prosecution of criminals who infringed the property rights of its members. The conviction of a burglar earned five guineas, with two guineas paid for the prosecution of anyone caught feloniously milking a cow! Civil registration of births, deaths and marriages was carried out by the parish, although in 1813 standardised national registers were introduced. Education was entirely voluntary and mainly organised by church and chapel. Responsibility for maintaining roads lay with the Justices and the parish whilst water supplies depended on the efforts of landowners, mine companies and private individuals. Housing depended on the same range of providers. Burials in Llandudno were controlled by the parish and restricted to St Tudno's graveyard until the Baptists acquired their own burial ground in Glanwydden in 1833. Between 1841 and 1852 Church burials took place in St George's graveyard. To discharge parish business regular meetings of the vestry, or executive committee, took place at the King's Head, on Old Road.

Nineteenth Century Llandudno

In 1801 the population of Llandudno was 318, in 1851 it was 1131. In 1801, 80% of the working population was engaged full time in agriculture and 20% in other trades and industries. By 1851 those proportions were reversed with less than 20% remaining on the land. The reopening of the copper mines radically altered Llandudno but perhaps the change was not so great as the statistics suggest. Llandudno's mines supplied industrial incomes without inflicting the scale of despoliation that afflicted English factory towns. The miners worked hard in difficult conditions but resolutely refused to labour underground for more than six hours a day. Most never lost touch with the land, and many maintained a few farm animals and cultivated a garden. All took time off to help with the harvest, to fish, to attend chapel or just to enjoy themselves whenever it suited them. Mid-nineteenth century Llandudno had changed but remained essentially a traditional Welsh-speaking community.

Chapter Twelve

Farming the Land

Cwlach Street was the miner's location of choice but was an unsuitable site for farming. Llandudno's nineteenth century agriculturists were to be found on farms scattered on the Great Orme and all across the flatlands as far as Rhiwledyn. Most farms were tenanted and rented from landlords. In nineteenth Llandudno that meant the Mostyns who owned far more land than everyone else put together.

Main Farming Zones

Substantial outlying holdings run in an earlier age by yeoman farmers or minor gentry, such as Cwm Howard and Marl, had lost land and drifted down the social scale as rapacious landlords of Gloddaeth had ambitiously expanded their Estate. The majority of Llandudno's mid-century farms were modest, workaday operations of between 10 and 100 acres. The farmsteads divide conveniently into three geographical zones; the rocky holdings of the Great Orme, the comparatively fertile farmlands of Bodafon and thirdly the low-lying, wind-blown, flat lands situated in between.

Great Orme Farms

Two old fashioned farms occupied the lands of the old Bishop's Palace, on the Great Orme, separated only by a stream of water flowing from the Tom & Jerry engine, and both, confusingly, know simply as 'Gogarth'. The larger, more north-easterly, 50 acre, holding, was run by Richard Jones whilst Mary Owen, farmed the smaller, 26 acre property. Although both Gogarths farmed land originally owned by the Church Richard Jones rented his land from the Gloddaeth Estate at an annual rental of £41 5s. Acres of Gogarth farmland were lost to the sea over the years and old Richard Jones could recall his father's complaints as his ploughshare struck the two large upright stones, 'Yr Hen Ddyn a'r Hen Wraig' (The Old Man and Old Woman). Yr Hen Ddyn a'r Hen Wraig remain but now almost disappear beneath incoming tides.

Wyddfyd had, in the mediaeval period, been a very important farm that gave its name to one of the Great Orme's three townships but nineteenth century Wyddfyd Farmhouse was no more than a small, single storey cottage with its landholding reduced to 28 acres. The ancestors of John Williams had occupied the farm for many generations and the family played a prominent part in the community. John's wife,

178

Elizabeth had a beautiful singing voice and the couple's son Benjamin became a hugely influential musician in the chapels. Besides running the farm John Williams also owned the shop in Old Road, run by his son and daughter, Dafydd and Jane.

The old farmhouse still exists, near the ski lift, and although no longer a working farm it is a valuable example of the type of agricultural dwelling that predominated in Llandudno before the hotels.

Penymynydd Ucha has been modernised and extended but previously looked much like Wyddfyd. Familiarly known as 'The White Farm', Richard Davies farmed 27 acres, rented from the Mostyns for £18 15s a year, within sight of neighbour, William Owen. 'The Pink Farm', more properly called, Penymynydd Isaf, the home of William Owen, father of Edward Owen, Tŷ Coch, 'Red House', extended to 12 acres.

No longer a farm, Tynycoed, 'Smallholding in the Wood', was formerly an important holding owned by the Williams family. From the late eighteenth century fields were leased to the New Mine company and by the mid-nineteenth only 14 acres were being farmed by Robert Jones but the early nineteenth century Estate owner, John Evans, retained a large portfolio that included Bodhyfryd. Tŷ Coch's farming activities were similarly curtailed by the expansion of mining and although Edward Owen nominally occupied twelve-acres the remaining agricultural land was remote from the house, with two fields on the Morfa and two at the top of Old Road. Wisely, Edward diversified into butchery beginning with the small shop described in the previous chapter.

Conveniently sited at the top edge of the village, Tyddynhwlfa, 'Wayside Smallholding', also operated as the Miner's Arms, but John Davies continued to farm 17 acres of land well into the 1850's.

Farms of the Flat Lands

Ty draw, 'House Beyond', was a very important farm in nineteenth century Llandudno with the farmhouse occupying a site behind the present Loretto College, Abbey Road. Much of the level land stretching from the foot of the Great Orme to the railway station and from the old St George's National School to the West Shore, some 106 acres, was fenced out into large fields belonging to Tŷ draw. According to Thomas Rowlands, David and Margaret Jones's farm was 'very carefully kept and well cultivated'. Tŷ draw supplied most of village with milk, butter and other farm produce and the Jones's were always willing to lend a hand to any villager fallen on hard times. They rented the farm from the Gloddaeth Estate for £68 10s per annum but were able to supplement

179

A Year Rent of Gloddaith Estate belonging to Sir Thomas Mostyn

N	Tenements	Tenants	Yearly Rents £	s	d	Rents rec'd £	s	d
	Llanrhos							
1	Maerddu	William Pritchard	210	"	"			
2	Gloddaith Issa	William Evans	54	"		74		
3	Pen Rhwllfa	Hugh Jones	9	9				
4	Tyn Bras	Anne Thomas	5	5	"			
5	Fynon Go	Robert Roberts	9	"	"	13	9	
6	Ty Celyn	Elizabeth Davies	9	2		11	12	
7	Hen du	John Thomas	5	5	"	8	12	
8	Gilfach	John Hughes	5	5		5		
9	Gwega	Barbra Hughes	5	5		1	15	
10	Glan Yfon	Owen Davies	2	15	"	2	2	0
11	Gesel Llangwstenin	David Hughes	13	11	6	13	10	10
12	Ty'r Onwen	Robert Williams	8	0		9	12	
13	Cae Cnaw	Samuel Davies	4	4		6	7	
14	Tyddin Gogarth	Richard Jones	45	"		55	4	
15	Pen Morfa	Thomas Evans	5	10	"			
16	Ty Draw	Anne Williams	70	"	"	86		
17	Ffrwd Penwinchel	Peter Jones	50	"	"	66		
18	Go Uch	Benjamon Edwards	4	"	"			
19	Tyn fron	Robert Williams	5	10	"			
20	Ty Gwyn	John Price	20	"				
21	Ty Newydd	Daniel Edwards	0	"	"	11		
22	Rost	Hugh Jones	2	2	"			
23	Whyfud	Roger Williams	0	"	"			
24	Pen y mynydd	Thomas Davies	15	"	"	15	13	
25	Pen y mynydd	Owen Thomas	11	"	"			
26	Maes fachrel	William Hughes	3	3	"	3	4	0
27	Bodafon	John Salisbury	90	"	"	120	15	1
28	Holland	Moses Nicholas	10	"	"			

their income by employing their horses in hauling equipment up the mines and ore down to the dressing floors and storehouses. 'Dafydd Jones kept five or six strong horses, which were kept busy supplying goods for the Old Mine and transporting copper down from the Old Mine to Morfa Isaf. About half a ton of copper was put in the cart and the rest of the load, packed in strong linen bags, was placed on a sledge drawn behind the cart which acted as a sort of brake when descending the steep and dangerous hill. Despite the pressure of his work with the horses, Dafydd Jones was seen on countless occasions, at great personal cost and inconvenience to himself, delivering coal or some supplies to his poor neighbours' (Rowlands).

Pwllygwichiad was the next biggest farm in this central area. Comprising 42 acres the farmhouse was sited near the Cenotaph and rented by Peter Jones from Gloddaeth for £52 10s a year. The farm's name, 'Pool of the Periwinkle' reminds us that it was situated on the seashore, overlooking rock pools. Pwllygwichiad's farmlands were in three parcels; land in the immediate vicinity of the house and outbuildings, fields just below Church Walks and a third block south of that middle section of Mostyn Street that includes the present library. It was here that Peter Jones ploughed out a surviving Bronze Age tumulus. Pwllygwichiad owned a lime kiln situated on the Great Orme, just above Cwlach Street. Lime was widely used in farming to neutralise over-acidic soil and break up clay. Nothing remains of the Pwllygwichiad kiln but other nineteenth century examples survive at Fferm; Tŷ Ucha, Penrhyn Bay; Ffolt and Bodysgallen.

Edward Jones grew 'splendid crops of oats and barley in Happy Valley' on his 25 acre Tŷ Gwyn farm, rented for £7 10s per annum. 'There was an old farmhouse and a narrow country road running in front of it to the present Happy Valley, which at that time belonged to the farm . . . Right in front of the house were the farm buildings, consisting of cow house, stable and a large barn where the Pavilion stands now, and between the barn and the sea there used to be a path, but the stormy sea soon undermined the ground and first the path disappeared, then the barn, etc until the soil was cleared right up to the rock.' After allowing Benjamin Edwards, of Plas, to graze his herd in Y Fach (Happy Valley) Edward Jones's interests turned to mining when a cow exposed ore beneath the sod. So after 1835 Tŷ Gwyn farm was transformed into Tŷ Gwyn Mine and Jones changed from agriculturist to shareholder.

William Jones of Bodhyfryd, 'Pleasant Abode', nominally held 24 acres of land but this was farmed by others and ownership of the land was retained by the Tyn y coed Estate and vested in his wife, heiress

Elizabeth Evans. The majority of Bodhyfryd's fields lay in the area between Old Road, Llywelyn Street, the foot of the Great Orme and the promenade but included two fields near the intersection of Market Street and Mostyn Street where ploughing competitions were sometimes held. William Jones was no farmer and had come to Llandudno from Flintshire, with his two brothers, John and Joseph, to take up ownership of the Tŷ Gwyn Mine. At first he lived in Tyn y Coed Farmhouse whilst his father in law, John Evans occupied the new, modern house, Bodhyfryd, that he built for himself. After Evans's death in 1840 William Jones and his family moved down to Bodhyfryd. William Jones was regarded as something of a gentleman by villagers, Bodhyfryd considered Llandudno's first mansion and his daughter, Ann, believed to own the only piano in the village. After his death in 1847 his image was dented when it was revealed that his personal assets were valued at £591 16s 2d but his debts amounted to £602 14s 10d, including £23 19s 6d owed to the King's Head, £15 16s 4d in unpaid bills from William Prichard's draper's shop and £6 13s due to Margaret Roberts of Tynypwll Farm for hire of her heavy horses for 'Team Work'.

Tynypwll, 'Smallholding of the Pool', was a small farm with the house standing in a tree-lined field between the Clarence Hotel and Upper Mostyn Street on the site now occupied by a row of single story buildings. Margaret Roberts farmed 11 acres but also maintained a peculiar menagerie that included a seagull, tame fox, goat, pet lamb and a monkey!

Farms Around Bodafon

The origins of Bodafon Farm were outlined in an earlier chapter but the entire holding, together with its outbuildings were transformed in the nineteenth century by the Mostyn Agents. In 1809 Sir Thomas Mostyn engaged land surveyor, John Maugham of Hitchin, to report on the condition of his Llandudno farm holdings. Maugham reported that, 'There are many parts of this estate . . . capable of very considerable improvement under judicious management, but the generality of the present occupiers being without judgement or capital very little benefit can be expected to result from them in their present situation.' To improve productivity and profitability he recommended Sir Thomas invest in improved land-drainage, modern agricultural buildings, farm consolidation and more accomplished tenants. All these measures were subsequently, if a little belatedly, enacted at Bodafon. The spur to modernisation was threefold; the 1829 appointment of Maugham as Chief Agent to the Mostyn Estate, the death of Sir Thomas Mostyn in

1831 and in the same year, the relinquishing of the tenancy by the widow of John Salusbury Davies whose family had farmed Bodafon since 1752.

In 1831 Maugham installed George Badcock, who had been appointed local land-agent for the estate as tenant at Bodafon. An office was added to the Hall enabling it to function as both farmhouse and Mostyn Estate Office. Opposite the Hall Maugham constructed a range of agricultural buildings designed 'upon the principle of a Manufactory', in accordance with the recommendations of his own 1809 report. Bodafon was transformed into a 'Model Farm'. As George Hiller observes, 'The principle was to make gravity move all the heavy material. There was a large granary on the first floor, which was dry and airy and there were three arches underneath to provide housing for cattle. On the western side there was a small shippon and the yards for cattle and horses were evenly distributed.' But reorganisation didn't end with the digging of new ditches, the erection of barns and the installation of a model tenant the adjoining farmlands of both Bryn y Bia, 'Hill of the Magpie', and Holland were also incorporated into the agricultural operation.

In 1831-2 George Badcock's holding comprised Bodafon's original 94 acres, plus 58 acres of Bryn y Bia land and a further 21 acres of Holland's fields. Badcock's holding also entitled him to graze sheep on the 214 acres of Gloddaeth Common and to take hay and grass from 17 acres of a meadow called Accra that lay at the extreme western end of the Bodafon farmlands. Llandudno's farmers and smallholders traditionally co-operated over the use of the vast, 70 acre, Accra meadow that they all considered ideally sited for hay production. John Maugham's 1809 assessment was not encouraging; 'The ground called Accra seems to be . . . completely impoverished by constant mowing and carrying away the produce.' Maugham wasn't impressed by the villager's co-operative efforts claiming nobody bothered to return nutrients to the soil, by manuring, that were lost through constant cropping.

Back at the Hall, a new coach house and servants' quarters were added and on 25th March 1833 George Badcock was delighted to convert his annual tenancy into a formal 21 year lease. Signed, on behalf of the Estate by Sir Thomas Champneys and his wife Charlotte Margaret Mostyn Champneys at an annual rent of £125 5s 0d. The duration of the lease must have appeared rather over optimistic as Badcock was then already 79 years old and had only the previous month buried his wife who was 23 years his junior! Badcock died in 1838 and was buried alongside his wife at Llanrhos but by then Bodafon had been transformed. But the 'principle of a Manufactory' wasn't applied to any other farm in Llandudno for the landlords had begun to entertain more ambitious ideas of property development.

Following Badcock's demise Bodafon was run for a few years by his widowed sister, Elizabeth Sutton, and her son, George, and his wife, Elizabeth but Bryn y Bia returned to separate operation. The 50 acres or so, of fields that constituted its farmland lay in the area now identified by various eponymous street names, Bryn y Bia Road, Close etc. A succession of tenants ran the farm until the holding was incorporated into the Bodafon operation in 1831. Between 1831 and 1838 the house was rented out separately and tenants included the family of Thomas Kendrick, whose brother, John, was born in Bryn y Bia Farmhouse in 1833. Just before Badcock died, the tenancy of the Bryn y Bia holding and house was granted to his nephew, John Williams, who, for the previous three years had assisted the Mostyn Agent and who duly succeeded him.

Williams was Caernarfon-born but had moved to Llandudno in 1835, marrying Jane Evans of Gloddaeth Isa the following year. In the 1841 census Williams described himself as a farmer and he appears to have run the holding with the help of a young farm labourer and a couple of female farm servants. However, as the Mostyn's resident Llandudno Land Agent he was also responsible for protecting the Estate's interest in the copper mines and promoting any other profitable enterprise that might arise. In 1849 John Williams moved to Bodafon Hall and reunited its landholding with Bryn y Bia where the farmhouse was once again let to a series of tenants.

John Williams proved a powerhouse of enterprise and administration and amongst his numerous offices he was a Justice of the Peace, a Poor Law Guardian for 34 years, for 27 years he was Chairman of the Board of Guardians and for 40 years he was Llandudno's Parish Clerk. He was also Agent for both the Old Mine and the Tŷ Gwyn Mine and for 43 years, Agent for Mostyn Estates. With John Williams in occupation Bodafon Hall was a hub of activity, bursting to the seams with an average of twenty people in residence. Beside John and Jane Williams and their six children there was Robert, John's brother who he employed in the Estate Office as a clerk, his sister Ann, who acted as housekeeper plus ten further employees. The latter typically comprised half a dozen farm servants, a bailiff, a dairymaid, a house servant and a nurse to look after William's young children.

Mid-nineteenth century Bodafon was a mixed farm with three-quarters of the land under cultivation, growing cereals and vegetables for both human and animal consumption. A small of herd of dairy cows was kept and a flock of sheep left to graze on Gloddaeth Mountain.

At the opposite, eastern, edge of Bodafon's fields to Accra was a small, picturesque thatched farmhouse called Adwy Rhydd, 'Ford of the Stream', that nestled in the fork of the present bridleway continuation of Ffynon Sadwrn Lane and Bodafon Lane. In the seventeenth century the land seems to have formed part of Bodafon's farmland but by 1738 Adwy Rhydd appears in the Gloddaeth Estate accounts as a separate, named holding occupied by Morris Price at an annual rental of £1 10s. In Maugham's 1809 survey the farmlands comprised just a couple of fields extending to about 3 acres. An enduring agricultural slump following the boom years of the Napoleonic Wars made it increasingly difficult to survive on such a small holding. In the 1840's tenant, Hugh Jones supplemented the family's income by working down the copper mine, meanwhile his widowed mother did most of the farmwork, including the dairying. Being a Llandudno miner didn't mean Hugh abandoned agricultural life for besides working his own holding part-time, as the Llandudno Advertiser recalled in 1899 'At harvest time it was a common sight to see thirty or forty stalwart miners in each field assisting the farmers to reap the corn and gather it into barns.' During the fifty-year tenancy of the Jones family Adwy Rhydd land was subdivided to create 7 small fields, all less than one acre, with five used for arable and the other two devoted to pasture.

Just north of Adwy Rhydd and adjoining the fields of Bryn y Bia the 10 acre holding of Shimdda Hir (Tall Chimney) framed the eastern farmlands of Bodafon township. The farmhouse stood on the site now occupied by the Craigside Inn and it first appeared in written records in 1792 in the occupation of Owen Thomas. In the mid-nineteenth century the property was owned by Llanrwst solicitor William Griffiths but let to and farmed by Ann Jones and her two daughters. When the elder daughter, Mary, married Eglwysbach sawyer, John Jones, in 1843 the couple took over the farm lease. Shimdda Hir farmed eight fields of which 3 acres were laid down to pasture and 5 acres used for arable.

Agriculture in the 1840's

Early Victorian Llandudno was no swampy wasteland incapable of pasturage or crop production. In the winter months the fields between the present Gloddaeth Avenue stretching across to Alexandra Road and Nantygamar Road remained wet and older villagers claimed the damp caused an illness they called the 'ague'. Efforts to improve drainage were attempted, initially by installing a ditch that emptied onto the West Shore. Around 1840 a team of men laboured for six months constructing 'Ffos Fawr', a huge semi-circular ditch that extended the agricultural drainage system around to Bodafon Fields but the problem was never

185

completely solved. Yet visitors often commented on the fecundity of Creuddyn farmlands. In 1811 Edmund Hyde Hall remarked that, 'the soil, where the rock does not force its way to the surface, is a fine deep loam, and upon it many spots are now enclosed and cultivated'. Bingley's 1839 visit prompted him to observe, 'at present it (Creuddyn) is . . . supposed to be some of the finest corn and meadow land in this part of Wales.'

Llandudno parish comprised 1757 acres of land of which 607 acres was cultivated for cereals, vegetables and fruit production, 295 acres of meadow and pasture land was devoted to grazing and hay production leaving 850 acres of unenclosed common land freely available for parishioners to exercise their 'commoner's rights'. Besides pasturage owned outright or leased from a landlord a parishioner was also entitled to graze animals on various parcels of common land contained within the parish. Common rights were determined and controlled more by tradition than by statute. If anyone took unfair advantage and attempted to allow too many animals to overgraze common pasturage then the matter would generally be settled by social pressure rather than resorting to law. Common land might offer the poor the chance to dig peat (turbary), take fish from rivers (piscary) or collect small branches of wood for repairing fences or fuel (estovers) and most crucially in Llandudno, the right to erect Tai Unnos.

Chapter Thirteen

Tai Unnos on the Morfa

Since time immemorial traditional Welsh communities accepted that if someone erected a house overnight ('Tŷ Unnos' = 'One-Night House') on land not already enclosed, farmed or claimed by someone else then they had the right to stay. The occupant might then freely enclose a small surrounding area of land to cultivate as a garden. As the Llandudno Advertiser recalled in 1899, 'in this way many a poor man had become the possessor of a freehold cottage and a nice plot of land'. For centuries enterprising individuals had erected Tai Unnos on obscure scraps of common land in Llandudno. Their priority was to acquire cultivatable land away from the gaze of the authorities. Ken Dibble has identified three surviving Tai Unnos in Nant y Gamar; Tan y Coed, Bron Gadair and Nant y Gamar Farm, where he suggests there are the remains of many more. Dibble also identifies a process whereby squatters were sometimes inveigled into paying nominal ground rent to the Mostyn Estate. The rental income was trivial but the transaction generated documentation later used by the Estate to claim legal ownership of the cottager's land. The squatters had no solicitors or land agents and their histories have been largely overlooked. Fortunately Llandudno's nineteenth century squatters didn't all seek to conceal their Tai Unnos. In the nineteenth century their location of choice was Llandudno Morfa which soon developed into a substantial and highly visible squatter community.

Self-Build Solution
Llandudno Morfa was that parcel of common land, 'Y Cyttir', that fronted the seashore between the cenotaph and the end of Vaughan Street. In the early nineteenth century it was described as 'a sandy, hilly expanse, similar to the West Shore'. It became a haven for squatters after the magnetic attraction of employment in the expanding copper mines disrupted the traditional pattern of Tai Unnos settlement. The agricultural quality of the holding was not a priority for mine-working squatters for they didn't have to survive on the produce of their land. Their priority was simply accommodation for themselves and their families. With the population of Llandudno doubling in the first thirty years of the nineteenth century there was acute demand for housing. Both mine owners and speculative builders failed to keep pace with the

187

demand so people solved their own housing problem by erecting Tai Unnos on the nearest available land to the village centre.

Llandudno Morfa

Morfa Common comprised 27 acres of rough grass and dunes, too dry for grazing but a popular summer playground for village children. Pwllygwichiad farm stood at the western end of the common whilst boundary with the adjoining parish of Eglwysrhos defined the eastern edge of the Morfa (Marine Hotel site). The outlying fields of Pwllygwichiad ran along the Common's southern boundary. To provide temporary shelter for incoming equipment and supplies and secure storage for copper ore awaiting shipment, a stone warehouse, Y Storws, had been erected on the land by the mining companies. The first Morfa Tai Unnos were erected alongside Y Storws, using the familiar warehouse name as a reference point for their address. So on 14th August 1825 schoolmaster Charles Bathgate and his wife baptised their son, William, at St Tudno's Church, registering their residence as, 'Y Storws'. By 1830 there were possibly three overnight houses on the Morfa, by 1841 this had expanded to about ten but within a decade the number doubled to twenty plus. Curiously the only Morfa Tŷ Unnos specifically cited by local historians, 'Tyn y Ffrith' (near Washington Hotel) wasn't amongst them. Tyn y Ffrith was not situated on the Common, it wasn't in Llandudno parish and wasn't even an overnight cottage but a long-standing, if somewhat dilapidated Mostyn smallholding situated in Eglwysrhos and paying the Estate an annual rental of £4 10s.

Process and Architecture of Tai Unnos

Like homesteaders of the American West, Llandudno squatters built sod houses to provide shelter. Barrow loads of turf were stacked up during the day to supply 'bricks' for their evening endeavours. Windows were prefabricated from timber and thatch gathered for roofing. If time permitted a fireplace and chimney of stone or plastered wattle was included. Refinements were added later once the occupant felt they'd established their right to stay.

Overnight Houses were also customary in England, 'During the first stages of industrialisation, mining communities sprang up among the pits which mined the outcrops on the moorland edge, and their inhabitants constructed their own houses, either by encroaching on common land as squatters or by paying a nominal rent to a ground landlord' (Laidlaw).

The architecture and construction of squatters' cottages were

188

determined by the local availability of building materials. John Taylor provides an early (1639) and interesting illustration, 'A great number of the inhabitants (especially the poorer sort) doe dwell in vallts, holes or caves, which are cut and digged out the Rocke: so that if a man be destitute of a house, it is but to go to Nottingham, and with a mattock, a Shovell, a Crow of Iron, a Chizell, and Mallet, and sauch instruments, he may play the Mole, the Cunny, or the Pioneer, and worked himself a Hole, or a Burrow, for him and his family.'

This cave option was also practised on the Great Orme until well into the Victorian era but Llandudno squatters generally opted for the traditional Welsh approach outlined by Iorwerth Peate, 'The intending proprietor and his friends proceeded . . . at nightfall, and with great activity, to cut clods of green sward. When a quantity of the turf had been cut . . . part of the company commenced building up the walls with the clods having been raised sufficiently high, the previously prepared roof was put on, and thatched with all speed so that the roof should be completed and smoke ascend through the chimney ere the sun rose.'

In 'Cwm Eithin', Hugh Evans of Llangwm provides a peek inside a typical north Wales example, 'There were several of these turf houses in the neighbourhood of my old home . . . in one of them . . . there was some kind of central partition which divided it into two rooms and the father had made a low loft over the sleeping room as sleeping quarters for some of the children'.

An old Llandudno resident recalled, in 1865, the outward appearance of the Morfa Tai Unnos, 'Huts built of earth and clay, white washed in front, with a small garden adjoining on both sides'. As the initial 1820's squatter's cottage went unchallenged the rate of settlement gathered pace and by 1850 a substantial community had developed.

The Morfa Community

Drawing on a variety of fragmentary primary sources it's possible to identify and even sketch in a few details of the lives of members of this lost community. In the 1840's a few individuals came and went but most families settled comfortably into their home-made houses and by the mid-century turnover was minimal. With few exceptions these cottages bore no names or numbers but I've enumerated each to identify their locations on the accompanying map of the Morfa. I introduce each example with a formalised table of biographical information, noting in turn: **name**, **age** (in 1850), **occupation** and **place of birth**. The future lives of these individuals and the subsequent fate of their community will be revealed in the final chapter.

189

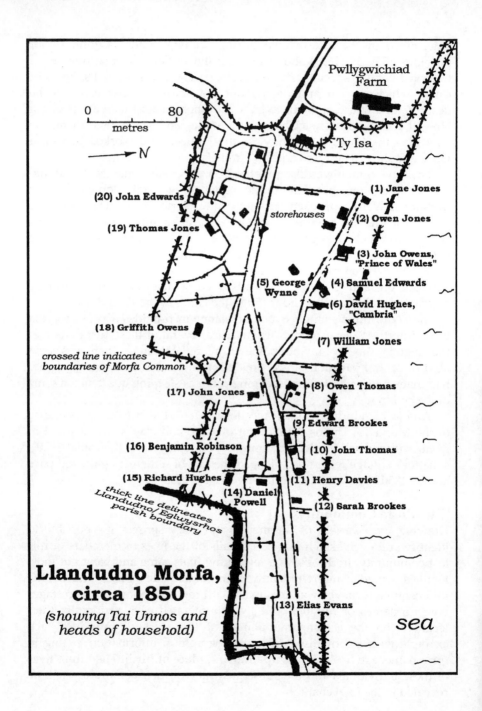

Pwllygwichiad Farm

0   80
metres

→ N

Ty Isa

(20) John Edwards

storehouses

(19) Thomas Jones

(1) Jane Jones

(2) Owen Jones

(3) John Owens, "Prince of Wales"

(5) George Wynne

(4) Samuel Edwards

(6) David Hughes, "Cambria"

(18) Griffith Owens

(7) William Jones

crossed line indicates boundaries of Morfa Common

(8) Owen Thomas

(17) John Jones

(9) Edward Brookes

(16) Benjamin Robinson

(10) John Thomas

(15) Richard Hughes

(14) Daniel Powell

(11) Henry Davies

thick line delineates Llandudno/ Egluysrhos parish boundary

(12) Sarah Brookes

Llandudno Morfa, circa 1850
(showing Tai Unnos and heads of household)

(13) Elias Evans

sea

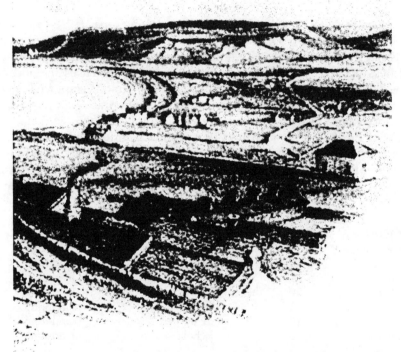

Llandudno Morfa, circa 1845, from above Plas Road,
with Pwllygwichiad Farm in left mid-distance and
Tabernacl Chapel nearer and to the right

1 MORFA

Jane Jones	51	widow	Rowen
Peter	28	miner/son	Gyffin
Thomas	27	miner/son	Gyffin
Hugh	26	miner/son	Gyffin
Elizabeth	23	daughter	Llandudno
Robert	21	son	Llandudno
William	19	son	Llandudno
Jane.	18	daughter	Llandudno
Richard	15	son	Llandudno
Annie	13	daughter	Llandudno
Edward	11	son	Llandudno
Francis	5	son	Llandudno

Jane was the widow of local copper miner Joseph Jones (1798-1848) who erected the family's Tŷ Unnos in the 1830's. Parish records reveal Hugh was baptised in St Tudno's Church on 5th September 1839 when their address was recorded as 'Storws bach'. In the 1841 census the address was described as Uch y don (Above the Waves) but this employed poetic licence for at the next baptism, in 1843, their home was again referred to as Storws bach. Joseph Jones was one of many Llandudno workers who assisted on the erection of the Conwy Railway Bridge in 1848. During construction work, despite being an excellent swimmer, Joseph was swept into the river and drowned. Thomas Rowlands recalled that Joseph's sons, Hugh and Richard both subsequently served as coxswains of the Llandudno lifeboat.

2 MORFA

Owen Jones	54	miner	Llandudno
Catherine	49	wife	Llandudno
John	24	miner	Llandudno
Catherine	24	daughter	Llandudno
Mary	22	daughter	Llandudno
Anne	16	daughter	Llandudno
Ellinor	11	scholar	Llandudno

Owen and Kitty Jones were amongst the best-known, and best-loved characters of old Llandudno and one of first couples to squat on the common. Mary Jones was born on the Morfa and baptised in St Tudno's in February 1828 and temporary resident Charles Bathgate, the schoolmaster, might have lodged here with the Jones's when his son William (who went on to become a Bangor fruit dealer) was born in 1821. Owen was the village pig slaughterer, a 'bright and cheerful old man with a ready answer to all who greeted him, Apart from the pigs he had not an enemy in the world. When he was seen going out after his shift, especially in the winter and the spring, it was obvious that one of these four-legged creatures was about to lose its life' (Rowlands). Catherine senior, or Kitty as she was known to villagers, ran a rival bakehouse to Marged Jones's village 'Typopty' and used a similar 'trumpeting' system, 'From the noise reverberating from the two establishments one could well imagine being in the vicinity of the walls of Jericho' (Rowlands).

3 MORFA

John Owens	52	miner	Llandudno
Alice	51	wife	Holywell
Thomas	16	farrier	Llandudno
Robert	14	scholar	Llandudno
Richard	11	scholar	Llandudno
Jane	7	scholar	Llandudno
Elizabeth	5	scholar	Llandudno
Alice	3	daughter	Manchester
Anne Jones	14	house servant	Llandudno
Anne Davies	27	visitor	Llandrillo
John Davies	32	visitor	Betws yn rhos
David Davies	29	visitor	Betws yn rhos

John and Alice set up home on the Morfa in the 1830's in a Tŷ Unnos they called Pen-y-Gro (Top of the Pebbles). 'When the Prince of Wales steamer commenced to run from Liverpool (to Menai Bridge) the name Pen-y-Gro was changed to the more aristocratic, Prince of Wales. In a short time the Prince of Wales was converted into an inn. Mr John Owen was the proprietor' (Roberts). Next the family began ferrying passengers from the boats to attract custom to their 'Prince of Wales Inn'. The place where the St George's Hotel now stands was then a prominent sand hill. 'The boatmen ascended this hill, often from which they had an uninterrupted view, and when it was time to meet the steamer they would call out from this hill with all their might, *This way for the steamboat!'* (Roberts). The Prince of Wales left an abiding impression on visitor, Richard Jones, returning to Llandudno after an absence of many years, 'The only house I remember was a long and low one, which was known as Caravansary (sic), Prince of Wales . . . It was a whitewashed place, where all travellers made their headquarters. To leave and reach the steamer we had to go into large whaleboats manned by big muscular men, who were strong enough to carry the people from boats onto dry land.'

4 MORFA

Sam Edwards	33	miner	Llandudno
Mary	28	wife	Llandudno
Owen	6	scholar	Llandudno
John	4	son	Llandudno
William	2	son	Llandudno

Sam Edwards was one of Llandudno's most devout Christians. 'He was baptised when about twenty years of age and continued without any wavering or flagging to the end . . . He was a thorough Baptist and had no sympathy for those that are anything or nothing . . . We remember to have heard one say of Mr Edwards that he went to a certain house in Llandudno and in that house there was a painting of the baptism of Christ, no doubt the best ever exhibited. When he saw it he fell down on his knees and burst into tears and explained, O! my great Lord!' A brave and accomplished swimmer William won widespread recognition for saving numerous people from drowning.

5 MORFA

George Wynne	31	miner	Llanrhos
Mary	25	wife	Llandudno
Anne	2	daughter	Llandudno
Elizabeth	1	daughter	Llandudno
John	1 week	son	Llandudno

As a young teenager George had followed his father, William, into the copper mines. His family then occupied Tan y stage, on the Great Orme. With ten people crammed into a small, single storey cottage when George married Mary in November 1842 it was obvious he had to move out and so the couple settled on the Morfa. Sadly their first born child, Anne, died in October 1850

6 MORFA

David Hughes	40	miner	Llandudno
Elizabeth	44	wife	Northop, Flint
John	18	miner	Llandudno
Edward	16	miner	Llandudno
James	14	miner	Llandudno
Jemima	12	scholar	Llandudno
Elizabeth	5	scholar	Llandudno

David Hughes, familiarly known to villagers as 'Dafydd Simon', was one of first settlers on the Common. All the couple's children were born in their Tŷ Unnos that like their neighbour's to the west, was early on extended to operate as an inn. After undergoing a similar process of evolution to the Prince of Wales, the Hughes's house was reborn as, the 'Cambria'. When, on September 9th, 1832 the couple baptised their first-born, John, at St Tudno's Church, they registered their address as 'Ystorws' and the father's name as David Hughes, alias David 'Simon', labourer.

'He was well-known to the visitors and all the habitues of the Llandudno beach. David Hughes, Cambria, was a character in his time . . . The old man could not express himself well in the English language; he used to tell visitors that *Edward* (his son) *had saved a man drowned*. On another occasion he was describing Edward thus: *Edward was a curly hat and straw head*. Another of his saying was, *David be me in the ground*, meaning that he would live after him. David Hughes in his young days was looked upon as the best fighting man in the village, and it is said that with a little encouragement he would hold his own against all-comers.' He also enjoyed a drink and jealous of the prosperity of shopkeeper William Prichard for a while, 'when well-primed, stand outside the shop and address the sign in some doggerel of his own composition' (Roberts).

'In those early days there were two rival boat companies on the beach, one headed by David Hughes and the other John Owen (Prince of Wales). It would be about the time of the Crimean War (1853-6) and both companies were nicknamed thus, David Hughes was called the Sultan and his men Turks and John Owen was called Czar and his men of course, Russians, and at times there would be much ado on the beach between the rival boat companies' (Roberts).

Despite his occasional wayward behaviour David Hughes was a shrewd businessman and in 1837 was amongst 250 local noteworthies who addressed a petition to the Poor Law Commission in London, pleading against Llandudno being incorporated into Llanrwst Union. They successfully argued for the creation of a local Union centred on a Conwy Workhouse.

7 MORFA

William Jones	52	miner	Anglesey
Elizabeth	53	wife	Llandudno
John	21	miner	Llandudno
Hugh	20	miner	Llandudno
Owen	18	miner	Llandudno
Robert	15	miner	Llandudno
Margaret	13	scholar	Llandudno
Henry	11	scholar	Llandudno
George	9	scholar	Llandudno

Thomas Rowlands remembered the old Cambria Inn and 'a little lower down lived William and Betty Jones'.

8 MORFA

Owen Thomas	41	schoolmaster	Anglesey
Mary (Ellen)	41	wife	Liverpool
Margaret (Alice)	1	daughter	Llandudno
Hugh Hughes	12	stepson, scholar	Llandudno

It's indicative of the high child mortality rate of the period that like other Morfa residents Owen and Mary's first-born, Margaret, died here aged only 4 years and 8 months on 29th July 1846. Her modest gravestone stands in St George's churchyard.

9 MORFA

Edward Brookes	29	miner	Flintshire
Jane	29	wife	Llanrhos
Mary	7	daughter	Llandudno
Thomas	5	son	Llandudno
John	3	son	Llandudno
Margaret	1	daughter	Llandudno

Edward Brookes married Jane Jones on 19th November 1840 when they were both living in the village. Together with Edward's brother and his wife the couple settled on the Morfa in 1843. Daughter Mary was born in the village but Thomas, John and Margaret were born here on the Morfa.

10 MORFA

John Thomas	33	miner	Anglesey
Mary	54	wife	Llanrhos

John Thomas was just one of a number of Amlwch copper miners who moved to Llandudno as the Anglesey industry contracted. His wife, Mary was the sister of Jane Brookes, next door, and little Mary Brookes regularly stayed overnight here with her auntie.

11 MORFA

Henry Davies	49	miner	Llandudno
Mary	48	wife	Llansantffraid
Thomas	21	miner	Llandudno
William	20	miner	Llandudno
Robert	16	miner	Llandudno
David	13	tailor	Llandudno
John	11	scholar	Llandudno

After living for a while at Lester Row, Henry Davies moved down to the Morfa, with his family, in about 1842 but tragedy soon followed. A baby boy, Hugh born here the following year, having been baptised at St George's Church on 1st December 1844, died just four days later. The oldest boy, Thomas began his working life as an agricultural labourer but soon decided to join his father and brothers in the copper mines.

12 MORFA

Sarah Brookes	**36**	**miner's widow**	**Conwy**
Margaret	9	scholar	Llandudno
Jane	7	scholar	Llandudno
Catherine	5	scholar	Llandudno
Owen	4	scholar	Llandudno
William	1	son	Llandudno

Sarah Brooke moved here with husband, William, in 1843, settling not far from his brother, Edward, at 'Number 9'. William Brooke was tragically killed in the mine and buried at St George's on the 2nd October, 1847 aged only 33 leaving Sarah to bring up the children.

13 MORFA

Elias Evans	**35**	**ag labourer**	**Betws yn rhos**
Anne	33	wife	Llandudno
Mary	6	daughter	Whitford
Catherine	1	daughter	Llandudno

Elias and Anne lost their little boy, John, aged two, in 1849, whilst they were living here on the Morfa. He was buried on 28th July in a little graveyard plot, marked by a simple memorial stone, at the northern end of St George's Church.

14 MORFA

Daniel Powell	**42**	**miner**	**Llandudno**
Anne	44	wife	Llandudno
Catherine	20	dressmaker	Llandudno
Richard	16	miner	Llandudno
Griffith	13	miner	Llandudno
Sarah	9	daughter	Llanrhos
John	6	son	Llanrhos
Daniel	3	son	Llanrhos
Jane	1	daughter	Llanrhos

'Daniel Powell was very well-known in the old times. He brought up a very numerous family, he being the father of 22 children . . . many stories of his wit are in existence among the older natives' (Roberts). Many claimed he was the funniest man they ever met but like David Hughes he was a dyed-in-the–wool Welshman who was never comfortable with the English language.

15 MORFA

Richard Hughes	34	miner	Anglesey
Elizabeth	31	wife	Llandudno
William	11	scholar	Llandudno
Catherine	10	daughter	Llandudno
Elizabeth	5	daughter	Llandudno
Hugh	3	son	Llandudno
Anne	1	daughter	Llandudno

Richard came to Llandudno in 1834 from Amlwch, seeking work in the copper mines. Around 1838 he married Elizabeth Jones, daughter of Peter Jones, Pwllygwichiad. After lodging for a while at the Miners' Arms they moved on to the Morfa. Elizabeth was born here on 11th January 1845.

16 MORFA

Ben Robinson	30	miner	Anglesey
Elizabeth	41	wife	Llandudno
Grace	3	daughter	Llandudno

Benjamin Robinson lived at Tan yr Allt on the Great Orme when he first arrived in Llandudno from Amlwch, describing himself as an agricultural labourer. The family set up home on the Morfa around 1842. Sadly first born baby Benjamin Robinson, aged two, didn't survive and was buried in St George's graveyard on 31st October 1844.

17 MORFA

John Jones	76	miner	Flintshire
Richard	30	miner	Llandudno
John	13	grandson/scholar	Liverpool

John Jones came to Llandudno to work in the copper mines, settling on the Morfa in the late 1830's.

18 MORFA

Griffith Owens	38	miner	Llandudno
Ann	27	wife	Llangystennin
Elinor	6	daughter	Llandudno
Margaret	4	daughter	Llandudno
Jane	2	daughter	Llandudno
Owen	1	son	Llandudno

Griffith Owens, 'a quiet Christian' (Rowlands) moved to the Morfa from Pen yr Ogof, where he had been a close neighbour of Thomas Kendrick around 1842. Baby Elinor was born here and baptised at St George's Church on 8th January 1844. The following year Margaret was baptised on the 21st December but several of the couple's children, Jane, Owen and Anne died in childhood. Griffiths Owen was one of the last of the working Llandudno copper miners.

19 MORFA

Thomas Jones	35	miner	Llandudno
Elizabeth	34	wife	Llandudno
Margaret	10	daughter	Llandudno
John	8	son	Llandudno
Owen	6	son	Llandudno
William	1	son	Llandudno
Elizabeth Jones	14	general servant	Llangystenin

Thomas Jones may have taken over the Tŷ Unnos erected by Samuel Jones who was here in 1845 when Thomas and Elizabeth lived at Cwm y Chimnel. Daughter Ellenor died on 30th April 1849 aged 2 years and 4 months then just over three weeks later William died aged 10 yrs 5mths.

20 MORFA

John Edwards	39	miner	Llandudno
Jane	38	wife	Flintshire
John	15	miner/son	Llandudno
Ann	6	daughter	Llandudno

John and Jane Edwards were one of the last couples to move on to the Morfa in the late 1840's.

A Local Squat for Local People

This snapshot reveals 20 Tai Unnos and 125 people (including 3 'visitors') occupying the Morfa, 11.5% of Llandudno's population squatting on just 0.015% of the 1757 acres that comprised mid-century Llandudno. Almost all heads of household, 90%, were miners (including 2 miner's widows), and most were born locally with Anglesey and Flint predictably providing the remaining miners and Betws-yn-Rhos supplying the sole agricultural labourer. If we go beyond heads of household and include all Morfa squatters we reach a total of 34 working miners. From this analysis we can see the squatter community was no opportunistic, transient, alien, intrusion but largely local people solving the housing crisis for themselves whilst working down the mines to provide for themselves and their families.

Some visitors looked down on the squatters' dwellings, 'Landing on the beach, there is little at first sight to attract attention . . . the few cottages on the strand have not the most inviting aspect and the visitor is glad to pass into the village which lies on the rising ground at the foot of the mountain on the right' (Liverpool Mercury 1849). Businessman William Bridge despised the, 'badly-built and dingy-looking cottages which now stud the beach' but scientist Michael Faraday visiting home-made homes near Beddgelert in 1819 saw beyond the superficial, 'The air of comfort about these little places is astonishing. A thousand conveniences present themselves, which have either been purchased at the expense of hard labour or contrived and executed with much judgement, and there appears to be no cessation in their endeavour to make all complete. It is true their means are very humble, and their production is too, but they have the true merit of being useful and they are the best ornaments cottages can have.'

Life on the Morfa

Morfa residents were alert to the dangers of their seaside location. 'Rumours often came of very high tides and threatenings of a flood from the sea, and in those times many of the cottagers carried what furniture and livestock they possessed on to higher ground on the side of the Orme; this proceding happened pretty often. On one occasion some neighbours were passing a certain cottage when they observed the owner putting the end of a rope fast to his chimney. When asked what he was about he answered, *I am fastening this rope to my chimney, the other end is fast to the water barrel, and when the flood does come I shall have a buoy on my house and will then know its position'*.

Despite having little land themselves squatters had access to a variety of food sources. They could even graze a few sheep on the scattered parcels of Llandudno common land. This was very popular as there were hundreds of acres of common grazing available on the Great Orme. 'In those days everyone had the right to keep a number of sheep on the mountain and paid a few pence a head to William Davies, Tai Newyddion, for shepherding'. A sheep fair was held every year on 22nd September when animals being sold were rounded up and herded into the old stone pens at the foot of Pendinas, near Wyddfyd. It was eagerly anticipated by everyone in Llandudno, with a brass band, stalls selling cakes, toys and ribbons and a great deal of drinking and carousing.

A Hazardous Harvest

In 1833 Samuel Lewis noted that collecting sea birds eggs was a popular if hazardous local pursuit. 'The north side of the Great Orme's Head is broken into craggy precipices of various elevations, which, during the breeding season, are the resort of various aquatic birds, among which are the gull, the razor-bill, the guillemot, the cormorant . . . and a small number of puffins . . . The eggs of the razor-bill are esteemed a delicacy, and the sale of them, generally at two shillings per dozen, affords a livelihood to several families employed during the season in procuring them.'

Robert Williams described, in 1835, how the eggs were obtained, 'The rock eggs, which are chiefly those of the guillemots and razorbills, are a delicious food, and great quantities are annually gathered. The bold adventurer is let down by a rope, which is fastened about his middle and planting his feet against the sides, and carefully shifting his hands, he gradually arrives at the haunt of the birds; having filled the basket, which is slung on his shoulder, he ascends to the summit of the cliff with the assistance of his partner who is stationed above. This is a dangerous employment, and there are several instances on record, where from the rope slipping or other casualties, lives have been lost, and the mangled bodies buried in the sea.'

Villager John Prichard recorded details of Dafydd Jones's attempt to collect eggs, 'The morning was so windy that it was dangerous to walk on the edge of the mighty cliffs. The brave lad was lowered by rope with his basket on his back over the highest cliff on Pengogarth, known as Henardd Uchaf, where the lighthouse now stands. He had been warned not to detach himself from the rope. Having reached the ledge where the eggs lay he collected as many as he could reach and saw many more at the far end of the ledge. The storm prevented him advising the men on the cliff top that he needed more rope, he released himself from it. He lost his grip and fell from the ledge on to Henardd Isaf, and in a second fall fell into the sea (and so) Dafydd lost his life.'

A traveller recalling an 1837 visit pithily concluded, 'The means of livelihood of the Llandudno people in those days appear to have been principally copper mining, sheep tending and the despoiling of sea birds' nests.'

Adventurous Epicures

Llandudno's sea cliffs provided another epicurean delight, samphire, which is now especially prized as an accompaniment to seafood. When Charles Darwin visited the village on the invitation of a character known as Old Price the pair employed an interesting method of collecting samphire from inaccessible cliffs on the Great Orme. Old Price noted, 'Here true Samphire (Crithmum maritimum) grows, which we used to get by shooting it down'! Darwin was an adventurous epicure, keen to consume rare or unusual delicacies. On another outing he surprised Old Price by his non-indulgence, 'The writer, in company with Charles Darwin, caught a Viper on the Warren about 1824, favoured by Wellington boots and very strong gardening gloves. Holding him short by the neck, we let him bite at the glove, and emit a drop of clear fluid along the fang, which sank instantly into the leather. When this had been done about five times, no more poison was left, and we killed, but did not eat him, a fact never satisfactorily explained.'

Rabbits and Wildfowl

The sand hills of both the north and west shores were home to thousands of rabbits that were eagerly consumed by villagers. Residents devised a semiformal system of entitlement to take rabbits (for the pot) from particular sections of the warrens, as they also did with grazing the Commons. When fields were flooded in winter geese, teal, mallard, widgeon and pochards were gratefully received. Rich pickings were guaranteed on Llandudno's eastern boundary where, according to George Porter of Pwllycrochan, 'In Old Price's youthful days we find the district between Llandrillo Church and the Little Orme a vast roadless marsh of reeds, bulrushes and ponds, the haunt and breeding-ground of countless water fowl.' Old Price claimed 'Afon Ganol eclipsed all over shooting grounds' and deplored the draining of wetlands. 'What will you say old boy, when every trace of the river shall have disappeared under the all-subduing ploughshare?'

Bounteous Botany

With little land for vegetables squatters collected a variety of local plants for the table. Lamb's lettuce, borage, lady's smock, and garlic mustard provided salads. Fungi from woods and fields were eagerly consumed. Alexanders made a good soup. Wood sorrel, fennel and chervil lent flavour to other dishes. Hazel nuts supplied a nutritious snack to anyone quick enough to reach them before the squirrels. Dewberries, blackberries, wild gooseberries and tiny wild strawberries were eaten raw and in fruit pies.

Cowslips made excellent wine and comfrey, dandelion and feverfew were essential ingredients in the folk pharmocology.

A Contented Community

Llandudno's squatters were sustained by making best use of a rich environment. Nominally miners many people also kept a few sheep, harvested wild plants, caught a few rabbits and collected and sold birds' eggs. If their homes were destroyed by high tides they helped one another construct a replacement from the materials to hand. Some visitors saw beauty in simplicity but others, imbued with the values of the factory age, could see no more than a village 'tenanted by Pigs and Peasants, who live in wretched huts and stys' (Alder) . . . 'a small village composed of a few miserable hovels, put together in the most primitive manner, and with the rudest materials' (Jackson).

Chapter Fourteen

Sailors, Wreckers and Smugglers

There were only four mariners in Llandudno according to the official 1851 census but according to Jackson the village was inhabited by 'fisherman and smugglers'. Like an iceberg, much of Llandudno's maritime activity was hidden beneath the surface. Villagers who worked down the mines were classified as 'Miners', although many also went fishing or owned shares in ships. Without Llandudno's extensive maritime links the copper mines couldn't operate. Ships brought in machinery and coal to power the pumps and exported ore to the smelters. A key maritime function was fulfilled by the Great Orme signal station and despite draconian punishments villagers continued to harvest the bounteous gifts that God, in his wisdom, caused to be cast upon their shores.

Fishing

Fishing nets could often be seen drying along the beach misleading visitors into believing residents spent all their time catching fish. In fact 'Llandudno miners besides following their ordinary occupations would also play the role of fishermen; in this capacity they caught herrings in the autumn and dredged for oysters earlier in the year. In order to find the oyster beds and the fishing grounds, they would use particular landmarks, and a most important one, being Abergele Church steeple. This being rather indistinct owing to the distance from Llandudno bay, in order to quicken the vision the west side of the steeple was whitewashed. The Llandudno fishermen were allowed the privilege of doing this for the purpose, and it is a fact that a party of Llandudno men would journey annually to Abergele and whitewash the church steeple so that it would appear more visible from Llandudno bay' (Roberts).

Herring, cod, whiting, mackerel and even the occasional dogfish, octopus and angler-fish were all caught in the bay and the 'Lark', a fishing boats jointly owned by a number of miners, was a familiar sight.

In the estuary fisherman netted excellent salmon and between January and April shoals of brwyniad, also known as sparling or smelt, were occasionally caught. A rare and mysterious fish, similar to the gwyniad, now found only in the depths of Llyn Tegid, it was said to smell of rushes and taste of cucumber.

When the shoals moved inshore amazing numbers of fish were

sometimes recovered from Clawdd-y-gored, an ancient fish weir on the site of the existing pier. As late as 1847 up to 10,000 herrings were left high and dry. The bottom part of this trap was reinforced with large boulders that ran out to sea with the end section curving around towards the present Queen's Hotel. 'The top part of the weir was made of rough wicker work and when the tides receded the fish would be left and caught in the north east corner' (Roberts).

Coastal Carriers

Coastal 'flats' that brought goods to Llandudno and carried away the copper ore were essential to the village's economy and way of life. With no proper harbour or deep-water anchorage these boats were designed with flat bottoms so that they could be beached at high tide and after unloading and reloading they would re-float on an incoming tide. Most landed near the present St George's Hotel, or if the wind was unfavourable on the West Shore. These old wooden sailing ships could typically transport about 50 tons of goods or copper ore, with the largest carrying 90 tons. The twenty boats identified below serviced the mines and village in the mid-nineteenth century but not all were based in Llandudno or operated at the same time and it was unusual to see more than five or six drawn up on the beach at any one time.

- **Argyle** – Conwy flat, Captained by Hugh Hughes, carried ore
- **Abbey** – Conwy built flat, 50 tons burthen, owned by Henry Hughes, brought general goods from Chester and Liverpool
- **Barbara** – Flat owned by William Jones of Tŷ Newydd
- **Conovium** – Owned by Captain John Parry and Co
- **Eleanor** – Coal carrying brig owned by Owen Jones, of Plas Ucha, and Company
- **Eliza** – Owned by Hugh Hughes, Gatehouse and William Parry, Tŷ Newydd
- **Five Sisters** – Conwy based flat, 50 tons burthen brought general goods from Chester and Liverpool
- **General Havelock** – Schooner jointly owned by a syndicate including Captain John Parry, John and Joseph Hughes (King William) and Job Jones (Great Orme Signal Station)
- **Hero** – Amlwch based ore carrier operated from 1823, 90 ton schooner reputedly so reliable it was not insured. Captain John Evans had been captured during the Napoleonic Wars. Captain split expenses and profits with owners. Mate got 48 shillings a month, ordinary sailor

40s. and board, boy 20s. and clothes. Evans died May 1830 and Francis Maden took over

- **John** – Flat owned and operated by the Tŷ Gwyn Mine Company, carried ore. Captained by William Hughes, Llathen wen
- **Lady Augusta** – Owned by Captain David Lloyd, briefly captained in 1857 by John Parry
- **Lady Champneys** – Flat owned by Tŷ Gwyn Mine Company, captained by Owen Hughes, carried 90 tons
- **Lady Willoughby** – Flat, home port Conwy, carried ore/coal
- **Lord Willoughby** – Carried coal/ore, based Conwy, schooner
- **Lovely** – Owned by Captain David Lloyd
- **Mary Ann** – Conwy based, brought in rope
- **Providence** – Conwy based brig, carried coal/ore
- **Rhuddlan Trader** – Home port Chester, carried coal/ore
- **Sarah Lloyd** – 33-ton sloop owned by Captain David Lloyd and registered at Beaumaris
- **Varchwel** – Caerhun sloop carrying coal/ore wrecked in Conwy Estuary in October 1844 when Richard Thomas of Conwy received a telescope from the RNLI for saving the life of John Wrench

Master Mariners

Captain David Lloyd (1818-75) and Captain John Parry (1820-1907) were Llandudno's leading mariners who captained and owned shares in numerous ships. Captain Lloyd was responsible for the construction of the only ship ever launched in Llandudno. When he retired from the sea he took out a lease on the Old Mine and embarked on the building of a boat named after his wife, the 'Sarah Lloyd'. Unfortunately the mines were then in decline and the Sarah Lloyd had to cast around for custom. Captain Lloyd's son John was, in 1861, tragically lost at sea off the Cape of Good Hope, whilst voyaging from Madras to Liverpool

Captain John Parry was born in Holyhead but moved to Llandudno, where all his children were born, in his youth when his father, Hugh, left Anglesey to work in the copper mines. John's brother also went to sea but died in 1851 whilst on a voyage from Brazil. Captain Parry's first voyage as Master was on the Conovium on June 8th 1848 when he carried paving stones from the West Shore to Liverpool. Soon after he was involved in a tricky incident aboard the Conovium, when it was blown ashore. 'In order to launch her back to the watery elements baulks of timber were fixed on the beach and about 40 horses on the sands in two rows were employed all doing their very best to draw the good ship out to where the tide would reach her. This scheme did not work although possessed of 40 horse-power and had to be abandoned. In a few days a Liverpool tug boat was acquired and at high water a tow rope was attached to the smack and after much manoeuvring the Conovium was once more in its own element.' Parry's 'General Havelock' was a particularly successful venture that carried ore from the mines, cement from Glasgow, timber from Liverpool and coal and bricks from Queensferry until it was blown onto the cob at Conwy by the 1859 storm that sank the Royal Charter.

Stormy Weather

'In order to provide against being driven ashore by storms two substantial moorings had been placed on the sands opposite the Grand Hotel; the sand was dug out and immense stones placed there to which was attached very heavy mooring chains. When a ship moored on the beach was caught by a nor' easter she would be made fast to this mooring in this manner; she would ride the gale out, although often heavy seas dashed against her. But occasionally when a sudden tempest arose half-a-dozen ships would be driven high up on the beach and left there until the next high spring tide would refloat them' (Roberts).

Another ship that failed to float away on a rising tide was the John. 'The flat was driven on to the rocks where the Grand Hotel is now situated. Owing to the wind changing direction very suddenly she could not work her way out into open water. The flat was well laden with copper belonging to certain parties, quite a dozen I think had parcels on board. These lots were not what you would call packed up, but placed on sheets one over the other. Under the circumstances it must have been difficult to keep the lots separate, but when the tide went out the owners each recovered his own and it was brought back to Glanymor in carts. No part of the valuable load was lost. The flat itself was damaged a bit, but was taken to Conwy and repaired there' (Hughes).

Servicing the Quarry Trade

'In the first half of the last (19th) century paving stones were shipped from Llandudno beach. The inhabitants would collect a large heap of stones; then a ship would arrive and load them, sail off with the cargo to the large towns of the Mersey and elsewhere. This process went on for many years, until at last the Government stopped the proceeding in order to protect the beach and foreshore . . . Two extensive quarries existed, one of each side of Happy Valley . . . The original idea was that of supplying stone for English manufacturers on the Mersey. For this purpose a stage was erected at the projecting point near the Marine Drive Lodge, the proprietor being Mr John Smith . . . Another stage for the same purpose was situated on the site of the Grand Hotel extending on to the plot of sand just in front. This was constructed by Mr George Brookes, Victoria Inn. Mr Brookes also made a road to connect this stage with the quarry, which is on the left side of Happy Valley. Many hundreds of tons of limestone were shipped from these stages. One of Mr Brookes's sons, John Brookes was master of a vessel which took a cargo of limestone from his father's stage. His ship was wrecked on the Hoyle Bank. After some days his remains were found on the shore, near Hoylake, and it is said there is evidence that he was not dead when he first reached the shore; everything of value had disappeared. He was interred in St George's Churchyard, March 9th, 1848 being 29 years old.'

'Perhaps it is not generally known that the stone used to build the masonry on which the Conwy tubular bridge are secured was quarried from the Great Orme's Head, the place where they were taken from is just round the first point of the Orme on the pier side; it is called Porthyheli; in a convenient spot a slip was made out of the rock through which the blocks of stone were slipped down to barges and then taken to Conwy. Mr Joseph Hughes (King William) was the quarry contractor' (Roberts).

Coastal vessels also transported products of other local quarries including fine sands and clays exported from Nant y gamar to Liverpool, Widnes and Runcorn for glass and tile making. In the quarry's latter years this particular trade was serviced by the Sarah Lloyd.

Passage to Liverpool

The first regular steamer service between Liverpool and Caernarfonshire began on 8th June 1822 when the 'Albion' sailed to the Menai Strait. Other vessels soon joined Albion on the route. All were wooden paddle-steamers, ranging from 150 to 200 tons, equipped with steam engines of 60 to 70 horse-power, and rigged to carry sail as well. Fares were expensive, with a first class cabin costing ten shillings, the equivalent of a labourer's weekly wage. There was a daily service each way between Liverpool and Bangor with intermediate stops at Hoylake, Orme's Head and Beaumaris but with no proper landing facilities passengers wishing to disembark at Llandudno had to endure improvised arrangements. If weather permitted boats could be rowed out to collect passengers. In adverse conditions Llandudno-bound travellers found themselves travelling on to Bangor or Beaumaris. Boats rowed out from the Morfa to ferry passengers ashore were operated by Llandudno's two rival Tai Unnos inns.

In 1843 the first iron paddle steamer appeared on the route, the 'Erin-go-Bragh'. Its arrival was recalled by an aged villager, 'On the slope, a little beyond the Baths Hotel (the old Pavilion site) . . . a crowd of miners could be seen anxiously looking towards the horizon . . . after a long and patient waiting, they saw the smoke, and then the hull, and in about three hours the never-to-be-forgotten 'Erin go Bragh' arrived. Two or three boats went out to meet her and brought ashore a number of boilermakers coming to work on the Conwy Tubular Bridge'. The Erin-go-Bragh was soon joined by the 'Prince of Wales' and 'Cambria', whose names were promptly adopted by Llandudno's Morfa inns.

The Prince of Wales was a 400 ton iron paddle-steamer built for the City of Dublin Steam Packet Company. She sailed between Liverpool and Menai Bridge on three days a week (illustrated), stopping in Llandudno as weather permitted. Competition on the route was fierce and by 1848 passengers could travel to Liverpool for two shillings and soon the rival companies were also offering free dinners on board and 3d back as you disembarked!

Not Waving but Drowning

Gazing out from the Great Orme villagers witnessed an almost endless procession of ships sailing to and from the Mersey, from ports around the world. The 280-ton Chester-built brig, Hornby, named after the family who owned her, set out from Liverpool on December 27th 1823, destined for Rio de Janeiro. Her Master was an irascible man named Captain Wade, who was fervently disliked at Beaumaris, where he had once lived. She carried a crew of thirteen, two passengers and a cargo valued at £60,000 on a voyage that left its mark on Llandudno. When the crew reached Point Lynas, on the coast of Anglesey, they met with strong winds from the north west which prevented them from seeking the shelter of Holyhead. For two days they tried to make headway, tacking back and forth between the Great Orme and Point Lynas. On the second night the Mate suggested to the Master that they should go into Beaumaris for shelter. But he got short shrift from Captain Wade who replied, 'I'd rather be at sea for ever than go there!'

The storm got worse and as they appeared in danger of being blown against the Orme, Wade directed crewman John Williams to loose the jib but once aloft Williams realised a collision was inevitable and leapt from the ship onto the rocky headland. 'Although in a very exhausted condition, the night dark, and the gale raging, he mustered his remaining strength and slowly climbed the rocks, until at last he was out of danger. Again he persevered and winded his way across the Orme. When the day was breaking he had found his way to the door of the smithy, which was

THE CITY OF DUBLIN COMPANY'S
Splendid and Powerful NEW IRON STEAMER the

"PRINCE OF WALES,"

Of 400 Tons Burthen, and 200 Horse power,

W. H. WARREN, R. N., Commander,

(Built expressly for the Station,)

Has commenced plying between Menai Bridge, Bangor, Beaumaris, and Liverpool, and will continue for the Summer on the days and hours following—namely:—

From Menai Bridge, MONDAYS, WEDNESDAYS, and FRIDAYS at 10 o'clock morning.

From George's pier-head, Liverpool, TUESDAYS, THURSDAYS and SATURDAYS, 11 o'clock, morning.

Cabin fare .... 6s.
Steerage do. .... 2s. 6d.
Children under 12 years, Cabin 3s. Steerage, 1s.6d.

Further particulars may be had on application to Mr. E. W. Timothy, or Messrs. R. and H. Humphreys, Menai Bridge; Mr. John Hughes, Ship-agent, Carnarvon; Mr. Robt. Pritchard, Post-master, Bangor; Mr. T. Byrne, Post-master, Beaumaris; or to Mr. J. K. Rounthwaite, at the Company's Office, 24 Water Street, Liverpool.

Menai Bridge, 20th April, 1846.

attached to the copper mine. The miners going to work found him there and did all they could to alleviate his plight. The miners on being informed hastened to the scene of the wreck, but found no traces whatever of the crew, who it is said all perished. Part of the ship was forced by the sea into a small opening in the rocks and remained stuck there for many years. This opening is called into this day Hornby Cave' (Roberts).

Rothsay Castle

A yet more avoidable disaster occurred on 17th August 1831 when the under-powered, clapped out wooden paddle steamer, the Rothsay Castle set out from Liverpool with 150 passengers anticipating a 'pleasure trip' to Beaumaris. The press described the Rothsay Castle as 'superbly fitted up for the accommodation and comfort of passengers' but already twenty years old and originally designed for service on the Clyde, when the ship first arrived in Liverpool it was in such obvious disrepair that many of the intended crew refused to sign on. Many timbers were rotten, there was a hole in the bottom of the hull, there was no signal gun and only one small, inadequately equipped lifeboat.

The ship was expected to sail at 10am but was delayed, first by bad weather and then because a Mr Forster of London insisted his carriage was hoisted aboard before departure. Eventually leaving at noon she ran straight into the full force of a NNW wind and a flood tide. The band soon joined the passengers in suffering abject sickness and profuse vomiting. A deputation of passengers, joined by Lord Derby's agent decided to beg Captain Atkinson to return to port, unfortunately they found him in his cabin dead drunk and fiercely abusive. At 10pm they arrived off the Great Orme having travelled 36 miles in ten hours. As they made for Beaumaris a fireman appeared on deck and announced there was two feet of water in the stokehold that would soon extinguish the boilers, depriving the ship of steam and losing all motive power! Passengers were ordered to man the pumps but like much else on board these proved useless. They then attempted to organise a bucket chain for bailing but were shocked to discover that the ship's only bucket had fallen overboard. Then the Rothsay Castle struck the Dutchman's Bank and began to break up. The iron funnel collapsed taking the mast with it, smashing into the hull and knocking the Captain overboard, to his death.

Just 23 people were saved. For days bodies continued to be cast ashore all along the coast of north Wales. Mrs Alice Tarrey was washed up onto Llandudno beach and buried on the Orme but the corpse of her two-year-old son John was swept into the estuary, landed in Glan Conwy and was buried in Llansantfraid Parish Churchyard.

Resurrection of Jane Tudor

On 15th February 1847 the 345-ton American barque, Jane Tudor, was
wrecked in heavy weather a short distance north of Gogarth farm on its
maiden voyage from Baltimore to Liverpool. 'It was Shrove Tuesday, the
good housewives of Llandudno were busy making pancakes when the
news was spread abroad that a three-masted ship was ashore; the
pancakes had to take their chance as everyone rushed to see the wreck'
(Roberts). Fortunately no lives were lost and the crew rather ingeniously
cut down the foremast and used it as a bridge to reach dry land on the
Great Orme. The wreck, together with its cargo were auctioned off to a
Liverpool man for £210, with the sails sold separately for £45, but the
following week it was sold on to two Conwy men. With the aid of two
Liverpool tugs they refloated and then repaired and reregistered the ship
and for twenty years it transported timber from Montreal to Llandudno.

Archiduco Palatino

A few weeks after the Jane Tudor struck the Gogarth side of the Great
Orme the Archiduco Palatino, en route from Constantinople to Dublin,
was grounded on the opposite side of the headland. 'Between ten and
eleven o'clock one very stormy morning scores of people were to be seen
running wildly towards the Fach or *Happy Valley*, shouting that a large
vessel was in the act of being blown onto the beach . . . driven by the
strong wind and waves on to the dangerous stones that abound below
the Valley. The vessel was a terrible sight, the sails torn and the signal of
distress flying between the masts . . . She was an Italian brig and carried a
crew of eleven men . . . a gale from the north-east was raging. The good
ship was forced ashore and grounded on the southern end of the old weir
wall just opposite the St George's Hotel. Great excitement prevailed, no
lifeboat was available, but the best boat on the shore, *The Lady Harriet*,
was at once manned. The brave and gallant crew consisted of John Jones,
Llwynon; Thomas Jones, Tanyrogo; Daniel Powell, Morfa; Captain
William Jones; John Davies, Tŷ Capel and Thomas Brookes, Victoria,
coxswain . . . Owing to the terrible state of the sea the boat was half
swamped and driven back ashore on her beam ends with great force
whilst preparing for another attempt. The sailors on board the wreck
launched their own boat and eight of their number got on board . . . Then
they were entirely at the mercy of the waves and hundreds of people on
shore, as if holding their breath, expecting every minute to see the boat
and its occupants disappearing in the storm. Eventually it got near the

shore and sank, but through the untiring efforts of the inhabitants five of the poor sailors were saved. The remaining three on board were also saved when the tide receded but neither the crew nor the inhabitants were able to understand each other as the Italians could not speak a word of English or Welsh. As a last resource an old sailor named Lewis Davies, Tŷ Ucha, was sent for and as he had sailed to foreign parts it was anticipated he would be able to converse with the shipwrecked mariners but it was of no avail and an interpreter was requisitioned from Liverpool... Among those that were saved was an Italian boy, his father having been lost in this wreck. This boy was harboured by a miner named Harry Davies, Morfa (of '11 Morfa', CD). The boy had endeared himself so much to his custodian that he was looked upon and treated as a son. Davies would not on any account part with the boy and some of his relations had to come all the way from Italy to claim and fetch him before Davies would relinquish his hold of the lad' (Roberts).

Burning of the Ocean Monarch

The most horrific maritime disaster witnessed by villagers occurred late in the morning on 24th August 1848 with the loss of the 'Ocean Monarch'. A few hours earlier Captain Murdoch had sailed out of Liverpool bound for the United States with 398 emigrants aboard, many of them Welsh. Five or six miles east of the Great Orme fire broke out, 'The flames were distinctly visible from Llandudno, where great excitement prevailed; fire was seen running up the rigging of the vessel. The Spanish yacht *Alfonso*, which was passing, bore down on the wreck and rescued many of the passengers. In the afternoon the *Prince of Wales* steamer on her way from Liverpool to Llandudno saved a few more, but the heat was so intense it was impossible to get near the wreck and the poor emigrants who had started out to the new country with such high hopes perished in the mad flames or threw themselves into the sea in sad despair' (Hughes).

The Ocean Monarch was entirely consumed by the flames, 178 lives were lost and Captain John Hunter of the Cambria was heavily censured for refusing to go to the aid of the stricken vessel. The Cambria was steaming by on her regular route from Beaumaris to Liverpool when Captain Hunter admitted he noticed the Ocean Monarch was on fire. Hunter claimed that he was carrying insufficient coal to effect a rescue attempt, he also considered the ship was already receiving adequate aid and did not wish to endanger the lives of his own passengers.

The Llandudno Advertiser later recalled, 'Following upon that awful night . . . the sea cast upon the shore the scorched and burned bodies for many weeks'.

Signalling Napoleon's Invasion

The Great Orme offered such a prominent lookout and deadly hazard to shipping it was early on adopted as an observation post and relay station. A signalling system, instigated by Prince William (later William IV) was installed by the Admiralty in 1804 to provide early warning of Napoleonic invasion. After a brief peace Britain was at war with France from 1803 until 1815. Napoleon was so confident of victory that, in 1804, he struck medals to celebrate the anticipated conquest. To allow Liverpool time to defend itself against an invasion fleet a chain of signal stations was established linking the port to Anglesey. Links in the chain stretched from a lookout at Holyhead via Point Lynas, Penmon, Great Orme, Cefn yr Ogof, Point of Air and Bidston to Liverpool. The Llandudno station was a simple wooden hut with a flagstaff and diagonal yard-arm. Uniform with other outposts, Llandudno was equipped with coloured flags and spheres for visual signalling and telescopes for observing ships and incoming messages.

The full complement of the station was a Lieutenant, a Midshipman and one or two seamen whose job was to keep a lookout and challenge suspicious vessels. Ships that were challenged had to make the 'private signal of the day' or be treated as an enemy. Packet boats, such as the Albion, were supplied with books of these secret code signals and specific action was prescribed should the French set foot ashore, as John Roberts recorded; 'Great fear existed among the inhabitants of the village, lest a French warship should visit the bay. The authorities had caused bonfires to be built on the range of hills from here to Chester, so that a signal could be given in case the enemy effected a landing. One of these bonfires was built on the summit of the Great Orme. During this excitement a suspicious-looking ship was anchored in the bay; the knowing ones said that the French had arrived and the preparations were made to light the bonfire, however this was not done that night. Next day the ship launched a boat and the crew commenced to row it ashore. The tension now was intense. They landed and to the great relief of the Llandudnoites they only came ashore in search of water. To show that the old people were not going to allow the French to land without some resistance, when this ship was in the bay, Robert Williams, Tynyfron, was observed one evening sharpening his pitchfork and when a neighbour enquired of him what he meant he said, *I'm making the points of this fork sharp and if any of those Frenchman land I shall pierce as many as I can with this fork.'*

Intelligence for Mersey Merchants

Napoleon's navy never reached Llandudno but observers may have suspected airborne invasion when, on the 1st October 1812, an alien balloonist penetrated Great Orme airspace. Fears soon evaporated as the airman was blown offshore and suffered the indignity of having his balloon fatally punctured by the bowsprit of a fishing boat!

Lingering fears of Napoleon disappeared with his death in 1821 but as Liverpool's shipping trade continued to expand the city's merchants realised there was profits to be had if they transformed the redundant Admiralty chain into a commercial signalling system. Export cargoes could be confidently arranged before ships berthed and importers assured of accurate delivery times. In 1825 Parliament passed an Act authorising the Trustees of Liverpool Dock to, 'establish a speedy Mode of Communication to the Ship owners and Merchants of Liverpool of the arrival of Ships . . . off the Coast of Wales by building, erecting and maintaining Signal Houses, Telegraphs or such other Modes of Communication as to them shall seem expedient . . . between Liverpool and the Isle of Anglesea'. Following an 1826 survey by Barnard Lindsay Watson, work began on modernising and supplementing the Admiralty chain, replacing the ball and flag signalling system with semaphore. Some of the stations were relocated but the Great Orme post continued to operate on its summit site. On 12th December 1826 a lease was granted to the Liverpool Dock Board by Mostyn Estates. It was only many years later that Board members discovered that the land actually belonged to the Bishop of Bangor and not the Mostyns who for decades had illegitimately demanded, and received an annual rental payment from them!

The LDB chain stretched 72 miles as the crow flies, from Holyhead to Liverpool, or 75½ miles via the signal stations. The first message travelled along the new system in 1827 informing Liverpool that the direction of the wind at Holyhead had changed from SW to W. The signal took just five minutes to reach its destination although it was a full hour before the changing wind direction was actually detected in Liverpool. Watson received a gold watch in gratitude from Sir John Tobin after a signal reached Liverpool informing him that his ship, Mayflower, had rounded Holyhead. Nervous of a long delayed arrival Tobin was on the verge of extending insurance on the ship's valuable cargo when this news saved him the unnecessary expense.

In 1836 Watson expressed concern at the neglected state of the Llandudno station. 'The house at Great Ormeshead is an old wooden building erected many years ago by Government . . . it is now in a state of decay as to render it, from the exposed situation, dangerous, it has just been temporarily strengthened by timbers, but should be rebuilt next spring – there is plenty of stone on the spot'. However it wasn't until 1841 that it was recorded that, 'The station is complete; dwelling house, signal room and outhouses; and the flagstaff erected, the old building taken down and the old telegraph masts taken to pieces'.

The first keeper employed by the Dock Board at Llandudno was Thomas Rogerson, who was appointed on 16th August 1827, he was succeeded in 1833 by William Williams, who in turn was replaced by Job Jones (1808-96). Jones was a popular incumbent who had first served at Llysfaen in 1839 but moved to the Great Orme on 6th January 1842, remaining until 1861 when he transferred to the nearby lighthouse. 'Mr Jones is remarkably courteous and intelligent; not only affording ready information to every inquirer, but kindly permitting visitors to watch his telegraphic operations, which at convenient opportunities he is always willing to explain; and to take a peep through his powerful telescopes at the sublime scenery of the district. A book is kept in which visitors are expected to enter their names and addresses. The solidity of the building – and it needs to be strong in such a situation does not more readily attract the stranger's notice than the domestic comfort and cleanliness of his dwelling, which are most creditable to the industrious management of his wife and family; every one of whom is also skilled in the use of the telegraph. A sheltered nook on the side of the hill near the Station is a favourite resort with picnic parties, combining as it does, welcome facilities for the enjoyment of the glorious prospects, and of the exhilarating recreations usually characteristic of such festive occasions. And here it might be proper to observe, that for the accommodation of visitors, Mr and Mrs Jones have set apart a comfortable furnished room, where tea is provided on the shortest notice and a supply of good lemonade, soda water and other beverages of the temperance class is always to be had' (Hicklin).

The Jones's visitors' book, ending June 1849, survives, showing over two thousand people had toured the signal station in the previous fifteen years. Jones also recorded details of other key village events, including the 1840 visit of the Bishop of Bangor on the day that he inaugurated St George's Church and the 1847 destruction of the Jane Tudor.

Wreckers and Smugglers

The wrecking of the Jane Tudor caused no fatalities to mariners but destroyed the lives of several residents of Llandudno. Whilst the authorities commended villagers for saving seamen Llandudno's determination to recover cargoes was severely punished. As far as villagers were concerned, life was sacred but cargoes cast ashore were fair game. Unlike the infamous 'Wreckers of Crigyll', on Anglesey, villagers never intentionally lured ships onto the rocks but if, by an act of God vessels were accidentally wrecked it was no more than 'harvesting the seas' to make use of goods washed ashore.

Customs Officers and Revenue men based in Conwy were regarded in Llandudno as unwelcome intruders and the story of their 1796 attack on a popular local smuggler named Simpson who was assisted by a youngster named Mark Bratts was long part of Llandudno folklore. Simpson and Bratts had run a lugger over to Holland and were returning with illicit duty-free goods when, as they approached the Great Orme they were chased by 'Typhon', a revenue cutter. As shots were heard people started to gather on the shore to witness the exciting events. As Simpson and his crew began frantically pitching kegs overboard Customs officers fired grapeshot into their vessel. When the smugglers refused to stop the Typhon fired a round of chain shot that sheared off their main mast. Quickly cutting this away and clearing a bar that held back the cutter the smugglers stepped ashore to cheers. As the boat was unloaded Bratt's betrothed, 16-year-old Jane Morgan, turned up to greet him only to learn that her beloved had been shot and killed by the 'Revenue'.

Llandudno's traditional contempt for Customs and Excise Officers was exacerbated in the early years of the nineteenth century when the deeply unpopular Lieutenant Wade of Beaumaris was appointed to command the Revenue's Conwy Bay cutter, 'Defence'.

Revenge of the Revenue Men
Wade was subsequently appointed Captain of the Liverpool brig, Hornby, and after it was wrecked on the Orme in 1824 his ex-colleagues ordered soldiers of the Welsh Regiment to Llandudno to guard the wreck. Billeted at the King's Head Inn they were unable to prevent Llandudno's enthusiastic looters stripping the ship's cargo of cloth. Nevertheless they tracked down the main culprits and marched them off to Caernarfon. Twenty-four villagers were arraigned on the charged of, 'Theft of cloth following the shipwreck of the Hornby' and eleven people were subsequently imprisoned;

- **Edward Williams**   12 months imprisonment
- **William Davies**   12 months imprisonment
- **William Davies**   9 months imprisonment with hard labour

- **Griffith Griffith** 6 months imprisonment with hard labour
- **John Griffith** 9 months imprisonment with hard labour
- **Edward Jones** 6 month imprisonment with hard labour
- **John Jones** 9 months imprisonment with hard labour
- **John Jones** 9 months imprisonment with hard labour
- **Robert Jones** 6 months imprisonment with hard labour
- **Daniel Owens** 6 months imprisonment with hard labour
- **John Roberts** 6 months imprisonment with hard labour

In pursuing the suspects Crown Official, Thomas Boardman shot and injured miner Robert Hughes, which resulted in a mutual prosecution but both were found not guilty and released.

Corn Galore

Despite the punitive sentences villagers continued to gratefully receive whatever God cast upon Llandudno's shores. In 1847 they enjoyed a bountiful corn harvest courtesy of the Archiduco Palatino. After the weather subsided Llandudno looked like a scene from Compton Mackenzie's novel *Whisky Galore*. The North Wales Chronicle observed, 'All work seems to be at a standstill, men, women and children have been fully engaged in robbing the vessel'. For 'this ship had on board a cargo of Indian corn, and the bulk not being of a substantial character, the corn was soon strewn by the sea about the shore in vast quantities. When the villagers saw this they assumed they had every right to collect it as animal food without harm to anyone until a party of soldiers on horseback arrived one Sunday to watch the wreck. They rode in from the direction of Conwy and at Llanrhos they met a Llandudno resident with a cartload of Indian corn. The cart was turned around and forced to unload near the spot where the parade is now, (after that many loads of corn were dumped there) and he was obliged to serve Her Majesty the Queen in Caernarfon Jail for many weeks. The arrival of the soldiers caused a sensation and in consequences there was a hurried heart searching . . . The officials kept a close watch but the villagers managed to avoid them and hide much of the corn in various places near their houses. The soldiers searched the houses for loot under the direction of an officer. At one house the owner remarked to a friend in Welsh, as the soldiers made a fruitless search, *The officer little knows what he is standing over*. What corn was collected from the wreck was hoarded on the beach and covered with a square sail of the wrecked vessel. So incensed were the miners that one night four of them took this sail, wrapped it up, and dropped it down a disused shaft. This theft occasioned another fruitless search, and later, when the soldiers had gone away the four culprits recovered their booty and shared the sail amongst them' (Roberts). Most villagers were delighted to have outwitted the authorities but Llandudno had, by 1847 fallen deeply under the influence of religious nonconformity and the Chapel Elders were not amused.

Chapter Fifteen

Declining Church and Aspiring Chapel

Following centuries of religious decline nineteenth century Llandudno erupted into open-air biblical debates, alfresco baptisms and a rash of church and chapel building.

The End of Anglicanism?

'At the very commencement of 1800 the only place of worship in Llandudno was St Tudno's Church on the Great Orme. Sundays were occupied by the young to romp and play, and the older ones looked on or lounged about the shore and hills . . . religion was at a low ebb.' The village had become centred on Cwlach Street so the population was little inclined to trek across the mountain to attend St Tudno's. The situation was yet more inconvenient for the curate, Reverend Robert Williams, incumbent 1795-1844, who lived across the water in Conwy. 'He was a parson of the old style, very innocent and kind to the people, but not a popular preacher. His congregation often consisted of not more than two or three. His sexton, John Williams, Wyffyd and Richard Jones, Gogarth were the only certain ones. Many anecdotes of him used to be related by the old people, most of them indicating the kind disposition and neighbourly habits. It was said he always left the funeral offerings behind him in the village; a good portion scattered among the children and the remainder at Tynyr hwlfa (Miner's Arms).' There wasn't a service every Sunday and until Telford's bridge opened in 1826 whenever the ferry didn't operate the Reverend Williams remained at home in Conwy. Llandudno villagers resented paying tithes to support a church they didn't attend and when a gale blew off St Tudno's roof in January 1839 the building was abandoned and Anglicans left without a place of worship. The prospects for the Established Church looked unpromising.

'Dippers' Come to Town

A similar decline in the fortunes of the Anglican Church occurred throughout Wales but elsewhere radical religious ideas took root. In 1776 Baptist missionaries from South Wales established a chapel at Fforddlas, near Glan Conwy, and Robert Roberts spearheaded attempts to carry the faith to Llandudno. Because of their publicly demonstrated commitment to whole-body immersion, villagers disparagingly referred to these Baptists emissaries as 'Dippers'. In 1789 Reverend Robert Roberts began preaching the 'good news' from the mounting block in the yard of 'Hen Dafarn'. 'Assuming there would be no objection to his preaching he asked permission from the fair, pleasant girl who kept house there and she was perfectly happy for him to do so, but her uncle, Owen Williams was not'. Owen ordered him to go but Roberts remonstrated, pointing out that, 'he had a right to preach and that his licence came from the same authority as the publican's licence. A heated argument developed between them and Owen Williams seized a pitchfork and threatened to stab the preacher. But Beti, his niece, stepped in and stood between the protagonists. She managed to persuade Owen Williams to go to the service in the parish church and so Robert Roberts had an opportunity to preach the gospel of Christ and Beti Williams accepted Christ into her life. She was baptised shortly after her friend Robert Edwards. For a short time the breaking of bread and preaching took place occasionally in the yard of the old tavern,' but soon the Baptists transferred their activities to Plas. Old Owen Williams had by then become intrigued by the Baptists' message and frequently walked down to Plas to hear more. Two Llandudno men, Robert Edwards, Llwynhelig and Richard Powell, brother of Daniel Powell, Morfa, were won over to the cause and baptised. And in due course old Owen Williams came to profess his faith.

In 1799 Owen Williams was baptised by Robert Roberts in the sea at West Shore, increasing Llandudno's complement of Baptists to four. John Roberts, Tynyffrith, recorded a typical Rev. Roberts ceremony, 'The people of the Creuddyn flocked to the shore and the Conwy people, their boats drawn in a semi-circle, covered the water. In the sea stood the baptised and the baptiser. The scene was new to the spectators from Conwy and in those days they were the most uncivilised wretches in Gwynedd. Had the occupants of Bedlam been present they could not have been noisier with their scornful and terrible shouting. *Silence in the name of the King of Heaven,* but this had no effect. *Silence in the name of George the Third,* he shouted again and pulled forth a licence from his pocket proclaiming. *This is an authority from His Majesty to conduct religious practices without hindrance from any of his subjects.* His manner and authoritative voice frightened them and he was able to proceed quietly and in a leisurely manner to explain the ceremony and officiate with becoming decorum.'

Margaret Owen – Rebel with a Cause

'Shortly after the baptism of Beti and Owen Williams God called another to his church. She was one of the most unlikely to come to the Kingdom . . . Margaret Owen, Plas Bach, was a strange character and was held in

Capel Ebeneser, erected 1814

Saint George's Anglican Church, erected 1840

fear and dread throughout the neighbourhood. She would defend herself with her fists against strong men and she feared noone. She earned a living selling white sand from Gloddaeth Mountain. At the time this sand was plentiful on the top of Nant y gamar and many thousands of tons of it was transported in ships . . . Margaret Owen travelled around the countryside selling this sand. It was used to scrub tables and other large items.' Everyone was amazed one, 'Sunday when she decided to accompany Robert Edwards and Richard Powell to the service at Fforddlas'. Questioning the pair about their ideas as they walked together the seven miles to chapel Margaret took an intense interest in the subsequent service. Afterwards chapel members 'decided that they had never met anyone so awkward and ignorant . . . a firebrand plucked from the flames . . . but on the other hand they found evidence of sincerity . . . and she was granted her wish to proclaim the Lord Jesus Christ at her baptism'.

Disaster struck at the end of 1801 when Robert Edwards and Owen and Beti Williams all decided to emigrate to America and Richard Powell abandoned the faith. 'All Margaret Owen's friends had gone away and she was left as the only member of the Baptist Cause in Llandudno and remained so for twelve years . . . During these years she walked many miles to and from Fforddlas . . . On her way she would call in all the other houses en route and invite people to the service . . . When she returned from listening to a sermon she took her testament in her hand and went next door to ask Benjamin Edwards or his wife or children to read the chapter she had heard . . . Margaret Owen had not the opportunity to learn to read her Bible, or any other book . . . but could memorise large sections especially from the Gospels, the Acts and the Epistles.' In 1812, after more than a decade of travelling alone, one Sunday morning, James Williams, Tŷ Isa asked if he might accompany her to Fforddlas, 'James, bach, I am pleased to see you' she replied, as tears rolled down her cheeks.

Trials and Tribulations of Tabernacl
James Williams was baptised later that same year and inspired by his conviction and enthusiasm by 1813 the cause had attracted sufficient members to seek a site for a chapel. This was no easy task as the Mostyns owned most of the land and expected their tenants to worship at the Established Church. Fortunately the Tynycoed Estate came to the rescue and offered some of their land. The Baptists claimed this was divinely ordained as, 'God's all-knowing providence has provided small estates in scores of places in order that a little of God's land should be available to

build places of worship in order to proclaim the unsurpassable wealth of Christ.'

Tabernacl Chapel opened its doors on 10th May 1815, it was a modest building 24 feet long by 21 feet wide and occupied an almost identical site to the existing chapel on the corner of Upper Mostyn Street and Llywelyn Avenue. Most villagers affectionately referred to Tabernacl as 'Capel Bach.'

Not long after opening the chapel the Baptists invited Christmas Evans to preach on Llandudno beach as John Jeffries, Tŷ Isa, was being baptised in the sea. Watching these events was Mostyn farm bailiff, Richard Williams and his wife who farmed Maesdu. The couple were won over, became members at Tabernacl and were duly baptised in the sea by Reverend Samuel Edwards. When John Phillips the Mostyn Agent found out he ordered Richard and his wife to abandon the faith but they refused and were forced to leave Maesdu.

A later Mostyn Agent adopted a more positive approach and instead of just bullying tenants attempted to bribe them towards Anglicanism. Spotting a potential advocate for the Establishment Cause he encouraged young John Williams of Efail-y-Waen, a Mostyn tenancy at Glanwydden, to study and offered to sponsor him 'to go to Tamworth to prepare for priesthood in the Anglican Church. He was on holiday and arrangements had been made for him to preach in St Tudno's Church on the mountain. On his way from Efail-y-Waen to St Tudno's Church he had to pass Capel Bach. He heard the sounds of worship and went inside and allowed the service in St Tudno's Church to take its own course. He was warmly greeted by the brotherhood and received sustenance for his body and a blessing for his soul in the worship in Capel Bach. He was not seen again in the Church of England.'

From the beginning Tabernacl proved a huge asset in recruiting members to the Baptist Cause and but it wasn't the first chapel in Llandudno, that honour went to the Calvinists.

Methodical Calvinists

Methodist preachers first appeared in Llandudno in 1806 at prayer meetings held at Tynyffrith, a small farmhouse sited near the Washington Hotel, at the invitation of Mari Roberts who had joined the Cause at Mochdre. Unfortunately Mari and her husband John leased their farm from the Mostyns whose Steward promptly ordered them to either evict the Calvinists or be evicted themselves. Mari Roberts courageously turned to organising outdoor venues so local prayer meetings could continue. Owen Owens, Pendyffryn recalled Philip

Hughes coming from Conwy 'with bread and butter in his pocket' to address a big crowd on the beach, delivering his sermon whilst perched upon a large rock. 'The service held on the sea shore was long remembered by the inhabitants and the conduct of the Steward talked of as a piece of impious tyranny.'

Fortunately in 1807 'God's all-knowing providence' kicked in again and the Calvinists were allowed to preach at Tynycoed. For a while the Baptists and Calvinist Methodists held joint meetings but when the Calvinists had expanded to fourteen members they felt confident enough to erect their own chapel. Once again William Jones of Tynycoed offered a site and in 1814 they opened Ebeneser, near the end of Bodhyfryd Road. 'A small and plain chapel, with a chapel house on one side, and a yard surrounded by a wall in front of the chapel'. Sunday services at the chapel were supplemented with Friday prayer meetings at Penymynydd Uchaf. Visiting preachers stayed with John Phillips at Penrhyn Old Hall who conveyed them to and from Ebeneser Chapel in his carriage.

There wasn't much progress in the early years of the chapel and by 1819 the Calvinists still only had 18 members. When the Reverend Moses Parry of Denbigh came to preach in 1824 he observed the Llandudno cause was 'dismal, and not on the increase'.

Arrival of Caersalem

Wesleyan Methodism was even slower to develop and it was more than thirty years after preaching began at Hen Blas in 1806 before the cause opened its own chapel. In the interim the Wesleyans used a succession of venues including George Brookes' house at Llwyn Helyg; Tanynant, Cwlach Sreet; Tabernacl Baptist Chapel; the wall outside William Pritchard's shop; Erw Coed, Bodafon and Tŷ Coed Bach, the home of Joseph Tamblyn. 'Tamblyn was born at Gwennap, Cornwall in 1811 . . . after his mother died when he was a child he moved with his father to Halkyn, Flintshire . . . In 1834 he moved to Llandudno on his appointment as *Pitman and Engineer*, receiving 15s. a week, the highest wage of any of the mine's employees . . . Because there was only one other Wesleyan in the vicinity of the Orme, Joseph Tamblyn first of all walked to worship at Bethel, Tywyn. But he was determined that Llandudno should have its own Methodist Society. The few Methodists who met at Erw Coed were too far from the bulk of the population'.

Tamblyn invited talented preachers to meetings at his own home and gradually he built up enough support to construct Caersalem Chapel, Cwlach Street. Opened on Good Friday, 1837, Caersalem measured 11 yards by 10 yards and seated almost 200 people and although initial costs were estimated at £150 expenses soared and soon the Cause was lumbered with debts of £450. John Wesley himself had been a Royalist and Tory and fortunately Llandudno's Wesleyans were socially a notch or two above the Calvinists and well able to settle such accounts. Besides the well remunerated Tamblyn, Caersalem's well-placed trustees included John Lester, husband of Elizabeth, a partner in the New Mine; John Owens owner of Gyffin Mill and a couple of wealthy Conwy businessmen; William Bridge, draper, stationer and property speculator and Edward Jones, twice Mayor of Conwy.

Not Yet Independent

Like the Baptists the Independents, who were also known as 'Congregationalist' were one of the original Nonconformist Causes. Yet they were slow to organise in Llandudno and ironically dependant on others to supply suitable preaching venues. The first Congregationalist to arrive in Llandudno was Thomas Jones, Frondeg who came from Flintshire to serve as Agent of the New Mine. He was joined in 1835 by Jane, the widow of Richard Rowlands, the Congregationalist Minister of Henrhyd. Her son Thomas, chronicler of village life, readily conceded, 'that the Congregationalists, during the time they were without a place of worship of their own, were accorded every facility, kindness and help from the other denominations. Despite this however they felt they were somehow homeless. This is how my mother felt. One day she went to Mr Jones and said, *Well Thomas, here I am with my children and there is no Congregational place of worship. I have decided, in order to avoid the danger of my children being raised without a spiritual home to devote myself and my children to the Wesleyan Cause. I have had a very kind letter from Mr Bridge bringing us to their notice.'*

Thomas Jones was reluctant to abandon the Cause and prompted Jane Rowlands to host fellowship meetings in her home at Frondeg Bach. 'Not long after starting the cause several outsiders came to reside here. They included Robert Meredith and Richard Davies from Newmarket, Thomas and Mark Hughes from St Asaph and several others . . . In those days we only held the Tuesday night fellowships and everyone worshipped with the different denominations on the Sabbath.'

'Congregational singing was immensely popular in those days . . . I remember in one meeting I had been conceited enough to consider that I understood music. An old member announced a six line hymn and as no one seemed prepared to start I pitched it myself. I soon realised my error. Instead of helping me the young members smiled and the older members looked profound and serious. I, meanwhile was forced to sing the whole verse on my own, the first and last solo I ever performed. To compound my discomfort instead of supporting me Joseph Jones asked, *What is that metre called Thomas? A special metre*, I replied. *A very appropriate name*, he said, *I never heard a metre so specialised. I would advise you to send it and every similar example to the same destination as the scapegoat was consigned to under the old Dispensation and never bother us with it again*. There was in the old meetings a very homely way of dealing with matters.'

We did not always enjoy an undisturbed fellowship. On one occasion when Mr R Meredith was discussing our verses the door opened and a man shouted, *Do you want any fresh herrings missus?'*

The congregation 'tried and failed to obtain land to build a chapel' and eventually 'Thomas Jones promised that if they did not succeed soon he would give a piece of the orchard and warehouse to the west of Frondeg to build a chapel'.

Overtures from Salt Lake City

By the end of the 1830's the Baptists, the Calvinists and the Wesleyans all operated their own chapels in Llandudno but the Anglican Church lay in ruins and the Independents still hadn't got their act together, then along came the Mormons.

The 'Church of Jesus Christ of the Latter Day Saints', or Mormons, began in Palmyra, New York State, in 1820 when an angel revealed certain truths to a fourteen year old boy named Joseph Smith. Smith started with just five followers but by the end of 1830 his energy and charismatic public speaking had turned this number into several hundred. Smith's successor, Brigham Young dispatched Mormon missionaries across the Atlantic to recruit converts for their new settlement at Salt Lake City. Around 1845 they arrived in Llandudno. 'Behind William Pritchard's shop was the garden of Tŷ Coch, and where Longton House now stands was a tall thorn hedge. It was under this hedge that the Mormons, or Latter Day Saints, congregated in the evening to conduct public services. On many evenings we stayed until ten or eleven o'clock listening to Thomas Parry and Samuel Jones debating with them . . . The Mormons claimed their leader, Joe Smith, had received new revelations from heaven in a forest in the American wilderness and that he could *speak with tongues* as the apostles had. They claimed that this miraculous gift was passed on to anyone on whom he or his disciples had lain hands. Samuel Jones argued with them on scriptural grounds . . . Thomas Parry issued a challenge to their chief apostle, John Parry . . . *Well John*, he said, you claim to be able to speak with strange tongues . . . *If you can speak Greek you must have received the gift from on high'* and he challenged the Mormon to translate a Greek testament. *'Ah,* said the apostle, *the Holy Spirit does not promise to allow us to speak with tongues in order to satisfy anyone's curiosity . . . An excellent excuse.* said Thomas, *You know no more about reading Greek than Ty'nyfron's cow knows how to knit socks'.*

'Between the Saints, Samuel Jones and Thomas Parry many entertaining hours were spent in the shade of the thorn hedge in the garden of Tŷ Coch.' A few villagers were inspired by the Mormon missionaries, including Peter and Elizabeth Hughes who followed them back to Salt Lake City where their Llandudno born daughter, Martha Maria, became the first female elected to the United States Senate.

Arise St George!

Just as the Nonconformists seemed to be gaining a monopoly on Llandudno's religious life the Anglicans opened St George's Church (illustrated), a beautifully impressive, conveniently sited building able to accommodate 450 worshippers. This ambitious venture was largely financed by the English owners of the Old Mine, Archibald and William Worthington. Designed in the Early English style by architect John Welch, St George's Church was consecrated by the Bishop of Bangor on 13th August 1840. A new rectory was erected next door providing the Reverend Williams with convenient on-site accommodation. Not that it was designed with him in mind for when the idea of building a new church was first mooted, 'some of the inhabitants thought it desirable to have a new parson and contemplated to petition the Bishop of Bangor to that effect. The old curate having learnt of the movement convened a vestry meeting and there told the dear beloved brethren that if they did want a more fashionable minister than himself they would certainly not like to see him in his old age after serving them to the best of his ability for so many years thrown to the street. He would be greatly obliged if they would give him a character (reference) so that he might apply for another place. The people's hearts were touched and a resolution was passed unanimously to give the old curate a good character, the same to be numerously signed and forwarded to the Bishop. This was speedily done and when the request for a new minister reached the prelate, his answer was that he had just received a most excellent character for the Rev. Robert Williams, and he felt sure he had no man in his diocese who could produce a better testimonial; therefore on no account could he think of removing such a minister. Robert Williams was allowed to finish his career in Llandudno.'

Unlike Llandudno's chapels, St George's Church was provided with its own, surrounding, burial ground. The nearest Nonconformist facility was miles away at the small Baptist graveyard at Ffolt, near Glanwydden, opened around 1832. Consequently, most local deceased dissenters left their bones in the graveyard of the Established Church whilst they journeyed onwards to heaven.

A more vital mid-century attraction to Anglicanism was offered by the fashionable Oxford Movement, led by Cardinal Newman. Worshippers who had felt the old Church of England had fallen into complacency and decay, were increasingly attracted back to the fold by Newman's ideas. But in Llandudno, after the modernisers failed to unseat Rev. Williams there was no danger of local Anglicans challenging traditional loyalties. After Rev. Williams died, in office in 1844, his successors continued to uphold the values of an Established Church. When the Honourable Edward Mostyn Lloyd Mostyn was threatened with bankruptcy and couldn't repay a debt of £26,000 owed to the Rector the reverend wrote back on 9th February 1853 with an illuminating proposition. The Reverend Evans (served 1850-57) offered to forget the debt and intercede on Mostyn's behalf with his other creditors, 'numbers of whom I know personally' if Mostyn would get him appointed as a magistrate. This partnership of political and religious Establishment was a powerful combination but Llandudno's Nonconformists were not easily intimidated and their chapels continued to develop and expand.

Dissenters Strike Back

In 1817 Llandudno's 40 Baptists were able to squeeze into 'Capel Bach' but by 1835 membership had expanded to 60 and so a bigger chapel was required. A fund-raising letter signed by Pastor John Griffiths and Deacons, William Thomas, George Brookes and James Williams explained; 'Christian Friends; Owing to an increase in the population and a spirit of hearing God's Word, our place of worship has become far too small . . . ' The enlarged Tabernacl, erected slightly south of Capel Bach measured 13 yards by 14 yards, seated 230, cost £290 to build and opened on 7th October 1835. In 1846 the Baptists organised 'the largest tea party ever held in Llandudno, and perhaps in the country. It was held on Whit Monday and it was the men, not the women, who played the greater part.'

The Calvinists' Chapel could similarly accommodate all eighteen members in 1819 but not the 1836 congregation of fifty so Ebeneser was also rebuilt (illustrated). The new chapel measured 16 yards by 12 yards, seated 240 and cost £236 to build. Visiting Calvinist preachers stayed with David and Margaret Jones at Tŷ Draw but were always invited for tea to Bodhyfryd by Mrs William Jones. The chapel's main preaching festival was a popular annual event in old Llandudno. It took place on Easter Monday and rows of stalls serving cakes and sweets were erected along the lane outside the chapel. 'Many from Conwy, Llansantffraid and other places came to Llandudno on that day.' Just across the lane was Tynypwll Farm whose pet lamb one day decided to join Ebeneser's congregation, 'it was a summer's day and the atmosphere heavy; the door of the chapel was open; a man was sitting on a bench situated on the floor of the edifice. He had fallen asleep. When in this state he was continually nodding his head. The pet lamb looked in and believed the man was nodding at him. Not able to withhold longer the lamb rushed into the chapel and butted the sleeper with such force that he fell on his back with his legs in the air, to the great discomfiture of the worshippers.'

The Wesleyans continued to prove especially attractive to Englishmen employed as specialists in the mines and Captain Vivian organised English language services. As Caersalem was adequate to the needs of the Wesleyan Methodist congregation it continued to serve the Cause without rebuilding. Meanwhile the Independents remained a small, dedicated and growing group although with no chapel of their own they occasionally relied on the hospitality of the other denominations. But all Nonconformist Causes benefited from the Temperance craze sweeping the country in the 1830's.

Llandudno Temperance Society

The first Temperance Society in Wales began at Holywell in 1832 and on 5th October 1836 a 'Llandudno Temperance Society' was formally inaugurated. All denominations took part and finances were accrued through collections, subscriptions and what was known as 'Casgliad Ceiniog y Mis', the Monthly Penny Collection. A large, decorative Llandudno banner was made that 'held a very favourable comparison to other banners in the area . . . The next step in the development of the movement was to hold Cymanfaoedd (hymn singing festivals) in the different districts . . . The Llandudno Society marched from time to time to Conwy and other places. In March 1838 it marched to Abergele, on another occasion the Society went to Glan Conwy, some on foot and some in carriages; a stately procession, they sang passionately all the way. In that Cymanfa some mischievious young man in the village took their carriages, one here and one there, throughout the area and they had much trouble in finding them. It was quite late when they reached Llandudno that night.'

About 1838 a Temperance Cymanfa was held in Llandudno on Morfa Isaf. Wagons served as platforms and the speakers included Richard Rowlands, father of Thomas the miner and author of 'Atgofion Hen Llandudno'. 'Some of the pioneer leaders in the village were William Wynne, Tan y stage; John Lloyd, Pen yr erw and Richard Jones; it is asserted that nearly every adult person in the place had taken the Temperance pledge . . . all the innkeepers in the village joined this movement with one exception. On one occasion two innkeepers were actually put to carry the banner in front of the procession. When one of these Temperance parades was marching through the streets there happened to be a great wild storm. Having occasion to pass the Victoria Inn the high wind blew a sign from the gable of this Inn on to the Old Road just as the crowd was passing; this created great excitement, and the refrain of the Temperance marching song:

'Mae banner dirwest ar y maes *(There is a temperance flag on the field*
A'r frwydyr fawr yn troi' *The great battle is turning)*

was pealed out with great enthusiasm by the crowd, who evidently believed that the happy time had arrived when all the beerhouses would crumble to the ground.'

'Y Diarddel Mawr'
Llandudno village in the 1830's and 1840's was a lively place with all denominations organising preaching, prayer and hymn singing meetings and festivals. A time of religious rivalry and competitive church and chapel building and re-building with congregations increasing and Christianity part of the warp and weft of everyday life and then, in 1847, disaster struck.

When the Archiduco Palatino was wrecked on Llandudno beach and almost everyone in the village enthusiastically helped themselves to its scattered cargo of Indian Corn the religious hierarchies took as dim a view as the civil authorities and retribution was swift and dramatic. Every single member of Llandudno's Wesleyan Cause was expelled, all but two of the Calvinists were similarly treated and only three Baptists survived expulsion. The effect was devastating, Nonconformity was almost destroyed and amongst villagers the event was long remembered and referred to with great resentment as, 'Y Diarddel Mawr' (The Great Excommunication).

Attendance at Church and Chapel

Expelled members were gradually re-admitted to their respective causes and a national census of religious attendance recorded in 1851 revealed Llandudno's denominations had revived. Separate counts of individual attendance at church and chapel, were recorded at services held in the morning, the afternoon and the evening. As officials of the respective meeting places compiled the figures themselves they were liable to inflate them to their own advantage and as some individuals attended more than one service the figures need to be treated with a degree of scepticism. All four of Llandudno's institutions held three services on census day apart from St George's, that abstained from afternoon worship, so the figures should be roughly indicative of the denominations comparative support. On census day St George's (Anglican) recorded a total of 185 worshippers; Caersalem (Wesleyan Methodist - incorrectly recorded as 'Zion') 180; Ebeneser (Calvinist Methodist) 400 and Tabernacl (Baptist) 482. Taken together (ignoring a degree of double attendance) the figures reveal a total attendance at religious establishments of 1,247 out of a total population of 1,131. Villagers were clearly keen on religion and despite Mostyn intimidation, they were overwhelmingly Nonconformist. The Anglicans had the largest and most architecturally sophisticated meeting place but were unable to lure miners back to the Established faith. St George's Church had twice as many seats as Tabernacl but attracted half as many worshippers. Nonconformism was winning the battle for religious supremacy but the Establishment was about to launch a counterattack through the schoolroom.

Chapter Sixteen

Schooling and the Blue Books

Residents of Llandudno village in 1800 had many talents but reading wasn't amongst them. It was said only three people in the parish could read and two of them had learnt elsewhere! The literate trio were Betty Lester, Tŷ Coch, who had been raised in Scotland; John Pierce, Tŷ Gwyn, a native of Flintshire and John Davies who farmed Tŷ Ucha on the Little Orme.

Precocious Pioneer of Pwllygwichiad

Village education in Llandudno begins and ends with Hugh Hughes (1790-1863) who founded the first Sunday School in his father, Thomas's, barn at Pwllygwichiad in 1801. Some of Hugh's inspiration seems to have come from frequent visits to the Calvinist chapel at Mochdre accompanying Mari Roberts, Tynyffrith, but much of the credit is due to his maternal grandfather, Hugh Williams of Meddiant, Glan Conwy. Williams not only educated Hugh Hughes but also ran a regular Sunday School at his farmhouse. When Hugh suggested starting a Sunday School at Pwllygwichiad it was probably his grandad's idea to ask Glan Conwy miller and Calvinist preacher, Cadwaladwr Williams, Felin Uchaf, if he would be their teacher. 'In those remote days this miller was considered a good scholar. He would walk from his home seven miles distant on a Sunday and return after, and with the help of a few others he was the means of establishing the Sunday School.'

Sadly Hugh Hughes's mother, Jane, died the following year and the family moved to Liverpool. The Sunday School then became a little irregular and may have lapsed for a while. Around 1807 the school transferred to the Lesters' barn at Tŷ Coch, which was more conveniently situated for the village. Eventually the Sunday School took up residence in the comfortable parlour of Hen Dafarn and according to villager John Prichard. 'At that time there lived there a bachelor called Edward Davies, commonly known as *Ned y Gadi*. He was the ugliest old man of body, face and mind that I ever saw. He was a blasphemer, swore constantly and possessed a lobster-like body. The reading of God's word and the worship killed off his swearing and I believe was instrumental in softening the ugliness of his body. It was at this place that Hugh Jones in one term progressed from his *A, B, C* to reading the Testament. This boy was afterwards the Reverend Hugh Jones, Ruthin, a well known Minister in his time. As far as I remember this was about 1814. Many Llandudno children learnt to read and write at this school.'

Penybuarth Miners' School
In 1811 historian Edmund Hyde Hall noted that 'by the miners assembled in the parish a school has recently been established and a master obtained for a stipend of £30 per annum.' The school was situated at Penybuarth on the Great Orme. The first teacher was John Rees and amongst his pupils was the John Prichard quoted above, who later became the first Principal of the Baptist College at Llangollen. Rees left after 12 months and was replaced by Frenchman Marcus Louis, who lodged at Pwllygwichiad, where he taught the farmer's son, Hugh Jones, to speak French. He also struck up a friendship with a local girl who worked there. They eventually married and moved away and the school then closed.

'Llandudno British School'
Having learnt English at Penybuarth and continued his studies at Toxteth Park School, Liverpool, in 1818 John Prichard returned to run a school at Llandudno's first Baptist Chapel. When Prichard left to prepare for the ministry at Abergavenny Baptist College in 1821 Mary Ellen was appointed as teacher. Under the sponsorship of the 'British and Foreign School Society', formed in 1808 to promote non-sectarian education, the school operated for alternate periods in the Baptist and Calvinist Chapels.

Supporters of the school, Thomas Jones, Frondeg; George Brookes, Victoria; Roger Lester, Tŷ Coch; John Smith, Siop; David Williams, Tŷ Draw and Tom Parry, Tŷ Gwyn tried to obtain a site to open a permanent, non-denominational school, but without much success. Eventually, with the help of the owner of the New Mine, Edward Lloyd of Cefn, a suitable site was obtained near Tabernacl and a wooden school building erected. John Roberts of Llanrwst, a teacher trained at Borough Road college, London was engaged and Llandudno's 'British School' (named after the national, sponsoring organisation) finally opened in 1844.

The Anglicans Strike Back
Nationally and locally Anglicans were alarmed at the prospect of primary education becoming the preserve of opponents of the Established Church and in 1811 set up the 'National Society for Promoting the Education of the Poor in the Principles of the Established Church'. The reactionary aims of the Society were boldly proclaimed, 'To

communicate to the poor . . . by means of a summary mode of education . . . such knowledge and habits as are sufficient to guide them through life in their proper stations'.

The religious doctrines of the Established Church had little appeal in Llandudno but villagers retained a reverence for the literacy of the Anglican clergy, 'We have heard one of the old people saying that he thought the Reverend Robert Williams was the cleverest and most learned man in the world because he had personally seen him in the King's Head writing a letter while at the same time talking with persons in the room.'

A Parochial School, sponsored by the Anglican Worthington family who owned the Old Mine and financed St George's Church, was opened in the village in 1837, on a site a little above Croesonen. Apparently two candidates were considered for appointment for the teaching post, a man familiarly know as 'Scwli Coch', on account of his red hair and John Williams, a learned author. 'Scwli Coch had served under Wellington and been a prisoner of war in France for many years. Rather than appoint John Williams 'the old soldier was appointed for the reason that he had better handwriting.' After a couple of years Scwli was succeeded by Harry Williams, who lodged at the George and Dragon.

When St Tudno's Church was wrecked by a storm in 1839 the pulpit was moved to this Parochial School where services were also performed until St George's Church opened the following year. To complement the new Anglican Church a beautiful architect-designed, stone built school, in the fashionable gothic style was opened a little further along the lane in 1846. Financed by a grant from the eponymous society, Llandudno's 'National School' cost £500 to build on land donated by the Mostyns. The building included a house for the headmaster and places for 120 pupils who were charged a penny a week for their education.

Political Interference in Education

Between 1800 and 1846 education in Llandudno had thus evolved through several temporary teaching arrangements to arrive in two purpose-built schools, backed by competing religious factions, Anglican and Nonconformist and each pushing its own political agenda. It was a pattern mirrored across the nation and it was almost inevitable that national politicians would seek to intervene and interfere.

Parliament, typically, launched its intervention via the apparently value-free mechanism of a 'Commission of Inquiry into the State of Education in Wales'.

The 1846 Commission was no simple fact-gathering exercise, like all government initiatives there was an underlying political agenda. The values of those supporting the Commission can be detected from their contemporary statements. An Anglican Curate quoted in the Government's 1842, 'Report on Children in North Wales Mines' said, 'I have observed that those who have had some education but were not religiously disposed were the most forward in producing a state of insubordination against employers . . . their knowledge seemed only to puff up the mind and to render it less subordinate to superiors.'

The chief instigator of the 'Inquiry' was Radical M.P. for Coventry, William Williams (1788-1865), an immensely rich cloth merchant. Proposing the Commission, in 1846, Williams advised his Parliamentary colleagues, 'An educated people could be governed easier and much cheaper (sic) than an uneducated, ignorant people.'

Employers wanted an educated yet servile workforce, Anglicans wanted children in Wales brought back into the fold of the Established Church, both considered use of the English language indicative of, and essential to, Civilisation.

The Commission's first Secretary, Sir James Phillips Kay-Shuttleworth, asserted in his 1838 'Report on the Training of Pauper Children' that education must aim 'to diffuse a grammatical knowledge of the English language, as the most important agent of civilisation'. Kay-Shuttleworth believed knowledge of English grammar would even civilise 'the coloured people of the colonies'.

Enthusiastic supporter of the Commission, Home Secretary, Sir James Graham considered the Welsh educationally and morally deficient, 'I regret to say that in some parts of the Principality the ignorance of the people not only lowers them intellectually, but depraves their moral quality.' Echoing and strengthening these claims the Honourable Edward Mostyn Lloyd Mostyn, M.P. advised the Commission that, 'the primary object (of Welsh schools) ought to be the means of gaining a knowledge of the English language, without which it is impossible for the labouring classes . . . to prevent the demoralisation consequent upon a state of ignorance.'

The Establishment believed the Welsh were ignorant and uneducated and that their lack of English led them into moral degeneracy. Nonconformist, Welsh-language education was in the firing line. Critics claimed the Commissioners under Kay-Shuttleworth were licensed to poke their noses into schools all over Wales praising Anglican education and damning the Dissenters. Curates and Rectors were expected to offer hospitality and provide gossip and slander on the morals of teachers and governors of Nonconformist schools, or at least that was claimed at the time. The constitution of the Commission certainly seemed to bear out the claims of the sceptics. All schools in Wales were to be inspected and written reports produced. Kay-Shuttleworth appointed three Commissioners who were given respective responsibilities for South, Mid and North Wales;

- Lord Ralph Robert Wheeler Lingen (1809-1905), Fellow of Balliol
- Jelinger Cookson Symons (1809-1860), Barrister, appointed Poor Law School Inspector 1848
- Henry R Vaughan Johnson, Called to the Bar in 1848, married the Lord Chancellor's daughter

All three Commissioners were male, all English, all Anglicans and all upper-middle class of similar social and educational background. They worked with remarkable industry, the Commission was formally instituted on 1st October 1846 and the 1,200 page, 3 volume-report published in the late autumn of 1847. Like other government reports it was bound in blue cloth. Its publication received a hostile reception in Wales where it was swiftly denounced as, 'Brad y Llyfrau Gleision' (The Treachery of the Blue Books).

Llandudno's Blue Book Reports

Llandudno came under the jurisdiction of Commissioner Johnson who appointed two assistants, Abraham Thomas and John James, to report on local schools.

John James, a cynical London-Welsh Anglican visited 'Llandudno National School', in Church Walks, on 13th March 1847. Of the 103 on roll 'there were 62 scholars present, 12 could read with ease, 3 repeated the Church Catechism correctly and out of 7 who could answer scripture questions, 2 excelled. 48 copies were shown me but there was not a good specimen among them. I examined 23 scholars in arithmetic and of these 4 could just work out an easy sum in simple addition . . . There was a class of 9 children between 8 and 11 years of age, no one of whom could read simple narratives . . . There were some English children but of the others only about 10 could understand and answer a simple question in the English language . . . The master was formerly a farming man . . . His knowledge of English is insufficient. He puts such questions as this, *How many parts of speech there are?'*

Abraham Thomas inspected 'Llandudno British School', 'not a quarter of a mile distant' on 12th March 1847. Thomas was a student from the Anglican college, St David's, Lampeter and is generally regarded as a more fair-minded reporter than most of his colleagues yet he pulled no punches at Llandudno. 'Of 110 children only 40 present. None could read well or write well upon paper . . . The first and second class were deplorably ignorant, they could not tell the number of Jesus Christ's disciples, how many gospels there are, or whether St Matthew was a man or woman. When examined in grammar the first class compared *good* and *bad* thus: *Good, gooder, goodest; bad, badder, baddest.* The monitors were rude, undisciplined and ignorant . . . The master was formerly a printer . . . his English was bad in grammar and idiom . . . He took no notice of the rude answers, which they made when he spoke to them; but allowed them to jump about the school from place to place and to play and chat with each other. It is difficult to conceive boys in school and subject to a master more rustic and offensive in their manners.

Hugh Hughes, Llandudno's Libertarian

The underlying prejudices and insulting tone of the Blue Books are apparent from these excerpts, and the damning effect of the full three-volume report can be imagined but Wales fought back. A highly effective campaign lampooning the Commissioners, their collaborators and their Inquiry was spearheaded by the man, who as a boy almost half-a-century before had initiated formal education in Llandudno, Hugh Hughes, Pwllygwichiad.

After moving to Liverpool Hugh had learned wood engraving and oil painting, specialising in portraits and topographical subjects. He toured Wales between 1819 and 1821 making sketches of memorable scenes, frequently returning to his grandfather's Glan Conwy farmhouse, Meddiant, to assemble a selection of prints into book form. Published as the 'Beauties of Cambria' and inscribed, 'Meddiant, 1823' the collection was widely acclaimed but his reputation was not confined to the aesthetic sphere for Hughes was an out and out radical. He enjoyed many commissions for portraits of Nonconformist ministers but after signing a petition, in 1828, supporting Catholic Emancipation he was expelled from membership of the Calvinist Methodists. He equally opposed tithes and all other aspects of Church Establishment and frequently employed his pen, and pencil, to promote a variety of radical, liberal causes. As a determined libertarian he abhorred the xenophobic, centralising, underhand authoritarianism of the 'Blue Books'. Through a series of lithographs, 'Pictures of the Million for Wales', published in the *Principality*, Wales's most successful English-language newspaper, he lampooned and lambasted the 'Blue Books' Commissioners, their collaborators and all their works. Hughes accompanied these cartoons

GATHERCOAL SCUTTLEWORTH'S FINAL CHARGE TO THE SPIES.

"The Whig Ministry are resolved to punish Wales for the dangerous example it gives, to the rest of the Empire, by its universal dissent from our Church! I now inform you, in confidence, that this is the real object of this espionage,—you are to help their lordships (of the Com. of Council) to make out a case against voluntary religion, by collecting such evidence of its connection with immorality, disloyalty, and barbarism, as will disgust the public mind of England, thereby preparing it to sanction the (despotic) scheme in contemplation for driving the Welsh back to the *true Church*. The use of the Welsh LANGUAGE being known to be favourable to the propagation of earnest personal religion, both the LANGUAGE and the NATIONALITY of the Welsh, as well as their religion, are to be destroyed! Your *professional*, with your personal *art*, will enable you to select such witnesses, and cull such evidence, as may secure our object without exciting suspicion. My lords have authorized me to assure you that you shall be made *gentlemen (!)* on your return."

GATHERCOAL SCUTTLEWORTH YN GOLLWNG YMAITH YR YSPIWYR.

"Y mae y Whigiaid yn penderfynu cosbi y Cymry am eu *hymacill-dwaeth*, yn yr hyn y rhoddant esiampl ddrygionus i'r deyrnas oll. Yr wyf fi am hyny yn dweyd wrthych chwi, yn *ddistaw*, mai gwir ddyben yr-yspiaeth hon yw, profi cysplltiad crefydd wirfoddol â *barbariaeth, anfoesoldeb,* a *gwrthryfelgarwch, fel y ffeiddier y fath* grefydd gan y Saison, (anwybodus) as fel y delont yn foddion i gymeradwyo y moddion (gormesol) a ddyfeisir, gan arglwyddi y Cyngor, i yrr y Cymry yn eu hol i'r "WIR EGLWYS." Ceir fod yr IAITH Gymreig yn wasanaethgar i daeniad crefydd bersonol; rhaid i chwi gasglu y fath dystiolaethau i'w herbyn, ac yn erbyn holl arferion cenedlaethol y bobl, fel y gellir dystrywio y rhai hyn GYDA'R GREFYDD. Cewch gan yr OFFEIRIADAU (gwrthodedig gan y bobl) y fath dystiolaethau ag sydd eisiau. Er mwyn cuddio ein dybenion ewch at rai o'r Ymnoeilldwyr, ond yn benaf at rai a cawir i chwi fel rhai lled hunerog. Rhoddwyd i mi awdurdod i addaw y gwneir chwi yn *foneddigion (!)* ar eich dychweliad."

Cardiff: Printed by D. Evans, at the "Principality Office."

with suitably satirical text (in English and Welsh).

Cartoons for the Million of Wales

In, 'The Origin of the Committee of Council on Education', number one in the cartoon series, Lord John Russell is standing, proposing the Commission to the Privy Council, who listen attentively from seats surrounding him. In the accompanying text Russell orates, 'My Lords . . . It appears from this letter, which was sent to me by the Rev. Chaplain of a prison . . . that few (children) can answer any religious question. *I asked a boy six years old (who had been very properly committed to gaol for looking over the stile at the Squire's game)* says the Rev. gentleman – *WHAT IS YOUR NAME? BILLY. WHAT DID YOUR GODMOTHERS PROMISE YOU IN YOUR BAPTISM? I HASN'T GOT NONE. WHO IS YOUR CLERGYMAN? DON NO. WHO IS THE BISHOP OF YOUR DIOCESE? DON NO. WHAT IS THE NAME OF THE SOVEREIGN OF THESE REALMS? DON NO.* (Sensations of astonishment and horror here seize their Lordships and their hair stands on end (depicted). Now my Lords . . . I propose the establishment of a Committee of Council to effect, covertly and by degrees, that which Parliament cannot accomplish by reason . . . (Shouts of Hear, Hear!.. Long life to Johnny! Long live Church and State!).

Following this parody of the Parliamentary appointment of the Commission in the next cartoon (illustrated) Hughes set out to ridicule the Commissioners themselves. Kay-Shuttleworth is depicted giving orders to his three Commissioners with the former wearing a coal scuttle on his head whilst the latter are seen to have asses ears protruding from beneath their wigs. In cartoon three we see sneaky school inspectors spying at keyholes, in four a Commissioner is smoking and drinking with a gentleman-clergyman whilst compiling notes for his formal report from the rector's prejudiced opinions on Nonconformist education. 'The Unlucky Visit', the fifth in the series, shows an inspector bursting unexpectedly into a classroom hoping to catch a teacher at his worst.

Unhappy Endings

Hughes's cartoons galvanised national opinion but were insufficient to ensure the long-term survival of Nonconformist schooling in his place of birth. The Blue Book Inspectors recorded an obvious gap between the quality of educational environment offered by Llandudno's rival schools. Where Inspector James noted that the Anglican school's 'building and furniture are very good', Inspector Thomas, at the British School, noticed that 'the windows of the school-room were broken . . . the neighbourhood of the school was in a disgraceful condition.' The contrast was obvious and the superior funding of the Anglican National School, supported as it was by the political and religious Establishment, enabled it to eclipse the education offered by the Nonconformist institution.

Pupils gravitated to the Church Walks school and around 1850 the British School closed. Sunday Schools continued to operate in Nonconformist chapels but in mid-century Llandudno the Anglicans monopolised formal full-time education.

Arch-critic of religious intolerance Hugh Hughes fared no better. He never returned to Llandudno and in 1869 died a pauper in Great Malvern, where he lies buried in an unmarked grave.

Chapter Seventeen

St George's Railway and Harbour

An isolated village at the tip of a peninsula with poor road links and no harbour seems an unlikely candidate for commercial port development but the 'Rocket's' 1829 success at Rainhill transformed the prospects for Llandudno. The following year Stephenson's engines were running on the world's first passenger railway, between Manchester and Liverpool, and schemes transforming Llandudno into the main railhead and harbour for traffic to Ireland were not far behind.

A Bridge Too Far?
Holyhead was the premier jumping off point for Ireland, with other ports offering a limited service, but in 1830 most passengers reached Anglesey by road and a rail connection posed new problems. Many doubted that existing technologies could enable the construction of a bridge across the Menai Straits capable of carrying a railway train. Weight was not the sole problem, experiments had shown crossing trains caused suspension bridges to oscillate dangerously. Alternative termini were therefore identified and connecting routes from England devised and compared.

Terminal Trio
In the early 1830's three possible Welsh termini emerged after consideration of the likely impact of railway developments on the conveyance of passengers, mails and goods to and from Ireland. The trio of possible ports along with their comparative merits and demerits were;

- Holyhead – shortest sea crossing but immense bridging problems
- Porth Dinllaen – fairly short sea crossing but difficult, mountainous rail route
- Llandudno – longest sea crossing but level, easily engineered rail route

Each of the three contenders had clear advantageous and disadvantages and each had its own lobby group of financial and political backers. In the second half of the decade the speed and reliability of the railways prompted the Post Office to transfer its Irish mail service from Holyhead to Liverpool. Holyhead realised it could no longer assume its supremacy in the coaching era would continue in the age of the steam railway.

Porth Dinllaen Project

At a meeting in Dublin on 9th August 1835 Henry Archer (1799-1863), manager of the Ffestiniog Railway and inventor of perforated stamps, proposed a rail and steamer link with London via Porth Dinllaen, near Pwllheli. The scheme was endorsed at a meeting in Caernarfon in January 1836 where it was affirmed that Porth Dinllaen was suitable for development into a harbour capable of sheltering the largest packet steamer. Following this a committee was appointed to seek the help of the Lord Lieutenant of Ireland in publicising the project in high places, and the eminent engineers, Charles Blacker Vignoles and John Urpeth Rastrick, were asked to survey possible routes from Porth Dinllaen through the Welsh mountains to join existing railways to the south.

Four routes were surveyed in the spring and early summer of 1836. Vignoles's preferred route ran through Shrewsbury, Llangollen, Bala, Barmouth, Tremadog, Porthmadoc to Porth Dinllaen. This was a little longer than his other options but the ruling gradient was only 1 in 150. A route through Ffestiniog included gradients of 1 in 16 whilst a line through Newtown needed a tunnel 1½ miles long under Carno Pass.

Holyhead Option

Government could hardly refrain from interfering in such strategically important planning and in December 1836 Commissioners were appointed to report upon and recommend a scheme of railways for Ireland. On 31st March 1837 they asked Vignoles to provide them with a report on possible connections between the Irish and English railway systems. Vignoles compared the viability of a Holyhead rail terminus with his earlier work on Porth Dinllaen. He noted that a direct connection between Holyhead and Chester required two lengthy tunnels at Penmaenbach and Penmaenmawr and a very difficult approach to Bangor that would be further complicated by an expensive disruption to property. If that wasn't damning enough 'the construction of a second bridge across the Straits of Menai is too great an undertaking to be seriously contemplated'!

If Holyhead was nevertheless selected Vignoles explained 'the present bridge across the Menai Straits must be made use of, the locomotive engines starting from, and stopping at each end'. The carriages would then, one-by-one be 'horsed' over the Menai Bridge, before being reconnected to a locomotive on the far side. Hardly an ideal arrangement and it is scarce surprising that Vignoles concluded by restating his previous support for the development of Porth Dinllaen.

When George Stephenson was subsequently invited to compare both

St. George's Harbour and Railway.

NOTICE IS HEREBY GIVEN,

THAT application is intended to be made to Parliament in the ensuing Session, for an Act for making, constructing, and maintaining a Railway from the Grand Junction Railway, near Crewe, to the Great Orme's Head, in the parish of Llandudno; and for making, constructing, and maintaining a Harbour by a sea-wall or breakwater in Llandudno Bay; also for making, constructing, and maintaining in, upon, over, and along such line, or bay, or breakwater, proper works and conveniences connected therewith, and to take such lands as may be necessary for that purpose, to be entitled Saint George's Harbour and Railway, and which said mentioned Railway is intended to pass through or into the several parishes, townships, cities, boroughs, and extra-parochial and other places of Llandudno, Llan-rhos, all in the county of Carnarvon; Llandrillo-rhos, in the county of Denbigh; Llysfaen, Is-y-iffordd, Pant, Isallt, Penmau and Rhwng y-ddwyffordd, or some of them, all in the county of Carnarvon; Llanddulas and Abergele, in the county of Denbigh; Rhyl, Rhyddlan, Prestatyn, Meliden, Llanasa, Gronant, Giwespyr, Picton, Whitford, Bychton, Eden-Owen, Mostyn, Holywell, Greenfield, Bagillt, Coleshill, Flint, Northop, Kelsterton, Wepre, Golftyn, Leadbrook Major, Leadbrook Minor, Hawarden, Sealand, Shotton, Aston, and Saltney, or some of them, all in the county of Flint.—St. Mary's, St. Werburgh's, St. John's, St. Oswald's, Hoole, Great Boughton, Littleton, Christleton, Rowton, Cotton Edmonds, Cotton Abbotts, Waverton, Halton, Foulk Stapleford, Huxley, Newton, Tattenhall, Clotten Hoofield, Tiverton, Beeston, Pickforton, Tilston Fearrall, Bunbury, Spurstow, Alpraham, Calveley, Haughton, Wardle, Cholmondeston, Stoke, Ashton-juxta-Mondrum, Poole Leighton, Woolston Wood, Wooleston, Alvaston, Beam Heath, Monks Coppenhall, Wistaston, Crewe, Shavington-cum-Gresty, Haslington, or some of them, all in the county of Chester.

AND NOTICE IS HEREBY GIVEN,

That power will be applied for in the said intended Act to deviate from the several lines of the said intended Act, for the line or lines of the said intended Railway and Harbour, for the making of which respectively, powers are so intended to be aplied for as aforesaid, as the same will be defined in the said application to Parliament, to any extent not exceeding one hundred yards on either side of such defined Railway line, Bay, Harbour, Land, Sea-wall, or Breakwater.

Dated this 1st day of November, 1836.

CAARLES ELKINGTON, Solicitor,
6, Furnival's Inn, London.

schemes he reached the opposite conclusion, coming down in favour of Holyhead. However he offered only a slightly improved system for crossing the suspension bridge over the Menai. Stephenson suggested that when a train reached the bridge its locomotives would again be detached but the carriages could be hauled across the bridge by ropes worked by stationary engines rather than towed by horses.

Llandudno Scheme

Meanwhile a group of businessmen formed the 'St George's Harbour and Railway Company' (SGH&RCo) to press the rival claims of Llandudno. Railway engineer John Jenkins was engaged to survey a viable north coast connection to Chester. Jenkins became an enthusiastic advocate of the St George's scheme, which he believed offered great potential as a harbour and a cheap, low gradient rail route. He claimed in the *Railway Magazine* that 'this route has met with the unqualified preference of a great majority of the most influential citizens of Dublin and that with their . . . support the company are now proceeding with vigour in the prosecution of their project.'

The directors of the SGH&RC were also encouraged by a meeting they had with the Chancellor of the Exchequer in January 1839 where they were assured that no public money given would be granted to support either of the two rival schemes. Furthermore recent events seemed to improve their prospects against the two other contenders. After gales damaged the Menai Bridge it looked even more unlikely that heavy locomotives would be allowed anywhere near it en route to Holyhead and the sinking of two vessels in the same gales added to the advantages of their scheme which included provision for a harbour of refuge. Full details of their scheme were set out in a comprehensive report and prospectus issued in October 1836.

'St George's Harbour and Railway Company'

The Company's prospectus is highly informative and worth quoting at length. The document is 'Dedicated to the Most Noble Marquis of Anglesea (sic)' and after listing its eight socially elevated patrons, including four admirals, four M.P.'s (1 overlap but no Mostyns!) it goes on to describe the scheme. 'The intended site of St George's Harbour is a bay formed by the bold, promontories called the Great and Little Ormesheads which stretch out from the coast of North Wales nearly two miles into the Irish Sea or St George's Channel; between these two gigantic piers is a noble basin of water covering a space of upwards of 1,000 statute acres, of from four to six fathoms in depth at low water.

It is intended to convert this bay (by means of a pier or breakwater on the outer or north-west side) into an asylum harbour for St George's Channel and to form a line of railway from thence along the coast of Denbighshire by Rhyl and Mostyn and along the banks of the Dee by Greenfield, Bagillt, Flint and Chester to join the Grand Junction Railway at Crewe Hall, near Nantwich in Cheshire. Thus forming a shorter and more direct line of communication between Dublin and London and the Midland counties of England and the Metropolis than any at present existing.'

The Company was capitalised at a million pounds and the prospectus invited the public to purchase its shares, priced at £100 each, £2 deposit, from John Pym, Company Secretary, Throgmorton Street, London.

Packet Station

The Company claimed 'in Holyhead Harbour there is only 11 feet of water at low water which limits the port to the use of steam vessels of small burthen and of comparatively little power.' In contrast, St George's Harbour will have 'a sufficient depth of water at all times of the tide to float steam ships of the largest class.' It accepted that the distance from Llandudno to Dublin is fifty percent further than the passage from Holyhead but asserted that the larger, more powerful vessels able to use St George's Harbour would be able to overcome this disadvantage by exploiting their greater speed. The Company suggested passage from Holyhead might take 8 hours and from Llandudno 7-8 hours.

'Members of Parliament, gentlemen on Parliamentary business or of the legal profession, the army and mercantile men will be conveyed by this route from the Metropolis of England to that of the Sister Kingdom in about eighteen hours . . . Mail and passengers leaving the railway station in London at eight o'clock in the evening would arrive, at the present rate of rail travelling, at St George's Harbour at six o'clock the following morning and be landed in Dublin, by powerful steam packets, at about two o'clock in the afternoon.'

Railway Line

The SGH&RCo extolled the minimal engineering works required to complete their proposed rail route. 'The whole line presents fewer obstacles or difficulties than have been found in the survey of any other of the same extent in the kingdom. Tunnels and bridges form a great item in the cost of railways . . . from St George's Harbour to Chester, with the exception of viaduct bridges across the rivers Clwyd and Dee and some small streams and canals no others will be required. There will be no curves or vertical inclinations upon any part of the line but such as accord with the most perfect economization of mechanical power and of the auxiliary power to be derived from the principles of gravitation.'

Besides simplicity of engineering St George's Railway offered a variety of attractive features. 'The railway will pass close to the bathing place of Rhyl . . . will cross the rich and beautiful Vale of Clwyd so much admired by tourists. And the country in the immediate vicinity of Conway is one of the most picturesque and interesting to the traveller in the Principality.'

'Vessels arriving from foreign ports, particularly the American packets can if the wind be unfavourable, land their passengers at St George's Harbour, who may by the railway reach their destinations before the vessel could get into the Mersey.'

Local industries would also benefit enormously from the railway. 'A prolific (copper) mine on the beach in Llandidno (sic), opened within the last two or three years is yielding to its proprietors nearly £20,000 per annum; the ore is now obliged to be sent to St Helen's or Swansea to be smelted, the latter a distance of 150 miles or more whilst there is a coal field within 20 miles of the mines. There are also other extensive copper mines near the Ormeshead which would be equally benefitted by the intended harbour and railway as coal for their steam engines or for smelting the ore may be brought by the railway at half its present freight . . . The towns of Abergele, St Asaph, Holywell, Flint, Mold and Wrexham being all contiguous to the railway will participate in its advantages and obtain an expeditious outlet for their mineral productions or manufactures.'

Commercial Port

The Llandudno railhead was projected to terminate at an enormous harbour constructed between the twin arms of the Great and Little Orme. Once completed St George's Harbour was proposed to fulfil three related functions; a commercial port, a harbour of refuge and a naval rendezvous.

'As a Harbour connected by Railway through Chester with the Grand Junction Railway to Birmingham and London, Port St George cannot fail to become a place of great commercial importance . . . The arrival of cattle, Irish produce and fish to Port St George destined to the manufacturing districts of the Midland counties of England to be transmitted by Railway and which now go by way of Liverpool could not fail to create an extensive traffic.'

Besides these imports the Company also identified bulk exports projected to pass through the port. Foremost amongst these was coal, which generally 'constitutes an important feature in the success of a railway.' Passing through Flintshire it was anticipated that the line would revive and enhance local exports of coal to Ireland. 'The freight on coals from the river Dee to Dublin is on average through the year not less than 8s per ton . . . Coals could be conveyed on the railway from Mostyn to Port St George at 2s per ton, 4s per ton would be ample freight from thence to Dublin which would effect a saving to the shipper or consumer of 2s per ton.'

'Limestone suitable for mortar and agricultural purposes is most abundant on the western part of the line of railway and can be worked at a very small expense . . . Chert accompanies the limestone strata in immense masses or rocks . . . (and) is useful for various purposes but especially for the manufactory of porcelain or Delft ware . . . Freestone suitable for buildings is frequently found . . . Mill stones are also found near the line . . . Brick clay is also plentiful . . . Slate of durable quality is also met with in several places . . . In the Ruabon Hills in Denbighshire and at Bromba (sic) near Wrexham (iron) ore of peculiarly excellent quality is obtained and several works are carried on with the most gratifying success . . . There are numerous (lead) mines and smelting works in Flintshire . . . Zinc ore is regularly raised over the whole of the lead district . . . oak timber of superior quality for ship building is plentiful in North Wales and in Cheshire.'

Asylum Harbour

The Company claimed there was urgent need for a 'harbour capable of affording shelter to a vessel in distress at low water or even at half tide (serving) Liverpool, the second port in the British dominions, which 13,941 vessels arrived at and the same number departed from last year . . . The formidable sand banks which stretch many miles out to sea, off Liverpool, debar all access to that port at low water and often prove the destruction of those who seek to enter in the darkness of night or during the violence of a storm, even in the day time at high water. An Asylum Harbour for vessels traversing the Irish Sea has been long contemplated and during the late war (Napoleonic) it was warmly espoused by the merchants of Liverpool but the frequent desertion of merchant seamen which then took place whenever a vessel touched a port or harbour on the coast, caused the project to be abandoned. The disadvantages of there not being a harbour of refuge on the Welch (sic) coast is admitted by all nautical men.'

'St George's Harbour will be almost unequalled, situated on a bold and projecting part of the coast; it will be accessible with all winds and with a sufficient depth of water, at all times of the tide, for ships of the largest size to run in, in perfect safety. The bottom is stiff clay and affords perfect anchorage.'

The 1,000 acres plus of the harbour would be bounded east and west by the twin limestone headlands, to the south by the beach and to the north by an enormous breakwater, 7,524 feet long, extending from the Great Orme, two-thirds of the way across the bay towards the Little Orme. This breakwater would be 196 feet wide at its base on the sea bed and taper to 16 feet wide at the top and with an average height of 60 feet.'

The SGH&RCo outlined the construction details. 'The Great and Little Ormeshead are two very high cliffs of rock, composed of loose masses proper for a breakwater or enclosing harbour . . . As soon as the line of the breakwater be marked or buoyed out stones may be blasted from the cliffs and be thrown down within the buoys until they rise above the water on which a tram road may be laid down and the breakwater carried on to the length required . . . a breakwater of a form and length . . . which in the opinion of scientific men would be an efficient one for St George's Harbour would contain 3,611,520 tons of stone. Which at an estimate given by experienced contractors would amount to, at 1s 3d per ton, £225,720 . . . It is (also) proposed to erect a tower on the Great Ormeshead with a distinguishing light at a sufficient elevation to be seen 30 miles out at sea, from all points of the visible horizon also lights on the breakwater to mark the entrance of the bay so that vessels may run in with safety either by night or day.'

Naval Rendezvous

'It will be borne in mind that at present there is neither a Dock Yard or Naval Depot in Ireland, North or South Wales or along the whole northern coats of England and Scotland . . . That from the Cove of Cork to the Mull of Galloway there is not a harbour in which a second rate man of war can float or enter with safety . . . That the mercantile navy of Ireland and that belonging to the north coast of England and Wales stand in need of protection by the Royal Navy in the event of war is evident from the fact that during the late war (of Independence) an American privateer came into the channel and in one night whilst a British fleet was lying at the cove captured or destroyed between that station and the port of Liverpool, ten sail of merchantmen.'

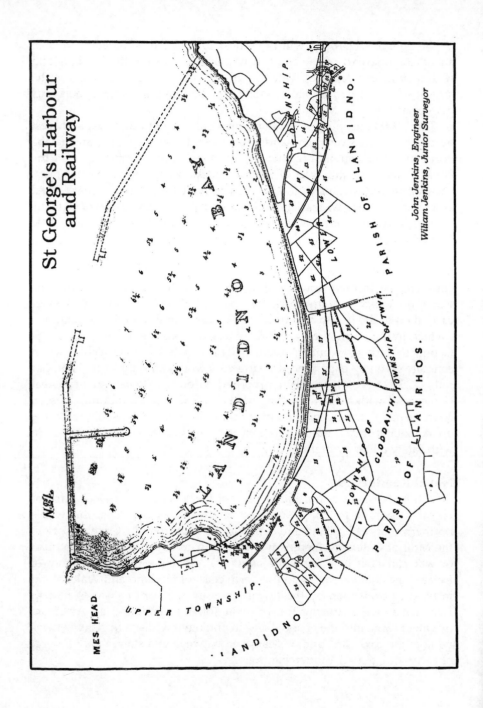

St George's Harbour
and Railway

John Jenkins, Engineer
William Jenkins, Junior Surveyor

Llandudno, Porth Dinllaen or Holyhead?

By the end of 1836 the three schemes had laid out their stalls and begun undermining the efforts of their rivals. Experts argued over the relative costs and benefits of harbours and railways whilst in the meantime the first national wave of 'railway-mania' came and went. In the Parliamentary session of 1840 not a single new railway company was incorporated and delays in developing a Welsh rail route to Ireland only encouraged the dominance of the port of Liverpool.

The deadlock was eventually broken in June 1842 when a select committee of the House of Commons was set up to examine the question of Post Office communication with Ireland. Although supporters of the Great Orme scheme continued to press the merits of Llandudno harbour they got short shrift from the committee who appeared from the beginning to favour Holyhead. Their logic was simple; as the speed of travel by railway was three times as fast as by steamer the shortest sea-route should be selected unless insuperable problems intervened.

William Cubitt told the committee that Vignoles' Porth Dinllaen line would inevitably get blocked by snow whilst George Stephenson reassured them on the viability of crossing the Menai. He patiently explained that each rail carriage weighed about five tons, equivalent to the weight of a coach and four horses. If drawn across the bridge by rope there would be no oscillation caused. He had laid out the line so that it could be carried either across the bridge or under one of the arches to a place at which another bridge might be made. He considered it perfectly safe to take the trains onto the end of the bridge and the delay caused by rope-hauling carriages across would only amount to about ten minutes.

After reviewing the evidence the committee supported the development of a rail route to Holyhead and with the guarded approval of Prime Minister, Sir Robert Peel, the scheme's promoters went full-steam ahead.

The Killing of St George

'The Chester & Holyhead Railway Bill' duly received Royal assent on 4th July 1844 and on 17th September the Treasury contracted for the CHR to carry the Irish Mails. The first sod was cut and the first shot fired at the Conwy tunnel on St David's Day, 1st March 1845 and thereafter St George appeared to be dead and buried. When the entire route was finally completed in 1850 Llandudno was by-passed and no harbour was ever constructed.

George Stephenson's son, Robert avoided the impractical rope-hauling of carriages across the Menai Straits by constructing a rigid railway bridge to a unique tubular design but other aspects of the Caernarfonshire section of the rail route proved as challenging as anticipated. In October 1846 heavy seas damaged the recently completed sea wall west of the Penmaenmawr tunnel then the following year the tunnel itself was found to be so full of fissures in the rock it had to be lined for half its length at great extra expense. Nevertheless the line brought prosperity to towns it passed through whilst Llandudno had to be content with daily horse coach connections from Conwy Railway Station.

Resurrection

Despite the lack of success of the original, 1836 proposals, in 1853 a more modest 'St George's Harbour Bill' was laid before Parliament. This bill proposed 'the making of a Harbour at Llandudno Bay in the County of Carnarvon between the points of land known respectively as Great and Little Ormes Head with a branch line of railway or communication to the line of the Chester and Holyhead Railway.' There were no ambitious aims to create the premier packet station for Ireland, no intention to construct an 'Asylum Harbour' or 'Naval Rendevous' just a commercial port connected to the mainline railway by a short branch line. The proposal included nine foolscap pages listing the port rates to be paid on an interesting variety of goods, including;

- Anvils   2s a ton
- Blubber   3d per 27 gallon barrel
- Chariots   15s each
- Dung   4d a ton
- Feathers   3d per 80lbs barrel
- Guano   2s a ton
- Ice   6d a ton
- Kelp   1s 6d a ton
- Oakum   2d a cwt
- Peats   4d for 800
- Snuff   6d a barrel
- Turnips   1s a ton
- Woad   2s a ton

With no commercial rivals anxious to strike down this St George's Harbour Bill it received the Royal Assent on 31st August 1853. However the Bill's backers lacked energy and determination and for years nothing was done to put its provisions into effect. St George may not have been dead but he was certainly resting.

Chapter Eighteen

Landlords of Gloddaeth

Llandudno village was a comparatively isolated community one step removed from the day to day demands of the wider world. External forces caused local religion and education to become increasingly contested and copper mining flourished as long as markets remained buoyant but of far more immediate and enduring import were the policies and demands of the Mostyn family, the landlords of Llandudno.

Power in the Land

In the Middle Ages the Mostyns tilted the balance of power in the Creuddyn in their favour and away from the Bishop of Bangor, and the Church, by fair means and foul. Of the 900 acres that comprised Llandudno Parish (excluding Common Land) the Mostyns owned 750 acres, over eighty-three percent, yet these figures severely under-represent their effective power. In 1796 the Mostyns owned 51,000 acres of which their Llandudno lands represented a mere 1.5% of their total landholding. Seated at the head of this vast empire was Sir Thomas Mostyn of Mostyn and Gloddaeth, the family's sixth Baronet. Over the years the Mostyns skilfully acquired Estates stretched across north Wales and beyond until they'd amassed thirty or so by the time of Sir Thomas. His own father, Sir Roger Mostyn (1734-96) had shrewdly added 22,000 acres through his marriage to Margaret (1744-92), daughter of Reverend Hugh Wynn, mother of Thomas, and heiress of Bodysgallen, Plas Mawr, Plas Hen and Corsygedol.

The portfolio of Estates inherited by Sir Thomas included commercial interests in the mining of coal, copper and lead as well as agriculture, forestry and shipping. The personal finances of the Mostyns dwarfed the entire economy of Llandudno. Should they attempt to direct the development of the village it would be difficult for the community to resist. Fortunately perhaps, Sir Thomas's interests lay elsewhere and apart from his agents imposing religious uniformity on Mostyn tenants his direct involvement with Llandudno was largely confined to squandering away the rents it yielded. Unfortunately his profligacy had dire consequences for Llandudno and it's fascinating to examine how this came about.

Sir Thomas Mostyn (1776-1831)

Born on the 20th October 1776, just twenty years later Sir Thomas Mostyn was elected a member of Parliament for the County of Flint. After it was, rather unsportingly, pointed out that he was underage and therefore ineligible he was obliged to step down. When he attained his majority the following year the legitimately elected candidate stepped aside and allowed Mostyn to assume his seat in the House of Commons. A position he retained, unopposed, until his death. He was also subsequently appointed Sheriff of Caernarfonshire in 1798 and Merionethshire in 1799.

Sir Thomas appointed John Phillips to manage his Llandudno affairs whilst he divided his time between three residences, Mostyn Hall, Mostyn; Swift's House, near Bicester and Park Place, St James', London. His Estates yielded an annual income of around £10,000 per annum, or £200 per week, whilst one of his agricultural workers received about 7s a week. For the labourer it was a struggle to survive on 7s. but for Sir Thomas it was an impossibility to rub along on only £200 for he had expensive predilections.

Pioneering Persecutor of the Fox

In 1796 fox hunting was the newly fashionably pastime for gentlemen who in an earlier age had amused themselves persecuting deer. Sir Thomas was every bit the fashionable Georgian rake, a determined bachelor whose life was dedicated to the single-minded pursuit of pleasure and his enduring passion was the ritual pursuit and killing of foxes. Sporting correspondent 'Nimrod' (1821) observed, 'Few men are better qualified to be at the head of a pack of foxhounds than Sir Thomas. A single man possessed of a fine fortune . . . the expense is not an object to him . . . no man is more fond of the sport.'

Mostyn's favourite hunting ground was the Oxfordshire farmlands around Bicester where the local hunt developed out of the informal activities of Lord Foley in the early eighteenth century. In 1778 his successor, John Warde, formalised proceedings, purchased a pack of hounds from the Honourable Peregrine Bertie, installed them at his new residence, Bainton Manor, Stoke Lyne and began the 'Bicester Hunt'. When Warde died in 1798 Mostyn offered to shoulder the enormous financial burden of maintaining the Bicester horses and hounds. He continued to operate from Bainton for a couple of seasons but meanwhile purchased 'Swifts House', an old coaching inn on the Bicester to Anyho turnpike road, had it demolished and in its place erected a 'Capital Hunting Residence' complete with 'excellent stables for 24 horses besides boxes, kennels, keeper's lodge, garden yards and 60 acres of grass and arable' (illustrated). 'The stables are uncommonly good and built to the form of a quadrangle with the huntsman's house, kennel, blacksmith's shop, etc on the outside; and as he (Sir Thomas) rents a manor surrounding the house, abundantly stocked with all kinds of game . . . no one lives better than Sir Thomas Mostyn' (Nimrod).

Mostyn soon became known as the 'Father of the Bicester Hunt' and he was encouraged and supported in this enterprise by members of another north Wales dynasty, the Lloyds. The Mostyns and Lloyds had been intermarrying since the sixteenth century and Llandudno's fate was to depend on their future relations. In 1800 three particular members of the Lloyd family, together with Sir Thomas 'formed a little colony of Welshmen in that neighbourhood' (Nimrod)

Sir Edward Pryce Lloyd (1768-1854), who had married Mostyn's sister, Elizabeth (1776-1842) in 1794 maintained a house near Sir Thomas, at Stratton Audley. His son, another Edward (1795-1884) grew up in the saddle to become an equally enthusiastic hunter. A contemporary noted, 'Sir Edward Lloyd is a good sportsmen, has a good eye to hounds and few men at his time of day, and of his weight, ride to them so well. His eldest son (Edward) promised to be a *first rate*.'

Sir Edward's brother, Reverend Griffith Lloyd completed the trio. 'Griff' enjoyed the living of local parish, Newton Purcell. According to 'The Druid' an appointment made to facilitate his hunting activities. Griff Lloyd had reason to be especially grateful to Sir Thomas for besides his Newton Purcell income he also enjoyed the living of Christleton, near Chester, an advowson in the gift of the Mostyns. To maintain both livings and a full hunt calendar Griff regularly commuted 120 miles each way by coach and chaise between Christleton and Bicester. The Newton Purcell rectory was in a ruinous condition and quite uninhabitable so Griff obtained a Bishop's license to reside with Sir Thomas at Swift's House, on condition that he properly performed his clerical duties. Although, according to the Rev. J C Blomfield, 'he would put off marriages and burials to suit the hounds'. Apparently 'he was only caught napping once and then he preached a Christmas Day sermon in February'. Popularly known as the 'black whipper-in', Griff was Sir Thomas' hunt deputy and principal adviser on kennel matters. According to Nimrod, 'Many of his (Sir Thomas') young hounds are bred in Wales and in one season he was known to have brought over fifty couples of puppies that had been walked by his Welsh tenants.'

Sir Thomas headed Mostyn Estates for 35 years and for 30 of those he was Bicester's 'Master of Foxhounds'. Although riding to hounds was a frighteningly expensive pursuit Sir Thomas adopted a singularly profligate approach. Where his successor as Master demanded an annual subscription of £2,000 from each member of the Hunt, Sir Thomas financed the entire enterprise himself. The 'Mostyn Hunt', as it was locally known, had no formal dress code but members generally rode to hounds resplendent in scarlet jackets. Favoured hunting companions of Sir Thomas received silver buttons bearing the monogram 'MH' though Mostyn reserved his most public expression of regard for a member of his kennels, to whom he erected an enormous, surviving stone obelisk at Bainton, bearing the inscription;

ERECTED IN 1812 BY SIR THOMAS MOSTYN, BART, M.P.
M.F.H. BICESTER HOUNDS, 1800 TO 1830
IN MEMORY OF HIS FAVOURITE HOUND
'LADY'

Sir Thomas' portrait of 'Lady', painted by William Bennett, still hangs in Mostyn Hall.

Horse Racing
At the end of each hunting season Sir Thomas travelled back to Mostyn Hall in a gig drawn by four hunters. At Mostyn he occupied himself with the activities of the Holywell Hunt Club. Founded mainly for social purposes at Holywell's White Horse Hotel in 1767, the club organised suppers, balls, gambling and racing and incidentally prohibited young bucks from marriage on pain of a £20 fine. In 1805 Sir Thomas acquired 18 acres of local common land from the Enclosure Commissioners so that he could provide the club with a convenient racecourse. The Mostyn family had long been patrons of the turf and maintained their own Spanish-style racing stable at Plymouth Copse Farm. Sir Thomas's own racehorses included 'Teniers', bred by Charles Day and a celebrated mare called 'Princess Royal'.

Each year, Sir Thomas also organised and sponsored 'The Mostyn Hunt Races' at Cottisford Heath near Bicester. The scene was recalled by William Wing, 'Dear, delightful, breezy, furzey, naughty old Cottisford Heath, how does thy name carry us back fifty years to the race course . . . replete as it was then with the smug, clean-shaved squires, parsons, farmers and traders from the towns and localities of Brackley, Buckingham and Bicester arrayed in deep white ties, kerseymers, top boots and blue and black coats; replete also with young farmers and farmers sons in bright green coats, resplendent with gilt buttons. How again our memory reverts to the spruce jocks in jackets of various colours the ladies in and on carriages, the grooms all important in their own eyes, the thickly packed pedestrians, the refreshment booths, the grandstand,

OXFORDSHIRE.
CAPITAL HUNTING RESIDENCE,

WITH CONVENIENT OFFICES,

Excellent STABLES for 24 Horses, besides Boxes;

KENNEL, KEEPER'S LODGE, GARDEN, YARDS,

AND ABOUT

60 Acres of Grass and Arable Land.

TO BE SOLD BY AUCTION,
By Mr. JOHN ROBINS,

Of Warwick House, Regent-street, at Garraway's Coffee House, 'Change-alley, Cornhill, London, on Thursday the 17th of June, 1830, at Twelve o'clock,—An eligible FREEHOLD ESTATE, Land Tax redeemed; comprising a commodious and conveniently planned HUNTING BOX, erected within a few years;—SWIFT'S HOUSE, the late Residence of Sir THOMAS MOSTYN, Bart. situate in the parish of Stoke Lyne, near Bicester, in the county of Oxford; containing an entrance hall, with viranda in front, breakfast parlour, inner hall, capital dining parlour and drawing room, all handsomely fitted up and finished in a suitable manner; on the first floor, four very excellent bed chambers and a bath room; six capital secondary bed chambers, and water closet. The domestic offices are enclosed from the house, and comprise housekeeper's room, with sink and water laid on, store room, larder, butler's pantry, with water laid on, store and plate closets, an excellent kitchen, scullery, with force pump, oven, servants' hall, shoe room, washhouse, a secondary staircase to a long passage, a convenient laundry, and five sleeping rooms for servants. In the basement, excellent cellaring for wine, ale, and beer. Detached, coal yard, wood house, knife and dust hole, slaughter house, with yard, smith's shop, capital brewhouse, with pump of water.

A capital kennel, with every necessary appendage, and grass yard for the run of dogs; huntsman's cottage, &c. The stabling is arranged with considerable judgment, comprising stalls for twenty-four horses, seven boxes, saddle and cleaning rooms, mess room, larder and scullery adjoining; three sleeping rooms for men; corn bins; chaff room; lofts and granaries; three coach houses, carpenter's shop, &c. a straw yard, with loose boxes; enclosed and open sheds for horses, and about FIFTY-SIX ACRES of Meadow and Arable Land all lying compact, adjoining the turnpike road from Bicester (from which it is distant about four miles) to Brackley and Banbury, and about sixteen miles from Oxford, in a county noted for field sports of all denominations and of such celebrity that requires no comment.

The Premises to be viewed by tickets, or by applying to Mr. King, at Swift's House, of whom particulars may be had; at the King's Arms, Bicester; Star and Angel, Oxford; Red Lion, Banbury; White Hart, Aylesbury; of Messrs. Bateman and Jones, Solicitors, Lincoln's Inn; at Garraway's; and of Mr. Robins, No. 170, Regent-street, London, of whom tickets for viewing may be had.

the extemporized stables whose walls were faggots of gorse and their roofs open to the sky, the gambling tents, the thimble-riggers . . . That looked for day, at the end of March or early in April, the last hunting day but one of the season, converted into a racing day.'

The most popular event of the meet was the 'Farmers' Cup Race' for which Sir Thomas provided a cup and a forty-guinea prize for the winner from amongst the field of non-thoroughbreds, ridden by a *bona fide* farmer residing within the geographical limits of the Hunt.

Gambling Clubs

In between summers spent at Mostyn Hall and the advent of the hunting season Sir Thomas occupied his mansion in the metropolis and Georgian London offered the fashionable set unparalleled opportunities for excess. The Prince of Wales (1762-1830), who became George IV, set the licentious tone for other drunken, whoring and gambling rakes to follow. Sir Thomas's London residence, at Park Place, St James's, was conveniently situated for the fashionable gaming clubs. Boodle's, founded 1762, at 28 St James's Street, was a Mostyn favourite much frequented by friend of the Prince of Wales and notorious Whig politician, Charles Fox, who narrowly escaped expulsion and disgrace when his father, Lord Holland, settled his £140,000 gambling debt. Brookes's, established 1778, at 60 St James's Street, was initially favoured by the Prince of Wales before he transferred his patronage to White's after his close friend, Jack Payne, was blackballed. White's, established 1698, faced Brookes's across St James's Street was Beau Brummell's favourite club until 1816 when he fled to Calais to escape creditors. Like Brookes', White's always kept an open betting book on the table for members to wager on matters of the most trivial or absurd nature. One member intent on helping a man slumped on the ground outside the club who seemed either dead or dead-drunk was ordered to leave him alone as the fellow's vital status was the subject of a current wager!

Besides these gambling dens in 1807 Sir Thomas was a founder member of another characteristically Georgian institution, the exclusive Bensington Driving Club. The object of the BDC was to provide an opportunity for gentlemen to emulate the dash and skill exhibited by drivers of Royal Mail Coaches. Prior to the founding of the BDC young bucks frequently bribed coach drivers to allow them to take over the reins of their vehicles and drive along the poor roads at breakneck speeds. The BDC was limited to a membership of twenty-five who met four times a year, twice at the White Hart, Bensington, near Oxford and twice at the Black Dog, Bedfont, near Hounslow, there was no annual subscription but members paid £10 on their election to the club. Members first wined and dined and thereafter 'dashed home in a style of speed and splendour equal to the spirit and judgement displayed by the noble, honourable and respected drivers'.

Despite his enormous income Sir Thomas's expenditure was yet greater. In 1818 Mostyn managed to keep at bay his immediate creditors by raising £100,000 from Messrs Coutts with a mortgage on his ancestral Estates. Unfortunately he continued to plough virtually nothing back into the farms and industries that produced the Estate's income and instead treated rental yields as entirely his own personal spending money. Depleting this with ease his indebtedness increased so that by 1829 the £100,000 owed had increased to £120,000.

End of the Line

On 17th April 1831 Sir Thomas Mostyn died at Park Place, unmarried and without legitimate heir. In accordance with his will he was buried with little ceremony, 'I desire to be buried in the family vault of Llanrhos in as private a manner as possible.' George Badcock the Mostyn agent in Llandudno faithfully recorded the modest funeral expenses;

	£	s	d
• four lengths of cloth for Jn Williams, Thos Lloyd, Wm Frankes and myself	4	24	0
• making up above into four suits of clothes	2	10	6
• cloth for the church	1	7	3
• ale for tenants attending the funeral		12	0
• refreshments for tenants attending the funeral		14	9
• mason for opening and closing the vault		6	0
• carpenter for opening and closing the vault		6	0
• cloth for cushion covers for church	8	3	1½
• tailor for making cushion covers in the church		9	0
• offerings for 25 tenants at 1s 6d each	1	17	6
• offerings for Thos Lloyd and Wm Frankes,3s 6d each		7	0
• offerings for Jn Williams and myself 7s 6d each	15	0	
• refreshments for tenants attending church on Sunday after the funeral	10	0	
	£41	**18s**	**5½d**

With no direct, legitimate heir Sir Thomas made provision in his will for his estate to effectively pass to his brother-in-law and old hunting companion, Sir Edward Pryce Lloyd. When Mostyn died Sir Edward was already 63 and his wife 56 so their older son, Edward, another of Mostyn's hunt companions, was the obvious heir apparent. With his parents' connivance he immediately began to operate as the power behind the throne.

As the end of the male line Sir Thomas included provision in his will to ensure the Mostyn name remained attached to the ancestral lands. Accordingly he required of individuals about to inherit 'all must take the name of Mostyn otherwise the estate is forfeited'. In 1831 Sir Edward Pryce Lloyd was therefore formally declared the first 'Baron Mostyn' and his son, who would soon determine the future of Llandudno, became the 'Honourable Edward Mostyn Lloyd-Mostyn.'

Legal Entanglement
In thirty-five years Sir Thomas Mostyn's profligacy had all but destroyed a property empire built up over five centuries. Radical rescheduling of debts and drastic reorganisation of assets was required if Mostyn Estates was to continue as a going concern. Financial stringency and personal austerity were essential but instead the family was plunged into costly internecine legal action. The problem arose because Sir Thomas's will included provision for his five surviving sisters and the eldest, Charlotte (1768-1845) was granted lifetime occupancy of Gloddaeth. Unfortunately her husband, Sir Thomas Swymmer Champneys (1769-1839) was an 'insolvent debtor' who was keen to raise cash by asset stripping the forestry around the house. On 16th February 1832 the first Baron Mostyn and his son applied for a legal injunction to stop them and this was granted on 20th February. This injunction from the Lord High Chancellor prohibited the Champneys from any further cutting of the oak, ash, beech, elm and other trees around the walks which 'had been laid out with great taste and considerable expense at Gloddaeth.'

Both parties returned to court in August contesting another provision of the will relating to £10,000 cash payments due to each of Sir Thomas's sisters. The Champneys unsuccessfully contended that Dame Elizabeth should be denied payment.

They were back in court yet again in January 1835 arguing over the terms of the renewal of the lease, from the Bishop of Bangor, concerning the 'Lordship, Manor and Lands of Gogarth'. This case dragged on for years with various claims, counterclaims and complications contributing to interminable and expensive legal wrangling. Matters were only finally resolved in March 1840 following the death of Thomas Champneys. In 1842 the family co-operated to promote a private Parliament Bill that overturned some of the more restrictive and costly provisions of Sir Thomas's will and steered the Estate in the direction of the overall control of the Honourable Edward Mostyn Lloyd Mostyn. This Act received the Royal assent on 30th July 1842. The following year the Mostyns finally renewed the lease on the Manor of Gogarth returning a semblance of legal order to the Estate.

Financial Meltdown

Sir Thomas was the main culprit in driving the Estate towards bankruptcy but his immediate heir and successor, Edward Pryce Lloyd-Mostyn made his own modest contribution. Between 1845 and 1849, the first Baron became the first head of the dynasty to embark on enlarging and extending the ancestral home since William Mostyn in 1576. It was a curious approach to rebuilding the family's finances. Lloyd-Mostyn engaged Ambrose Pointer, the first President of the Royal Institute of British Architects to completely rebuild the ancient hall, add a new library, construct Drybridge Lodge and erect a new church.

His son, Edward Mostyn Lloyd Mostyn was a less sober individual than his barrister father and his pattern of irresponsible spending would have warmed the heart of his dear deceased Uncle Thomas. Having hunted at Bicester with Sir Thomas in his youth he was also a member of the Holywell Hunt Club and founder of the 'Flint and Denbigh Foxhounds'. He was a keen follower of the turf and his horse 'Peter the Great' won the Stand Handicap, one of the last races held under the auspices of the Holywell Hunt Club before the gentry switched their patronage to Chester racecourse, where Lloyd-Mostyn then, in 1843, became a race steward. Lloyd Mostyn paid Lord George Bentink £100,000 for a stable of thoroughbreds that included the filly 'Queen of Trumps' which won the 1835 Oaks and St Leger and was never beaten. There was also 'Surplice' the winner of the 1848 Derby and 'Seventy-Four' which came second in the first Grand National in 1835.

Lloyd Mostyn also enjoyed the card tables, and evenings in London were gambled away at Boodles, even occasionally addressing his correspondence from the club.

Moral Bankruptcy

The Mostyn inheritance included more than crippling debt, there were also tragic consequences of Sir Thomas's uncaring sexual behaviour. The Mostyns were prepared to resolve financial matters in open court but were anxious to suppress knowledge of Sir Thomas's abusive behaviour. Now almost two hundred years after the events it is difficult to piece together stories intended to be kept secret for ever but documents record at least three cases in which Sir Thomas appears to have behaved abominably towards women; the cases of Mary Browne, Mary Wyatt and Elizabeth Mostyn.

In a letter dated, 24th July 1821 the Reverend William Frederick Browne, Launton, near Bicester, charged Sir Thomas Mostyn with the accusation that 'You have positively seduced my daughter and violated her person . . . have most cruelly beat her and treated her ill'. Rev. Browne's three page epistle left little room to doubt the seriousness and extent of his allegations. Browne claimed Mostyn;

• had abused his social position to take advantage of a vulnerable young woman
• had sexual intercourse with Mary Browne
• sought to avoid his moral responsibility and legitimise the liaison
• violently beat Mary Browne in an attempt to drive her away

Reverend Browne, then rather surprisingly, stated the only way that Sir Thomas might escape social opprobrium was to marry Mary but Mostyn refused. One might suspect Browne and his daughter of being no more than a pair of blackmailing 'gold diggers' were it not for the fact that as Browne noted in his letter his 'rank in life' was 'not much inferior' to Mostyn's. Rev. Browne was not merely Rector of Launton, a position he had held for 42 years, but one of the largest landowners in the area, immensely rich and well educated, well connected and a Justice of the Peace.

Born 1755, William Browne was educated at Westminster School and Christ Church College, Oxford. In 1779 Browne took over the living of Launton from his clergyman father and in 1785 was also appointed a prebendary of Wells Cathedral. He continued his studies and by July 1800 had added both 'Bachelor of Divinity' and 'Doctor of Divinity' to his academic credentials. He was a keen countryman who continued to expand the family's landholding, purchasing local farms as they came up for sale. He farmed these in conjunction with his glebelands.. He was an enthusiastic sportsman and his name appears on the list of persons in the county paying the Game Duty every year from 1785 until he died. He had nothing to gain and everything to lose by accusing the Master of Foxhounds of cruelly violating his daughter.

Of Browne's four children, one boy died in infancy, two married most respectably; William Frederick married the daughter of Sir Hugh Dalrymple and served with great distinction at Waterloo whilst Ann married Moses Williams Staples Esq. of Furnival's Inn, London. Mary meanwhile remained at the rectory with her father.

Neither Browne nor his daughter had any reason to contrive their accusations and nothing suggests they were prone to such irrationally. On the contrary, circumstantial evidence points towards the truth of their outrageous claims.

In a furious letter sent to Sir Thomas from Launton on 6th August 1821 Browne details how Mostyn had attempted to prevent Mary from speaking out, after beating her himself he had decided to 'order his servants to use her ill and one in particular to ride over her.' Mostyn's scheme was apparently thwarted and Mary rescued as 'the principal inhabitants in the street thought it necessary to order their servants to protect her'. Determined to suppress Mary's accusations and 'not finding that he could succeed by such measures (Mostyn) contrived by stratagem to get her into prison'.

Both Browne and Mostyn referred the matter to their respective solicitors whilst simultaneously embroiling friends and relations in bitter recriminations. Mostyn's nephew, Edward Lloyd (later Lloyd Mostyn) engaged in particularly ill-tempered communications with Browne's son, just recently retired from the military. Only the eventual intervention of the Earl of Jersey had any emollient effect. As a keen huntsman and the largest local landowner (Browne had the second largest holding), 'Jersey', as he signed himself, was well known to both parties and sensitive to the immensely destructive effect their prolonged dispute was having on the social life of the county. In a letter from London dated 6th July 1822 'Jersey' informed Mostyn that, 'When I first saw Dr Browne he seemed determined, if possible, to drive you out of the country.' He went on to advise Sir Thomas to ensure that his associates, particularly his nephew Edward Lloyd, kept their noses out of the affair if there was to be any hope of calming things down.

Mostyn slowly slipped off the hook, he had managed to rally powerful allies and after Jersey's intervention Browne abandoned hope of forcing Mostyn to follow other disgraced rakes abroad. Shocked by Mostyn's aggression, Browne plaintively inquired of Jersey whether 'Mutual civility was not expected in a fox hunting country?'

Mary never married but moved away from Oxfordshire and in 1837 Rev. Browne 'Died by Visitation of God' at her residence, 36 York Square, near Regent's Park, London, but that wasn't the last time serious accusations were levelled against Sir Thomas. Almost to the day he died, in April 1831, he was fighting off charges of sexual impropriety. In a letter received by Mostyn at his Park Place address on 4th February 1831 he was charged by a Martha Wyatt with dishonouring the name of her sister, Mary. Martha insisted that Mostyn's behaviour had provoked lascivious speculation and unseemly betting amongst the young rakes, which as you 'well know is death to a woman's reputation'. Again it is conceivable that the accusation is unwarranted but there is the further case to consider of Sir Thomas's illegitimate daughter.

Even whilst Mostyn was denying illicit sexual congress with Mary Browne he was paying the financial penalty of a previous illegitimate relationship. Sir Thomas acknowledged the offspring of this earlier intercourse financially but denied his daughter love and official recognition. The identity of the child's mother remains a mystery but his daughter's name was Elizabeth Mostyn. Born around November 1808, when Mostyn was 32, nothing is known of Elizabeth's early life until 1821 when we find her in Boulogne where she has been lodged away from the prying eyes of polite society. Elizabeth was cared for by two English spinsters, Catherine and Margaret Cruikshank, who ran the boarding school she attended. Elizabeth remained with the Cruikshanks at Boulogne from at least 1821 until Mostyn's death ten years later. Throughout the decade she continued to write to Sir Thomas, whom she addressed as 'Papa'. Mostyn's occasional replies have not survived but he routinely settled the Cruikshanks' account which were variously delivered to him at Bicester, London or Mostyn.

From Catherine Cruikshank's June 1822 letter we learn that Elizabeth was fluent in French, Italian, and English but Italian was her favourite language. She had made great progress with the piano and earnestly begged Mostyn's permission to be allowed to play the harp. The following year Elizabeth was delighted when Sir Thomas agreed to pay for her portrait to be painted and sent to him at Swift's House. She later unsuccessfully appealed to him to send her a likeness of himself but never reproached him for her exile or his estrangement. In desperate need of approval and affection she generally signed off with, ' . . . to my very dear Papa. Your affectionate daughter Elizabeth Mostyn.'

In Elizabeth's last surviving letter from Boulogne, dated 13th November 1830, she again unsuccessfully begged for a likeness of her father, a few months later he was dead.

In his will Sir Thomas Mostyn bequeathed £20,000 'to my natural, or reputed daughter, Elizabeth Mostyn' but as a bastard she inherited no land, title or family. Fortunately she was befriended by a fellow pupil at Boulogne, Elizabeth Clarke, whose father, solicitor, Edward Hyde Clarke welcomed Elizabeth Mostyn into their family home in Leamington Spa after Sir Thomas's death. By June 1831 she was living with the Clarke family at 18 Clarendon Square. In Leamington Elizabeth Mostyn met and married, on 8th June 1840, wealthy, well-connected landed proprietor, Charles Clement Brooke. In August 1841 she bore him a son, Charles Hyde Brooke, whose middle name touchingly recognised her debt to the man who had kindly rescued her from the anonymity of exile abroad. It seemed, at last, life was eventually bringing happiness and love to Elizabeth but it was not to be and within a year she was dead.

When Elizabeth died the £20,000 owed to her from Sir Thomas Mostyn's will was assigned first to her husband and after his demise to trustees acting for her only child, Charles Hyde Brooke. Charles spent years trying to extract this legacy from the Mostyns but the family convinced the courts they were unable to pay, despite retaining control of a vast property portfolio. In 1865 Elizabeth's son abandoned all hope of ever gaining his rightful inheritance and sailed to the antipodes to serve the Anglican Mission to Melanesia. He was probably inspired to pursue this course by his mother's old friend, and Charles's namesake, Edward Hyde Clarke, a lifelong campaigner against slavery and colonialism.

Charles had a troubled missionary career and eventually fled from Melanesia after being caught engaging in improper sexual conduct with local schoolboys. He never married and when he died in November 1926 his estate, worth only £619 8s 5d, passed to fellow clergyman Edward Arthur Hort.

Charles Hyde Brooke's death passed unnoticed by the landlords of Gloddaeth. To the Mostyns, Elizabeth and Charles were an embarrassing and inconvenient offshoot that had long ago been effectively snipped from the family tree.

Chapter Nineteen

Edward Mostyn's Cunning Plan

When Victoria ascended the throne in 1837 Mostyn ownership and control of Llandudno looked uncertain. Unpaid creditors threatened to break up the family's property empire and liquidate the assets. 'On the tenth day of January, one thousand and forty three . . . a Petition for Adjudication of Bankruptcy hath been filed against Edward Mostyn Lloyd Mostyn . . . under which Petition the said Edward Mostyn Lloyd Mostyn hath been duly found and declared bankrupt.'

A Cunning Plan

Thrift and economy didn't appeal to the Honourable Edward Mostyn Lloyd Mostyn (1795-1884) but fortunately he had a cunning plan, a way to pull a rabbit from a hat, to liquidate other people's assets and turn them into cash for himself. He planned to evict the families living on Llandudno Morfa and acquire the land for himself. The Tŷ Unnos tradition recognised their right to stay but Mostyn knew the courts wouldn't protect them. To ensure his own title to the land would be recognised by the courts he embarked on a scheme the family had practised elsewhere, a Parliamentary Enclosure Bill. He would get Parliament to pass an Act that extinguished all existing rights and entitlements of Llandudno's Commoners and transferred ownership of the village's Common land to freeholders, of which he was by far the most powerful. Freeholders would receive a share of the 955 acres of Llandudno Common land in rough proportion to their existing landholding in the parish. In 1843 more than half of Llandudno parish was Common land and of the remaining 900 acres of freeholds, Mostyn owned 750 acres, over 83%. A successful Enclosure Bill would double the Mostyns' Llandudno landholding. The big losers would be the families settled on the Morfa who would lose their homes, their land and along with all the other villagers the right to graze animals on the parish's other scattered parcels of Common land. An Enclosure Act would destroy the old village of Llandudno but first it would have to gain Parliamentary approval.

Gentlemen's Agreement

In an earlier age landlords simply hired thugs to drive the poor from the land and Estate building by force was routine but that was not the way of

Edward Mostyn Lloyd Mostyn (1795-1884),
Painted by Hugh Hughes of Llandudno, c.1835

the Victorian gentry, at least not in this corner of the Empire. Parliamentary democracy employed subtler, more gentlemanly methods of driving the poor from the land. On 12th July 1843 was published, 'An Act for inclosing Lands in the several Parishes of Eglwys-rhos, Llandudno and Llangwstenin in the County of Carnarvon . . .' (illustrated). Such procedures were by then commonplace and Parliament passed an average of one a week. Llandudno's Enclosure Bill was no different from any other and was rubber stamped as routinely as its predecessors.

The squatters weren't immediately evicted as the Enclosure process was quite elaborate. Firstly an Enclosure Commissioner was appointed, 'Mr Richard Yates of Whittington in the County of Salop, Gentleman.' Yates then drew up accurate maps of the Creuddyn's three parishes, detailing the ownership of each landholding shown. This Enclosure map was eventually completed in 1847 and was followed by a process of allotting the Common lands between the freeholders identified on the associated map schedule. This allotment was completed on the 25th April 1848 (with minor later modifications). Mr Yates' redistribution of Llandudno's 955 acres of Common was as follows (excluding trivial allocations);

- William Jones of Tyn y Coed, 2 acres
- Rector of Llandudno, 5 acres
- William Griffiths of Shimmdda Hir, 6 acres
- Sir Richard Bulkeley Williams-Bulkeley, Baronet, 14 acres
- Bishop of Bangor, as Lord of the Manor, 18 acres
- Thomas Peers Williams of Marl, 23 acres
- John Lloyd Jones of Gogarth, Tŷ Coch etc, 45 acres
- Edward Lloyd Mostyn Lloyd Mostyn. 832 acres

As these allotments were not granted in single blocks some freeholders subsequently exchanged plots between themselves to create more unified holdings. By the following year Mostyn had shaped a Llandudno holding that suited his development aims. A prospectus was drawn up, and on Tuesday 28th and Wednesday 29th August 1849 at Plas Mawr (not the advertised Castle Hotel) an auction was held of, 'Leasehold Building Land, in 176 Lots, at Llandudno, on the Estate of Gloddaeth, belonging to the Honourable E M L Mostyn, M.P.' (illustrated).

Fashionable Bathing Resort
It's widely accepted that Edward Mostyn's idea of developing

ANNO SEXTO & SEPTIMO

VICTORIÆ REGINÆ.

▼▼▲▼▲━▲━▼━▲▼▼▼▼▲▼▼▲★▲▼▲━▲━▼▲▲▲▲▼▼▲▼▼▲▼▼▲▲▼▼▲━▲▼▲★▲▼▲━▲▼▲▲

Cap. 14.

An Act for inclosing Lands in the several Parishes
of *Eglwys-rhos*, *Llandudno*, and *Llangwstenin* in
the County of *Carnarvon*, and in the Parish
of *Llandrillo* in the Counties of *Denbigh* and
Carnarvon, or either of them.

[12th *July* 1843.]

WHEREAS there are within the several Parishes of *Eglwys-
rhos*, *Llandudno*, and *Llangwstenin* in the County of *Carnarvon*, and in the Parish of *Llandrillo* in the Counties of
Denbigh and *Carnarvon*, or either of them, divers Commons, Com-
monable Lands, and Waste Grounds, Heaths, Open and Common and
other Fields and Waste Lands, and other Common Lands and Waste
Grounds, which lie intermixed in small Parcels, and are inconveniently
situated for the Use and Enjoyment of the several Proprietors
thereof and other Parties interested therein, and in their present
State are incapable of any considerable Improvements: And whereas
the Right Reverend *Christopher* Lord Bishop of *Bangor*, in right
of his Bishopric, is or claims to be Lord of the Manor of *Gogarth*
in the said Parish of *Llandudno* t And whereas the said *Christopher*
Lord Bishop of *Bangor*, in right of his See aforesaid, the Honourable
Edward Mostyn Lloyd Mostyn, Sir *Richard Bulkeley Williams
Bulkeley* Baronet, Dame *Margaret Mostyn Champneys* Widow, Dame
Silence Erskine Widow, *Thomas Peers Williams* Esquire, *Lloyd Hesketh*

[*Private.*]　　　　　　　5 d　　　　　　　*Bamford*

Llandudno as a bathing resort was first suggested to him, in 1846, by Owen Williams, a visiting Liverpool surveyor and estate agent. Williams certainly claimed to be the inspiration behind the idea but this is a naïve simplification. There is no need to look to Williams, or anyone else, for Mostyn's inspiration. The family had not only already been involved in developing Rhyl into a bathing resort and achieving this through the Parliamentary Enclosure mechanism but Edward Mostyn himself had been directly involved in the process. It didn't require an enormous leap of imagination for him to wonder if he might attempt a similar scheme 15 miles along the coast at his Gloddaeth Estate.

On 11th June, 1794 four members of the Mostyn family, along with others, published and promoted a Bill for enclosing, draining and developing Rhuddlan Marshes. This was followed in 1807 with a notice inserted in the 'Chester, Cheshire and North Wales Advertiser' offering for sale 20 acres of 'rich common marsh in eligible situation for sea bathing'. Rhuddlan Morfa was transformed into the nascent Rhyl with a 'Baths Hotel' erected in the 1820's. In 1839 a further big land sale took place at Rhyl's 'Mostyn Arms Hotel'. The Honourable Edward Mostyn Lloyd Mostyn chaired a meeting at the hotel in 1846 inviting subscriptions for the levelling of sand dunes and laying out of terraces for the better enjoyment of visitors. In another prescient move, on 28th May 1852 Rhyl's developers successfully promoted an 'Improvement Act' for the town's transformation to be carried forward by 30 'Improvement Commissioners'.

When Edward Mostyn promoted Llandudno's Enclosure Bill in 1843 he already entertained ideas of developing a bathing resort but was aware of other possibilities. Whether Llandudno was to become a commercial port or a watering place Mostyn was sure to profit enormously. Despite a general slump in agriculture, land values in Caernarfonshire had risen by more than 40% since 1815, higher than any other north Wales shire, except for Anglesey, and with the coming of the railway, land prices were bound to rocket.

Imaginary Harbour and Truncated Railway

By the late 1840's Mostyn pursued a bathing resort scheme as the most profitable option but did not abandon the possibility of combining this with a commercial port development. Fully ten years after the passing of the Enclosure Act, with fashionable hotels already arising along the seafront, Edward Mostyn still considered it worth pushing a new 'St George's Harbour Bill' through Parliament.

A widely promoted print of 1853 illustrates how Mostyn intended to bring the railway right up to the seafront so that it connected with a commercial landing place. As building work progressed on hotels, shops, roads and services for the new resort the option of combining this with an unsightly harbour development proved increasingly impractical. By the end of 1854 a commercial port development was no longer a realistic possibility. The St George's Harbour Railway Company did erect a simple wooden pier, in 1858, to comply with the terms of the 1853 Act and formally protect its legal right to erect a harbour but by then this was no more than a pipe dream. The Company's own railway, opened in the same year, accepted reality and halted far short of the pierhead at the opposite end of town.

Clearing the Commons

Whilst Mostyn's advisors devised detailed plans for his new resort he had to first ensure the land was cleared before development could commence, especially the prime plots along the seafront. Unfortunately, in 1849, as the land was being sold from beneath their feet there were over 120 people living on the Morfa, in 20 houses. By census night, in 1861, everyone had gone, their houses demolished and cleared away, and in their place stood fashionable seafront hotels. Parliament might have granted Mostyn and his fellow MP's the right to evict cottagers from their homes but Enclosure Acts enforced elsewhere, such as Rhoshirwaun in 1802, Llandeiniolen in 1808 and the Llyn in 1812 were forcibly resisted by squatters facing eviction. Physical resistance might have been expected from Llandudno's community of miners who had a tradition of standing up to Customs Officers, Revenue Men and domineering mine owners yet the Morfa cottagers offered no violence as their homes were torn down.

Squatters' Fate

After their eviction the only heads of household who abandoned Llandudno were those visited by the Grim Reaper. Most continued to call themselves miners for more than a decade although the mines were in terminal decline. We can obtain a quick snapshot of the squatters' fate by examining their records in the 1861 census; (key; W=widow, min=miner, Bk=Back)

Morfa – Head of House	1850 job/age	1861 address	1861 job
1 Jane Jones	miner's wid,(51)	20 Madoc St	pauper
2 Owen Jones	miner, (54)	3 Wyddfyd Cots	miner
3 John Owens	min/publican, (52)	Lloyd St	innkeeper
4 Sam Edwards	miner, (33)	Mostyn St	town labourer
5 George Wynne	miner, (31)	Mostyn St	min/publican

6	David Hughes	min/publican, (40)	Lloyd St	boatman/pblicn
7	William Jones	miner, (52)	(W, Penybuarth)	deceased
8	Owen Thomas	schoolmaster, (41)	15 Madoc St	miner
9	Edward Brookes	miner, (29)	5 Madoc St	quarryman
10	John Thomas	miner, (33)	(W. 5 Madoc)	deceased
11	Henry Davies	miner, (49)	Bk. Brynwythen	miner
12	Sarah Brookes	miner's wid, (36)	16 Madoc St	charwoman
13	Elias Evans	agric lab, (35)	14 Madoc St	stonemason
14	Daniel Powell	miner, (42)	11 Madoc St	carter
15	Richard Hughes	miner, (34)	13 Madoc St	miner
16	Benj. Robinson	miner, (30)	12 Madoc St	miner
17	John Jones	miner, (76)	------------------	deceased
18	Griffith Owens	miner, (38)	17 Madoc St	miner
19	Thomas Jones	miner, (35)	2 Wyddfyd Cots	miner
20	John Edwards	miner, (39)	Mostyn St	baker

The most striking feature of the 1861 evidence is that 50% of the Morfa households moved to Madoc Street into properties built by the Mostyns to accommodate workers required to service the new resort. Compared to other working class streets, like Somerset and Bodafon (now Row), the Madoc Street houses were less basic, more spacious and more airy. Originally they even had small front gardens and there's no doubt that the Mostyns had learnt from enclosure evictions elsewhere. In Llandudno they employed a skilful blend of legal imposition and practical inducements to winkle squatters out of their homes, offering them leases on Madoc Street properties for a token 5s a year. A few Morfa residents preferred to make their own arrangements and moved nearer to friends and family on the Great Orme, but five determined squatters refused to be gulled into giving up their prime freehold plots in exchange for a cheap rent and a life of wage slavery. John Owens, Sam Edwards, George Wynne, David Hughes and John Edwards all successfully held out for commercially valuable sites in the new town.

John Owens, 'Prince of Wales' and David Hughes, 'Cambria' had, of course, already built up successful pub businesses on the Morfa and both were able to continue, transfer and expand their trade, under the old names, onto sites on Lloyd Street. The Cambria Inn was situated on the NW corner of Lloyd and Mostyn Streets and the enormous Prince of Wales was situated almost opposite on the corner of Lloyd Street and Somerset Street. Nevertheless the attractions of business weren't sufficient to prevent John Owens' sons, Owen and William, from emigrating to America in the spring of 1849. They were accompanied by almost forty other residents of Llandudno who sailed from Liverpool on

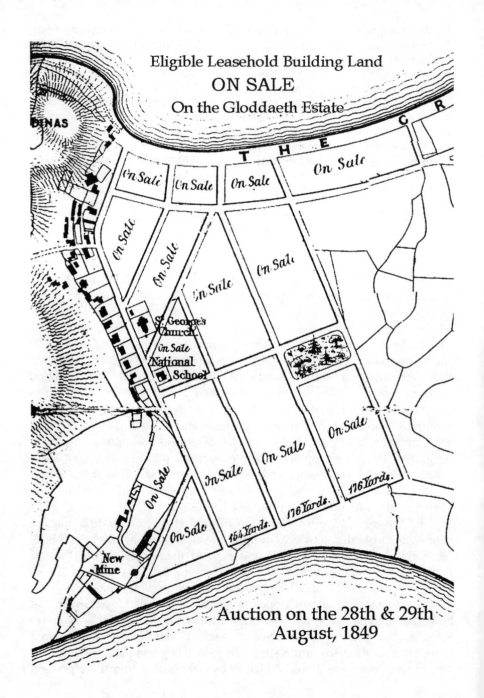

Eligible Leasehold Building Land
ON SALE
On the Gloddaeth Estate

Auction on the 28th & 29th
August, 1849

274

the 1st May aboard the 'Jamestown', embarking five weeks later in New York. Previous experience in the copper mines even encouraged a couple of the party to join the California goldrush.

George Wynne also opened licensed premises at Temple House, Mostyn Street but this was a less successful venture than the Cambria and Prince of Wales. Samuel Edwards and his wife, Mary developed their Mostyn Street, 'Mona View', property into a very successful lodging house business. John Edwards' bakery shop at Roche House, Mostyn Street was one of the most enduring businesses in town, later branching out into groceries and confectionery it was operated at 85 Mostyn Street by successive generations of the Edwards family. Some of the families lodged at Madoc Street began to dip their toe into the business world as copper mining contracted. The abolition of import duties in 1848 made the mines uneconomic and encouraged the development of vast, open-cast copper mines abroad. Edward Brookes developed a career as a carriage proprietor, Daniel Powell and his wife opened up their Madoc Street home as a lodging house whilst Griffith Owen turned his house into a grocers' shop. Despite suffering two extraordinary tragedies Sarah Brookes' daughter, Catherine, who was actually born on the Morfa in 1844, founded and operated one of Llandudno's most successful bathing machine businesses (illustrated). When she was an infant her father was one of the few men killed in the copper mines and when she married carriage proprietor John Davies he was killed by lightning whilst driving around the Great Orme.

Richard Hughes became Madoc Street's richest resident after his enforced career change, from miner to building contractor, reaped huge dividends. Amongst Hughes' prestigious projects foremost was the construction of the Marine Drive around the Great Orme, which earned him enormous admiration for his demonstrable surveying and engineering skills. When he died in 1897 he left behind the impressive sum of £2,383 19s 6d.

Twilight of Old Llandudno

The 1843 Enclosure Act sealed the fate of old Llandudno but the village survived more or less intact for ten years. The turning point came in 1853 with four key events;

- Closure of the Tŷ Gwyn Mine
- Prolonged strike at the Old Mine
- Crucial parish meeting
- Building of the first seafront hotel

Expenses on the Marine Parade Llandudno for
the Month ending 18th Octr. 1851.

			£ s d
William Roberts Labourer 24 days @ 1/8 pr day			2 - 0 - 0
John Roberts — Do. 24			2 - 0 - 0
Owen Thomas — Do. 24			2 - 0 - 0
James Jones — Do. 24			2 - 0 - 0
Robert Jones — Do. 24			2 - 0 - 0
Gabriel Williams — Do. 24			2 - 0 - 0
William Thomas Cartage 1 Team 18 days @ 4/-			3 - 12 - 0
Richard Owen Do. — 1 - " - 18 - "			3 - 12 - 0
William Williams Do. 2 - " - 18 - "			7 - 4 - 0
Robert Williams Labourer 23 days			1 - 18 - 4
Robert Jones " — 23			1 - 18 - 4
William Pritchard — 23			1 - 18 - 4
William Pritchard — 12			1 - 0 - 0
Robert Evans " — 13 "			1 - 1 - 8
Thomas Pritchard superintending 24 days 1/-			1 - 4 - 0
David Lloyd 14000 Bricks to Close up Shaft @ 5/ pr M			3 - 10 - 0
170 Loads of Gravel @ 4d pr Load			2 - 16 - 8
400 Oak Poles @ 3d pr yard			5 - 0 - 0
			46 - 15 - 4
Thomas Williams 4 Weeks affording surveyors &c			2 - 0 - 0
			£48 - 15 - 4

The Above a/c examined &
found correct 3rd Nov 1851
     his
   Thomas X Pritchard
     mark

       Bodafon Conway
       3rd Novr 1851
Dear Sir
  I send you Above expenditure on the
Parade for the Month ending 18 Octr 1851 The Amount of
which be pleased to remit by Friday I am Dear Sir
      for J. Williams yours obdt
          Robert Williams

Contractor Thomas Pritchard's monthly account for making
up Marine Parade, October 1851. Submitted for payment to
John Williams, Mostyn Agent and Robert Williams,
the Office Clerk (and John's brother).

The Tŷ Gwyn Mine had been highly productive but flooded in both 1844 and 1850, and on the last occasion the sea had burst into the workings so unexpectedly that miners had to flee leaving their tools and drills underground. Considerable expense was expended pumping the mine dry and sealing fissures along the foreshore but flooding remained an expensive problem. With the price of ore falling an angry meeting of shareholders agreed in 1853 that the game was up and the mine had to close.

In March 1853 the Old Mine was sold to a company who employed 'John Taylor & Sons, Mining Engineers' to manage the works. The new managers decided to increase profitability by ending the miners' flexible work pattern. Llandudno miners had traditionally started and ended the working day when they wished, averaging about 6 hours labour a day. This allowed them time for smallholding, fishing, feasting and socialising and distinguished their lives from those of the wage slaves of industrial England but it didn't appeal to John Taylor & Sons who reported, 'So contrary was this system to any known to us in any copper mine in Great Britain, or in any mine whatever where we are concerned, either as partners or as managers, that we decided at once to take a stand against it, and to insist on a full eight hours' work per diem . . .' As a result the miners 'stood out and resisted our rules almost throughout the whole of the year. As the autumn came on a few offered to work and we induced several strangers to the neighbourhood to take bargains, but winter had almost come upon them before the main body of old and accustomed hands offered to take their bargains upon tribute, in conformity with the regulations which we had laid down.'

On 6th October 1853 a Llandudno parish meeting, chaired by Edward Mostyn Lloyd Mostyn agreed to apply to Parliament for a local 'Improvement Act'. This would provide for the creation of a Board of Commissioners empowered to push through the measures necessary to transform a rural village into a modern town, paving, lighting, sanitary works etc. It was identical to the procedure that Mostyn had already promoted in Rhyl.

Before 1853 the only buildings erected along the seafront were the humble dwellings of the Morfa squatters. In 1853 the site previously occupied by John Owen's long, low, whitewashed Tŷ Unnos pub, the 'Prince of Wales' was cleared and the magnificent St George's Hotel was erected in its place. It was a potent symbol of the new Llandudno.

Progress and Change

Thousands of years of history created Llandudno village, its unique culture and close-knit community. A single Act of legalised robbery transformed Llandudno into the playground of the fashionably rich. Some villagers welcomed Llandudno's social elevation whilst others regretted their close-knit community had given way to the materialistic values of the market place. Many people made money but the financial benefits of the Enclosure Act overwhelmingly accrued to the Mostyns. It's often claimed that the Mostyns saved Llandudno from economic collapse but the truth is the reverse.

In volume one of 'Llandudno and the Mostyn Influence', (jointly published by Mostyn Estates) Ron Williams tells us, 'it is futile to attempt to apply the social and other judgements of the end of the 20th century to the situation of 150 years ago. The process of enclosure was sanctioned by the law of the land and the Mostyns as the local landowners were entitled to take advantage of the fact for whatever intended purpose' yet in volume two he claims 'It is the historian's prerogative – and perhaps his (sic) duty for he has all the benefits of hindsight – to comment on and assess the value of the actions taken in the distant past.'

Williams was right the second time, history is not a mere chronicling of events, but an attempt to identify and evaluate causes and effects. We aim to understand the perspective and motivations of people in the past and evaluate these against contemporary concepts and values.

Williams' post hoc justification of the Mostyn's Enclosure Act rests on three contentious assertions;

- 'The process of enclosure was sanctioned by the law of the land'
- 'the Mostyns as the local landowners were entitled to take advantage . . .'
- 'for whatever intended purpose'

'Sanctioned by Law'
Williams claims that enclosure was sanctioned by law but Mostyn's action contravened the ancient Welsh law of 'Tŷ Unnos'. Edward Mostyn did comply with the terms of the 1843 Act of Parliament but then he was the very MP who personally steered it through Parliament. Although Parliament had purportedly been made more representative by the Reform Act of 1832 it provided for precious little representation from the ordinary people of Llandudno for out of a population of a thousand only 10 people had the vote. There was a property qualification for the franchise and to stand as a Parliamentary candidate the law required an annual income of at least £600 when the average Llandudno miner earned £35. The House of Commons was consequently a gentleman's club overwhelmingly (70%) composed of the owners of great landed

279

estates (the comparable figure for the Lords was 100%). Even the Chancellor was honest enough to admit that although the Reform Act allowed more urban representation it enhanced 'the aristocratic share by increasing the influence of the great landed proprietors in the counties'. The Lord Lieutenant of the County was invariably a landed magnate and the squirearchy were the local magistrates.

Parliament and the law were hardly neutral arbiters on Enclosures. Their values are revealed in a Board of Agriculture report, of 1794;

'Let those who doubt go round the commons now open, and view the miserable huts and poor, ill-cultivated, impoverished spots erected or rather thrown together . . . which by loss of time both to the man and his family affords them a very trifle towards their maintenance, yet operates on their minds as a sort of independence; this idea leads the man to lose many days work by which he gets a habit of indolence; a daughter kept at home to milk a half-starved cow, who being open to temptations soon turns harlot, and becomes a distressed ignorant mother instead of making a good useful servant...'

It doesn't require 150 years hindsight to identify the inherent injustice of a legal system that condemned people to death or transportation for petty theft yet provided the very mechanism that enabled landlords to steal the homes and land from beneath the feet of the poor.

'Entitled to Take Advantage'
The claim that the Mostyns were 'entitled' to take advantage of the Enclosure Act cleverly elides two different interpretations of the word. Asserting their 'legal' entitlement would amount to no more than re-stating the obvious truth that the law was on their side. To claim there was any 'moral' entitlement would, on the contrary, be laughable.

A verse published in 'Tickler Magazine' on the 1st February 1821 neatly parodied the ethics of enclosures;

'The fault is great in man or woman
Who steals a goose from off a common
But what can plead that man's excuse
Who steals a common from a goose?'

'Whatever Intended Purpose'
One might also question the validity of Mostyn's exploitation of the Enclosure Act mechanism, for Parliament initially devised and justified this procedure on the grounds that it would increase food production. By enclosing and more intensively farming common land agriculture was

DEATH OF AN OLD INHABITANT.

—We regret to announce the death, which took place on Sunday, of Mrs. Catherine Davies, 18, Madoc Street. Mrs Davies linked the past of Llandudno as a pleasure resort with the present, for she was a daughter of the late Mrs. Sarah Brookes, who was one of the first to cater for visitors who desired to bathe in the sea in the early days. In those days van proprietors and their clients became friends, and their coming each year was preceded by letters announcing dates, etc. In that way Mrs. Davies, who carried on the business, became on friendly terms with quite a host of friends, many of whom have written letters of condolence to her daughters. Mrs Davies was born in April 1844 at one of the long since demolished cottages known as Morfa Isa. Her husband, the late Mr. John Davies, was one of the Ty Capel family. She is survived by three daughters, i.e., Mrs. S. J. Jones, 18, Madoc Street; Mrs. M. Davies, 1, Glanywern Cottage, and Mrs. C. Holland, 2, Queen's Cottages. The funeral took place at Llanrhos on Thursday, the Rev. J. F. Reece officiating.

intended to become more efficient but Mostyn was bent on property development not farming. In reality the law was there to serve the gentry and the Mostyns were no more cynical in exploiting its provisions than their Parliamentary colleagues.

Of course it is convenient for those who come out on top of any social change to depict the process as natural and inevitable but the transformation of Llandudno was neither. It was imposed through an act of legalised theft perpetrated by a powerful family that was both morally and financially bankrupt.

Only Memories Remain

It is glib and unfair to conclude as Williams and others have done, that the absence of violent resistance is evidence that villagers happily accepted the evictions and destruction of the old way of life. Villagers simply resigned themselves to what they considered inevitable. They realised resistance would be viciously suppressed and attempted to secure the best deal they could for themselves and their families. Their response was typical as landscape historian W G Hoskins makes clear, 'In most places the legalised theft was carried through without any active threat from the illiterate and cowed peasantry'. Hoskins emphasises 'it is almost impossible to convey to modern minds the full significance of common lands for the old peasant or thrift economy which made use of all the resources of the neighbourhood and was very nearly self-sufficient.'

Most villagers were less dramatically confronted with the changes than the squatters on the Morfa. Many residents on the Great Orme continued to occupy the same houses and only slowly, as the new town developed, did they begin to realise their traditional, Welsh way of life was disappearing forever. Some welcomed the transformation, whilst others, like Thomas Rowlands, were initially impressed but lived to regret the loss of the old ways. In his 'Adgofion am Llandudno' Rowlands proudly observed, 'The tiny cottages scattered over Morfa Isaf have given way to the hotels, shops and boarding houses of the Parade, Mostyn Street and other wide roads that cannot be bettered anywhere in the United Kingdom. The carts of John Williams, Hen Ferry; Thomas Owen, Gyffin and the carriages of John Edwards, Tan'rallt are now things of the past'. Yet when he died in 1902 his obituary described how he had become more and more disenchanted with the changes, 'He thought he saw all around him in Llandudno a slackening of fibre, a departure from former ideals, an adoption of alien habits which his soul abhorred.'

Llandudno had become the 'Queen of the Welsh Resorts' but some of her subjects still grieved for her lost youth and innocence. When Robert G Owens returned to Llandudno in 1911 after emigrating to America in 1849 he was interviewed by a reporter from the Llandudno Advertiser who noted that, 'Frankly speaking he is disappointed for he would like to have seen the place as he left it when a boy and a map of which he carries in his mind. The homely cottages he remembers are no more, and Mr Owens regrets them. But he still finds a few with whom he played as a boy . . . The majority however, like the cottages have gone and only memories remain.'

CHRONICLE OF CREUDDYN HISTORY

350 million BC	Llandudno submerged beneath warm tropical seas
30,000 BC	Ice, a thousand metres thick, covers the Creuddyn
10,000 BC	Stone Age hunter-gatherers shelter in Llandudno caves
6,000 BC	Neolithic farming commences in the Creuddyn
2,000 BC	Copper mining begins on the Great Orme
500 BC	Iron Age Celts erect Pen-y-dinas hillfort
47	Deceangli tribe surrender to invading Romans
410	Roman army finally withdraws from Britain
490	Birth of Maelgwn Gwynedd
856	Rhodri Mawr defeats a Viking fleet off the Great Orme
993	Last Viking raids on Gwynedd
1078	Robert of Rhuddlan captures Deganwy Castle
1093	Gruffydd ap Cynan kills Robert of Rhuddlan at Deganwy
1170	Death of Owain Gwynedd
1213	Llywelyn ap Iorwerth recaptures Deganwy
1252	Borough of Deganwy granted a Royal Charter
1282	Edward I defeats and executes Llywelyn ap Gruffydd
1350	Black Death kills everyone in Deganwy
1401	Glyndŵr rebels burn down the Bishop's Palace
1457	Mostyn family marry into the House of Gloddaeth
1536	'Act of Union' subsumes Wales within England
1539	Thomas ap Richard ap Hywel anglicises name to 'Thomas Mostyn'
1585	First book produced in Wales printed on the Little Orme
1593	William Davies hanged, drawn and quartered
1650	Archbishop John Williams dies at Gloddaeth
1692	First recorded copper mining lease
1748	Mines reported as flooded and abandoned
1761	Great Orme copper mines reopen for regular production
1789	Baptist sermons begin in yard at Hen Dafarn
1790	Radical artist Hugh Hughes born at Pwllygwichiad farm
1801	Population of Llandudno 318
1802	Death of Thomas Williams, the Copper King
1804	Signal station erected to warn of Napoleonic invasion
1806	Calvinists at Tynyffrith threatened with eviction by Mostyn agent
1807	Pyllau works formally adopts the name of the 'New Mine'
1809	John Maugham surveys Mostyn's Llandudno estates
1811	Population of Llandudno 452
1813	John Davies of Bodafon killed in Great Orme mine works
1814	First (Calvinist) chapel opens in Llandudno

1815	Tabernacl Baptist Chapel opens
1817	Mostyn farm bailiff evicted from Maesdu for Nonconformity
1818	Sir Thomas Mostyn raises £100,000 mortgage with Coutts
1821	Population of Llandudno 509
1822	Porthyrheli quarried for stone for Conwy bridge
1823	Hornby wrecked and eleven villagers subsequently imprisoned
1824	Charles Darwin 'botanises' on the Great Orme
1826	Liverpool Dock Trustees establish 'Ormeshead' signal station
1827	Tom & Jerry pumping device installed at Gogarth
1831	Population of Llandudno 662
1835	Tŷ Gwyn Copper Mine opens
1836	Saint George's Harbour Company Bill
1837	Wesleyans open Caersalem Chapel on Cwlach Street
1838	Llandudno's first Post Office opens
1839	Storm blows the roof off St Tudno's Church
1840	Opening of St George's Church
1841	Population of Llandudno 1047
1842	Penmorfa mining adit completed
1843	Llanduno, Llangystennin and Eglwysrhos Enclosure Act
1846	St George's National School opens in Church Walks
1847	Blue Book Commissioners visit Llandudno's two schools
1848	Enclosure Allotment
1849	Llandudno land auction held at Plas Mawr
1851	Population of Llandudno 1,131
1852	First seaside villas erected on North Parade
1853	Strike at the Old Mine and closure of Tŷ Gwyn Mine
1854	Opening of St George's Hotel

Bibliography, Notes and Acknowledgements

Recommended General Publications

- Proceedings of the Llandudno and District Field Club – (1906-56) 27 volumes plus supplements
- Transactions of Llandudno and District Historical Society – (1986 to present) 6 volumes to 2005
- Published journals of the Great Orme Exploration Society (GOES)
- *'Gathering the Jewels'* is a key web site for many visual aspects of Welsh history

Bassett & Davies   *Atlas of Caernarvonshire* (1977)
Bezant Lowe, W   *The Heart of Northern Wales* (2 volumes, 1912 & 1927)
Davies, John   *A History of Wales* (1993)
Draper, Christopher   *Walks With History – Llandudno* (1999)
Evans, Gwynfor   *Land of My Fathers* (1974)
Lynch, Frances   *A Guide to Ancient and Historic Wales; Gwynedd* (1995)
R.C.A.H.M.   *An Inventory of Ancient Monuments; Caernarvonshire* (1956)

CHAPTER 1. An Ancient Landscape; 350 million BC

The geological collection amassed by the Field Club may be consulted by application to the Curator of Llandudno Museum (LM), Gloddaeth Street, Llandudno

Ashton, W M   *The Evolution of a Coastline* (1920)
Bevins, R E   *Mineral Treasures of Wales* (1994)
Lamb & Sington   *Earth Story* (2003)
Millward & Robinson   *Landscapes of North Wales* (1978)
Roberts, Neil   *The Holocene, an Environmental History* (1997)

CHAPTER 2. Stone Age Hunter-Gatherers on the Great Orme; 10,000 BC

Key paleolithic artefacts have been acquired by the British Museum (BM) where the decorated horse jaw is on public exhibition. It may also be viewed on the BM web site.

Barton, Nick   *Ice Age Britain* (2005)
Green & Walker   *Ice Age Hunters, Neanderthals and Early Modern Hunters in Wales* (1991)

Prior, Francis   *Britain BC* (2003)
Sieveking, G de G   *The Kendrick's Cave Mandible* (British Museum
                        Quarterly, 1971)

CHAPTER 3. Llandudno's First Farmers; 6,000 BC

Llety'r filiast is the key site and can be visited without charge at the end
of Cromlech Road. Blodwen, the neolithic skeleton found on the Little
Orme can be seen at Bacup Museum where she remains the guest of the
local historical society

Darvill, Timothy   *Prehistoric Britain* (1992)
Dibble, Kenneth   *The Lady of the Little Orme* (1997)
Lynch, Green & Davies   *Prehistoric Wales* (2000)

CHAPTER 4. Bronze Age Copper Miners; 2,000 BC

The Bronze Age copper mine on the Great Orme is as archaeologically
important as Stonehenge and a visit is essential. Numerous important
artefacts are on display at the mine and in Llandudno Museum.

O'Brien, William   *Bronze Age Copper Mining in Britain and
                        Ireland* (1996)
Pearson, Michael P   *Bronze Age Britain* (2005)
Roberts, Nyda   *The Bronze Age, A Time of Change* (1994)

CHAPTER 5. Pen Dinas Hillfort and the Roman Occupation; 500 BC

Pen Dinas can be visited at any time, free of charge. The gold stater is on
display in Llandudno Museum along with the Iron Age harness piece

Arnold & Davies   *Roman and Early Medieval Wales* (2000)
Davies, Oliver   *The Copper Mines on the Great Ormes Head* (1949)
Hogg, A H A   *Hill-forts of Britain* (1975)
Ogden, William Sharp   *A Find of Roman Bronze Coins on the Little Orme*
                        (AC 1909)

CHAPTER 6. Maelgwn and the Age of the Saints; 410

Deganwy Castle can be visited at any time, free of charge. There are
interpretative boards on site. The Tyddyn Holland stone can be inspected
in Llanrhos Church and on the opposite side of the road Ffynon Santes
Fair can be visited.

Edwards & Lane   *Early Medieval Settlements in Wales AD 400-
                        1100* (1988)

Gwyn Davies   *A Light in the Land, Christianity in Wales 200-*
                     2000 (2002)
Nash-Williams, V E   *The Early Christian Monuments of Wales* (1950)
Parry, Tom   *Llys Helig* (1996)

CHAPTER 7. Viking Raiders and Norman Colonisers; 950

St Tudno's Church is a key site with much twelfth century stonework, a font of the same period and two contemporary intricately carved stone coffin lids on display inside.

Boon, G C   *Welsh Hoards 1979-81* (1981)
Charles, B G   *Old Norse Relations With Wales* (1934)
Davies, R R   *Conquest, Coexistence and Change; Wales*
                     1063-1415 (1987)
Davies, W   *Wales in the Early Middle Ages* (1982)

CHAPTER 8. Medieval Life in Gogarth and Gannoc; 1284

This is the earliest period in which documentary evidence directly informs our understanding of Llandudno's past. Relevant leases and other documents relating to the township of 'Kyngrayader' and the Manor of Gogarth can be consulted at the University College of North Wales archive (UCNW), Bangor. Archaeology nevertheless retains a crucial role and the ruins of the Bishop's Palace, although on private land, can be seen from the Great Orme above, or the beach below. Viewing is not only essential but urgent as this immensely important site is threatened with obliteration by a destructive combination of erosion and property development. The mediaeval plough marks and hut platforms on the Great Orme also merit attention (and protection from ignorant car parkers!)

Alcock, Leslie   *Excavations at Degannwy Castle* (1967)
Aris, Mary   *Historic Landscapes of the Great Orme* (1996)
Carr, A D   *The Black Death in Caernarfonshire* (2000)
Davies, Henry Rees   *A Review of the Records of the Conwy and the*
                     Menai Ferries (1942)
Hague, Douglas B   *The Bishop's Palace, Gogarth* (1957)

CHAPTER 9. Uchelwyr to Country Gentlemen; 1536

Of the five gentry halls depicted only Penrhyn Old Hall (a public house) and Bodysgallen (a hotel and restaurant) are easily accessible although a visit to Gloddaeth (a private school) and Marl (a local authority education centre) might be possible on application to the Principals.

Llangystennin Hall is now a private residence and access is therefore unlikely.

Crean, Patrick J   *A Life of the Venerable William Davies* (1985)
Gruffydd, R Geraint   *Argraffwyr Cyntaf Cymru* (1972)
Jones, John Gwynfor   *The Welsh Gentry, 1536-1640* (1998)
Lewis, Edward A   *The Decay of Tribalism in North Wales* (1903)
Lloyd, George   *Beacon Watch Towers on the North Wales Coast*
                          (AC 1964)
Robinson & Williams   *A Nation Under Siege, The Civil War in Wales*
                          (1991)
Tucker, Norman   *North Wales & Chester in the Civil War* (2003)
Wicklen Stanley I   *Cave Printers of the Little Orme* (nd)
Williams, Glanmor   *Wales and the Reformation* (1999)

CHAPTER 10. Reopening the Copper Mines; 1761

For anyone with a particular interest in mining membership of the Great Orme Exploration Society is essential. GOES explores, preserves, researches and publishes all matters relating to Llandudno's copper mining industry. Their publications can be consulted at Llandudno library. The books noted below by Don Smith and C J Williams are particularly recommended.

Dodd A H   *The Industrial Revolution in North Wales* (1933)
Hyde Hall, Edmund   *A Description of Carnarvonshire, 1809-11* (1952)
Smith, Don   *The Great Orme Copper Mines* (1988)
Thomas, Peter D G   *Politics in Eighteenth-Century Wales* (1998)
Williams, C J   *Great Orme Mines* (1995)

CHAPTER 11. Heart of the Village; 1800 . . .

A stroll along Cwlach Street provides an excellent introduction to the layout of the old village. The reminiscences of John Roberts printed in occasional articles published in the Llandudno Advertiser, mainly in 1910-11, are invaluable. They can be viewed on microfilm at both Llandudno Library (LL) and Conwy County Archive (CCA).

Rowlands, Thomas   *Adgofion am Llandudno* (1893)
'Gwnodl'   *Llandudno, Its Origin, Rise and Progress* (1865)

CHAPTER 12. Farming the Land

Various Mostyn estate maps, surveys and rental lists provide evidence of the early part of the nineteenth century and the tithe map, enclosure allotment map and their accompanying schedules provide information on landholdings in the mid-century. Farmhouses surviving from this period that can be seen from public footpaths include Penymynydd Ucha and Isaf, Wyfydd, Tynycoed, Bodafon, Tŷ Ucha, Fferm, Bryn Gosol and Cwm Howard. Meticulous published studies by Kenneth Dibble on *Bodafon (1993)*, *Nany y Gamar (1990)*, *Rhiwledyn (1995)* and *Penrhynside (1999)* provide a wealth of detailed information on agricultural holdings in areas neglected by other historians.

Gibson, J   *Agriculture in Wales* (1879)
Lowe, Jeremy   *Welsh Country Workers Housing 1775-1875* (1985)

CHAPTER 13. Tai Unnos on the Morfa

The publications listed below provide useful background information on Tai Unnos but there are no published accounts of the Morfa community. The most important, though difficult to reconcile, primary sources are;

• Map and schedule published by the St George's Rail & Harbour Co. in 1845
• Tithe map and schedule, 1845
• Enclosure map and schedule, 1847
• 1841 and 1851 census records
• The recollections of Thomas Rowlands and John Roberts (publication details above)

Evans, Hugh   *Cwm Eithin* (1931)
William, Eurwyn   *Home-Made Homes, Dwellings of the Rural Poor in Wales* (1988)

CHAPTER 14. Sailors, Wreckers and Smugglers

Primary sources on maritime Llandudno are particularly disparate but the first two secondary accounts cited below are recommended places to start, otherwise it is necessary to collate scraps of information from Quarter Session records, newspaper accounts and reminiscences. The archive of the Mersey Docks & Harbour Board is accessible at the Merseyside Maritime Museum, Albert Dock, Liverpool. The Llandudno signal station was demolished a century ago but the surviving station at Llysfaen was almost identical and can be seen from the public footpath. Job Jones's visitors' book can be consulted at (CCA).

Frank Large   *Faster than the Wind, the Liverpool to Holyhead Telegraph* (1998)

Jones, Ivor Wynne   *Shipwrecks of North Wales* (1973)
Wilson, Geoffrey   *The Old Telegraph* (1976)

CHAPTER 15. Declining Church and Aspiring Chapel

Only Caersalem, the Wesleyan chapel survives as originally built although it is no longer used for religious purposes. Records of Ebeneser, the first Calvinist chapel, can be seen at (CCA), including details of the baptism of 'Thomas Cynric' (Kendrick) in 1821.

Prichard, John   *Cofiant Mr William Prichard* (nd)
Roberts, John   *Hanes Bedyddwyr Cylch Llandudno* (1926)
Roberts, J Roger   *Ebeneser* (1975)
Rowlands, Thomas   *Adgofion am Llandudno, a Dechreuad Achos yr*
                        Annibynwyr yn y Lle (1992)
Williams, B & J Tudno   *Methodistiad Dosbarth Llandudno* (1926)

CHAPTER 16. Schooling and the Blue Books

Establishing a reliable chronology of early schooling in Llandudno is fraught with problems and I present this account with no great confidence. It is difficult to reconcile inconsistent reminiscences and primary documentary evidence appears entirely absent. St George's School (1846) is the earliest school whose history can be accurately identified.

H.M.S.O.   *Report of the Commissioners of Inquiry into the*
                        State of Education in Wales (1847)
Llandudno SBPT   *St George's National School* (2003)
Lord, Peter   *Hugh Hughes* (1995)

CHAPTER 17. St George's Harbour and Railway

Numerous maps and documents published by the company survive and their old seal can be seen (on application) at the National Rail Museum, York. Remnants of structures eventually erected by the company in 1858 can still be detected at Llandudno Railway Station (an original low-level platform) and under the existing pier (wooden stumps of the original pier).

Elis-Williams M   *Packet to Ireland* (1984)
HMSO   *An Act for the Construction and Maintenance of*
                        Harbour at Llandudno (1853)

St George's H & R Co   *Report Submitted to Parliamentary Select*
Committee on Harbours of Refuge and
Shipwrecks, Port Charges of Liverpool etc (1836)

CHAPTER 18. Landlords of Gloddaeth

The published sources below offer much useful information although strictly from the landlord's viewpoint. Literally thousands of primary Mostyn documents can be consulted at Flintshire Archive, Hawarden and UNCW. Frustratingly, I have failed to discover many details of the conception, birth and upbringing of Elizabeth Mostyn and would welcome any information readers might uncover.

Carr, Raymond	*English Foxhunting – A History* (1976)
Hiller, George	*Your Obedient Servant, the History of an Historic Welsh Estate* (2003)
Ll Mostyn & T Glenn	*The Mostyns of Mostyn* (1925)
Williams F Ron	*Llandudno and the Mostyn Influence* (1996)

CHAPTER 19. Edward Mostyn's Cunning Plan

The lives of Morfa residents can be tracked through the 1861 and later censuses, trade directories and Llandudno Advertiser obituaries. Some old-established Llandudno families retain a lingering sense of injustice and resentment against the Morfa clearances and supplied details of the fate of their evicted ancestors. Either by accident or design the fine detail of the physical clearances is not well documented and the exact chronology can only be discerned by inference. (CCA) holds several small maps extracted from leases and mortgage deeds, illustrating aspects of the development of the Morfa and the general transition from the layout of Llandudno village to the street system of the modern bathing resort.

Parry, R	*Llandudno; Its History and Natural History* (1855)
Prebble, John	*The Highland Clearances* (1986)
Roberts, R Alun	*Welsh Homespun* (1930)
Ward, Colin	*Cotters and Squatters* (2002)

Acknowledgements

More people than I can list here contributed to this book. Some offered the fruits of original research, some permitted the reproduction of illustrations, some argued me out of intemperate judgements whilst my partner, Anna Jeffery, patiently read, re-read and improved innumerable ill-punctuated drafts. I owe a particular debt of gratitude to Tom Parry who provided invaluable leads when my own efforts ran aground and to Pat Tucker for her skill and patience in tracking down Sir Thomas Mostyn's Oxfordshire activities. I would also like to take this opportunity to thank Bob Barnsdale Denise Hallsworth, David Haynes, Paige Lau, John Lawson Reay, Ian Reed, Ron Williams and the archivists of UCNW, Conwy, Flintshire, Gwynedd and Lambeth Palace and the reference library staff of Leamington Spa and Llandudno.

Index